Markets and Politics in Central Asia

Over a decade ago the countries of Central Asia – Kazakhstan, Kyrgyzstan, Tajikistan, Turkmenistan, and Uzbekistan – emerged from the former USSR to become independent countries. In the infancy of these new states' independence, significant structural economic reforms were undertaken, but the methods employed varied greatly.

In this comparative study of economic and political development in Central Asia, Gregory Gleason brings a clear, lucid analysis of the impact of the economic reforms on the countries' political liberalization. Generalizing from the experience of the Central Asian states, the book argues that economic reform and political liberalization should be viewed as an interconnected process, linked in terms of policy cycles. Breaking with traditional analyses, this provocative book shows how markets and politics are closely related in Central Asia.

With separate chapters on each country along with comparative, analytical sections, this authoritative book is an essential contribution to an ongoing debate. Students, academics, and professionals interested in transition economies will find this book useful, interesting, and enjoyable.

Gregory Gleason is Professor of Political Science and Public Administration at the University of New Mexico, USA.

Economies in transition to the market
Edited by Professor Josef C. Brada
Arizona State University and
Professor Paul G. Hare
Herriot-Watt University

Volume 1
Unemployment in Transition
Restructuring and labour markets in Central Europe
Tomasz Mickiewicz and Janice Bell

Volume 2
Markets and Politics in Central Asia
Structural reform and political change
Gregory Gleason

Markets and Politics in Central Asia

Structural reform and political change

Gregory Gleason

Routledge
Taylor & Francis Group
LONDON AND NEW YORK

First published 2003
by Routledge
11 New Fetter Lane, London EC4P 4EE

Simultaneously published in the USA and Canada
by Routledge
29 West 35th Street, New York, NY 10001

Routledge is an imprint of the Taylor & Francis Group

Typeset in Goudy by
Newgen Imaging Systems (P) Ltd, Chennai, India
Printed and bound in Great Britain by
Antony Rowe Ltd, Chippenham, Wiltshire

British Library Cataloguing in Publication Data
A catalogue record for this book is available from the British Library

Library of Congress Cataloging in Publication Data
Gleason, Gregory
Markets and Politics in Central Asia : structural reform and political change / Gregory Gleason.
p. cm. – (Economies in transition to the market ; 2)
Includes bibliographical references and index.
1. Asia, Central – Economic conditions – 1991– 2. Asia, Central – Economic policy.
3. Asia, Central – Politics and government. I. Title. II. Series.

HC420.3 .G57 2003
330.958–dc21 2002032460

ISBN 0–415–27396–X (hb.)

Contents

Tables

Acknowledgments

This is a book about the relationship between economic and political reform. It is a book about the initial stage of the transition from communism to national government in the countries of Central Asia. The transition began about 1990 and accelerated during the mid- to late 1990s. During this period I had the opportunity to observe close at hand key aspects of the transition from communist to post-communist rule in the countries of Central Asia. Like most things human, the experience was imperfect. I witnessed the euphoria and great expectations that many of the people of the region had for the dawning of a new era. I witnessed many aspects of the process by which change occurred. I witnessed the frustration and disappointment that grew as many of the goals that seemed so easily attainable in theory proved so elusive in practice. But in addition to the disappointments there were also very positive moments. In the midst of great adversity, I witnessed human decency and determination that went far beyond what I had a right to expect. I was frequently asked – asked by people who really needed to know the answer – what the relationship was between economic reform and political change. I offered the textbook definitions that were available at the time, but I was not always satisfied with the answers I gave. It was this experience that sent me back to the drawing board to organize my thoughts and summarize my understanding in the form of this book.

Field research for this book was undertaken during the period 1997–2001. Research on this book was facilitated by assistance from of the Academies of Science of Kazakhstan, Kyrgyzstan, Tajikistan, and Uzbekistan, by the Kazakhstan State Academy of Management, the Eurasian Institute of the Market, Tajikistan State University, and by Almaty State University. I am indebted to the Soros Foundation, the International Research and Exchanges Board, the American Councils for International Education, and the Bureau of Educational and Cultural Affairs of the US Department of State for generous support that made field research possible. I am grateful to Paul Davis and Sean Roberts of the United States Agency for International Development, Vivian Walker of the US Department of State, and David J. Green of the Asian Development Bank for encouragement and support. I am grateful to Martin Spechler of Indiana University and Michael McKee of the University of Tennessee for advice and comments.

My greatest debt is to the Central Asian scholars and policy makers who freely shared data, insights and, in my more fortunate moments, tea and pilaf. I am particularly grateful to G. Abdulova, T. Abdushukurova, B. Atabaev, A. Bolotbaev, G. Ileuova, N. Khan, A. Muhidov, G. Mutanov, M. Olimov, M. Pikulina, S. Primbetov, F. Seitova, B. Suzhikova, R. Zhalimbetova, and the late Bakhrom Tursunov.

Notes on sources

The Central Asian countries – Kazakhstan, Kyrgyzstan, Tajikistan, Turkmenistan, and Uzbekistan – occupy a territory of some 3,994,400 sq. km, or about 25 percent larger than the area of all the countries of the European Union. Each of the Central Asian states has an official national language, but numerous other languages are used in speech and writing. The Russian language was the official government language and was widely used in the area before 1991, but its use has rapidly diminishing since independence. Sources used in this book include materials in the indigenous languages, Russian and English.

Formal discourse in Central Asia is riddled with nuances created by the intersection of coexisting and competing cultural influences. The very names of the country and the peoples that inhabit them have to a certain extent been dynamically determined. For instance, the official name of Kazakhstan during the Soviet period was "the Kazakh Soviet Socialist Republic" with the word *Kazakh* being rendered in a way convenient for speakers of the Russian language. After Kazakhstan became independent, some people argued in favor of changing the name to *Kazakstan*, dropping the "kh" combination in favor of a direct translation from the Kazakh language. But because the 'kh" in Kazakhstan is actually neither a "k" nor a "kh" but a distinctively different sound, it would be more faithfully rendered as a "q." Hence the country should be spelled *Qazaqstan*. This strange concoction was fortunately abandoned, but no clear consensus on transliteration has emerged. Thus Kazakhstan may be written either as *Kazakstan* or *Kazakhstan*. Transliteration is to some extent merely a matter of style. So I have opted in favor of the simplest style. For example, I use Akaev instead of Akayev. I use this convention throughout the text with the exception of direct citations.

Statistical materials on economic indicators are drawn primarily from the *Asian Development Outlook 2001* published by the Asian Development Bank. Additional statistical materials are drawn from the International Monetary Fund periodic country reports or from other intergovernmental organizations. These sources are identified within notes at the end of the appropriate chapters rather than listed in the general bibliography.

Statistical materials on governance and political indicators are drawn primarily from *Nations in Transit 2001* published by Freedom House, New York, from the annual Corruption Perception Index published by Transparency International (TI) Berlin, and from the Governance Research Indicators Dataset maintained by the Governance Group at the World Bank Institute. Evaluation materials on elections are drawn from periodic reports of the Office for Democratic Institutions and Human Rights of the Organization for Security and Cooperation in Europe (OSCE). Assessment materials on civil and human rights are drawn from the annual and periodic reports produced by Amnesty International, Freedom House, Human Rights Watch, and from the annual Country Reports on Human Rights Practices issued by the US Department of State.

Contemporary news sources, both printed and electronic, constitute an important source of information regarding economic and political institutions and policies. Many of the news references are ephemeral in nature. These sources are typically cited in the text and footnotes at the end of chapters but not in the bibliography, which is reserved for more analytical sources. The most commonly used news sources are cited in the text as follows:

CACI, Biweekly Analyst, Central Asia and Caucasus Institute, Washington.
Eurasianet, Central Eurasia Project of the Soros Foundation, New York.
Interfax, Interfax News Service, Moscow.
IWPR, International War and Peace Reporting. The electronic information service of the Institute for War and Peace Reporting, London.
NIT, Nations in Transit 2001, Freedom House, New York.
Newsline, The electronic information service of Radio Free Europe/Radio Liberty, Prague and Washington.
TI, Transparency International, Berlin.
WPS, What the Papers Say, Media Monitoring Agency, Moscow.

1 Economic and political reform

Free markets and democracy are related. Open markets and open minds mutually reinforce one another. It is natural then on theoretical grounds to conclude that the shortest paths to democracy and free markets for countries with distorted economies and authoritarian politics should be economic and political reform programs that are parallel, complementary and contemporaneous. Yet empirical observation does not offer much support for this conclusion. Some countries succeed in economic reform, but not in political reform. Some succeed in political change, but fail to make progress in economic development. The countries of Latin America in recent years have enjoyed comparatively good success with democratization, yet they have been less successful with economic liberalization. During the same time period many Asian states have had relatively good success with economic reform but have been less successful in democratization. In some African states political reform has not been accompanied by economic progress while in others political reform is championed as the cause for economic progress. In Russia political reform preceded market reform, but at least in the early stages of Russia's reform heavy doses of "shock therapy" produced ample shock and only modest therapy. At the same time, China made great progress in economic reform; but China's reform was adopted, at least in part, as a deliberate strategy to forestall political change. If democracy and market freedom are so closely related theoretically, why is the empirical relationship between political and economic liberalization so complex and varied?

The countries of Central Asia – Kazakhstan, Kyrgyzstan, Tajikistan, Turkmenistan, and Uzbekistan – emerged as independent states from the disintegration of the USSR in 1991. For over a decade these five countries have been striving to carry out market and political reforms. These republics were previously integrated into the broadly uniform network of Soviet political institutions and economic relationships. From this single point of departure, these countries have pursued reforms that took them in very different directions. What can the experience of these countries teach us about the relationship between markets and politics in Central Asia? Answering this question is the principal aim of this book. The book seeks to explain the relationship between market reform and political change in the specific circumstances of the Central Asian countries.

A secondary goal of this book is broader. In today's tightly interconnected world of global markets it has become apparent that those countries that can find the winning formulas for matching open markets with open political institutions are likely to be hastened along in their overall development efforts. Those states that fail in this undertaking are likely to find that they run the risk of falling further behind in development efforts. In other words, globalization appears to have the effect of rewarding countries that can globalize effectively while punishing countries that do not. The "Washington consensus" – the proposition that the economic reform packages of the Washington based international organizations represent international standards and best practices – has been understood by many policy leaders in the emerging world to constitute the winning formula for unlocking the benefits of globalization. This is why many political leaders in the emerging markets of the world find it so perplexing that simple formulas for balancing economic and political reforms do not readily emerge from the broad comparative picture. Policy leaders would like to think that the right policies, the right policy mix, the right tempo of change, and the right styles of implementation can lead to increased prosperity, increased opportunity, enhanced political stability, and to greater participation in the international community. Conversely, policy leaders assume that competing policies or policies that create invidious competition and even conflict with a country's neighbors are likely to lead the country into counterproductive efforts, forestalling economic progress and complicating political development. What can the experience of the Central Asian countries teach us with respect to the timing, phasing, and tempo of economic and political reforms geared to achieving the desired results and avoiding the undesirable? The secondary goal of this book is to answer this general question by drawing out the implications of Central Asia's recent experience for political and economic theory.

In years past "Soviet Central Asia" was seen as one region. When the individual countries emerged after the breakup of the USSR, however, it was not long before they begin to exhibit substantially different tendencies. It was therefore a mistake, prominent in the social science literature regarding these countries and the societies of Central Asia prior to the collapse of the USSR, to assume that the countries were homogeneous with respect to potentialities. Yet the fact remains that the countries emerged from a single, highly uniform framework of formal political and economic institutions. Consequently, we can use the point of independence as a baseline against which to measure the effect of institutional and political change. What accounts for the divergence in outcomes in countries that have similar cultures, and similar institutional starting points? Of course, a sample of five countries is too small to enable us to draw any rigorous statistical conclusions.[1] But this does not mean we cannot benefit from systematically exploring the outcomes. In the treatment presented in this book, our goal is to explain political reform. In other words, the success of the countries at achieving political reform is regarded as the thing to be explained, the dependent variable. The success of the countries' differing economic reform strategies is the independent variable.

In assessing how the contrasting economic strategies of the states differentially affected their progress toward liberalization and democratization it must be acknowledged that in absolute terms, progress toward democracy in all the Central Asian states has been limited. The Central Asian region was previously governed by leaders of the Communist Party of the Soviet Union and each of the Central Asian republics was administratively managed at the apex of power by a local communist party first secretary. By the end of the first decade of independence, the parties and the party secretaries of all the Central Asian countries had been replaced and the post-communist governments were ruled at the apex by "presidents."[2] In all cases these were leaders who came from the former Soviet *apparat* or high rungs of the Soviet establishment. All the countries had established "presidential systems," giving the presidents the power to rule by decree with the force of "constitutional law." While all of the countries had conducted elections, none of the governments could be said to have fully conformed to international standards for free and fair elections. Three of the governments had former communist leaders who extended their mandate in extra-constitutional ways. None of the governments had what could be described as an independent judiciary. None of the governments had established a deliberative legislature with true powers of the purse. Even in the most open and liberal of the countries – Kazakhstan and Kyrgyzstan – the parliaments had been routed by presidential decree. Judging by the benchmark criteria for measuring democratic progress used by international human rights monitoring organizations, none of the Central Asian states had realized the full potential for democratic change during the first decade of independence.

If we conclude that the Central Asian states have made limited absolute progress toward establishing sustainable systems of democratic governance, we must also acknowledge that important relative differences did exist among the Central Asian states. The status of democratic reform was quite different in all the states. The differences among the states was represented in a range of substantive policy categories including human and civil rights, treatment of dissidents and opposition, rule of law and adjudication of dispute, tolerance for religious, ethnic, and territorial differences, the character of the business environment, and the treatment of non-nationals. The different countries of Central Asia have valued these political goals differently and pursued them with varying degrees of enthusiasm. But there has been no such disagreement with respect to the goal of economic development. In this connection, all of the Central Asian states are united by a common purpose. All of the states have sought the goal of economic development.

This book analyzes the relationship between economics and politics. We begin by noting that countries may deliberately undertake efforts to spur economic and political improvements or they may find themselves thrust by necessity into circumstances of economic and political change. The former case we usually refer to as reform; the latter case we tend to characterize simply as change. For our purposes in this book we analyze economic reform – the "structural reform" of the book's title – as consisting of steps that improve the country's management of markets. Thus, we use the concepts of economic reform and structural reform interchangeably in the analysis that follows. We use the concept of "governance" to refer specifically to the package of policy correctives that is undertaken to improve rules, policies, procedures, enforcement mechanisms, and other public institutions that support market transactions. Understood in this way, governance is a specific aspect of structural reform.

For the purposes of this book, we maintain a distinction between the concept of governance and the much broader idea of government itself. Governance deals explicitly and exclusively with those policy changes that affect how markets function in a given society. In contrast, government deals with the totality of public decision-making. The actions of government influence a broad sphere of activities ranging from ideological or normative concerns to social and cultural issues. Government often involves decision-making that has or is intended to have little direct impact on how markets function. Moreover, while economic reform refers specifically to the steps the political leadership of a country takes to change the country's economic policies, government reform refers to the steps the political leadership of a country takes to change the nature of the government and political processes of the country. Government reform is therefore always self-referential to some extent. To carry out a true government reform, it is the government itself that must adopt the rules to determine what rules government will use in its actions. Economic and political reforms are obviously linked. But how they are linked is more subtle than is generally supposed.

Policy cycles and political alignment

We can be confident that free markets are associated with democratic politics. Classical liberalism argues that markets and politics are linked in a fabric of closely related and necessary institutions. Classical liberalism argues that these institutions are designed to facilitate and protect the freedom of choice and the freedom of action of individuals, groups, and firms within a society. The fundamental principle of liberalism, as Freidrich Hayek argued, is "that in the ordering of our affairs we should make as much use as possible of the spontaneous forces of society, and resort as little as possible to coercion" (Hayek, 1960, 1972: 17). Freedom of choice is exercised in the sphere of material exchange within markets. Freedom of choice is exercised in the sphere of political exchange within democratic institutions.

When people are free to choose the relationships into which they enter, the transactions they undertake, and the substance of the exchanges in which they are involved, their actions are apt to be an accurate reflection of their true preferences. When people are free to choose the interactions into which they enter without coercion from higher order administrative structures, when they are free to decide for themselves the terms of the exchanges into which they enter, when they are free to decline to enter into transactions they view as unattractive, their behavior is much more likely to accurately reflect their true wants and desires. When people become accustomed to exercising consumer sovereignty within the marketplace of goods and services, it is natural for them also to come to expect a similar range of choice in the political marketplace of ideas. When people make virtue out of industriousness, self-reliance, prudence, probity, and stewardship, it is natural for them to come to believe that these same values should be practiced in the public sphere. When people exercise the right to make the most important decisions affecting their own welfare and bear the responsibility for the results of those decisions, they also come to expect honesty, accountability, efficiency, and effectiveness from their public institutions and public officials. Free markets make free minds. Free minds are the essence of democracy.

How precisely are free minds and free markets related? What is the foundation for the strong intuition we have that market behavior and political behaviors are related? Many explanations have been suggested for this. If people are free to act in markets, there may be some spillover effect into their political life. Some social learning may take place in economic life that is carried over into the realm of political choice. The habits of thought and practice instilled in market relations may infuse political life. People may begin to see their interests in terms of the latitude of choices open to them. They may begin to see other people in similar situations as having similar interests. The coalition of interests that emerges in market situations may reinforce democratic pluralism through facilitating interest group behavior. Yet these and other parallels between market and political behavior may constitute merely incidental association. Can we reason on the basis of close incidental association that free markets and free politics are causally related?

The experience of European and North American countries does indeed suggest that there are strong causal links between the spheres of economics and politics, but it does so in ways that are by no means always apparent. Reflecting on the relationship between politics and markets, Charles Lindblom, observed (Lindblom, 1977: 5):

> We understand liberal democracy so poorly that we do not know – neither economists nor political scientists have produced more than speculative essays on the question – why it is that liberal democracy has arisen only in nations that are market oriented – not in all of them but only in them. The tie between market and democracy is on many counts an astonishing historical fact. We understand neither markets nor democracy well if we cannot explain it.

Lindblom's celebrated treatise on political economy, *Politics and Markets*, is an effort to identify the causal linkage explaining the "astonishing historical fact" that liberalism has emerged only in contexts where markets function and are protected. He speaks of political systems that are based on multiple and competing centers of authority, or "polyarchies." These polyarchic systems are based on rules that form the foundation of the competition for power.[3] Lindblom concludes that polyarchy is the product of a benign collusion between business interests and political leadership. Lindblom argues that polyarchy is "tied to the market system not because it is democratic but because it is not. If all past and existing polyarchies are dominated by business and property, it is to the dominating minority that we may owe its ties to the market system" (Lindblom, 1977: 169).

Getting to the bottom of Lindblom's "astonishing historical fact" is of great interest to economic and political theorists intent on understanding the experience of the highly developed, democratic, market-oriented countries. But explaining this historical fact is far more than that for the developing countries and emerging markets. For them it is an urgent necessity and perhaps an issue of national survival (Carothers, 1999). If economic reform and political reform are related, these countries need to know why and how. In *Politics and Markets*, Lindblom explains that a bargain is at the heart of the relationship between market conditions and democratic process in the advanced countries. Lindblom argues that a compact between, on the one hand, business and property and, on the other hand, the society's political leadership representing the broad public interest, is responsible for keeping markets free and keeping politics polyarchic while, at the same time, sustaining political stability. Lindblom's compact explains why the most developed societies continue to exhibit great resilience and public support even though they do not always measure up to their own democratic political rhetoric.[4]

Economic and political reforms are different undertakings. Economic reform seeks to change the capacity for system output. Political reform, in contrast, attempts to change the political rules of the game. To the extent that economic reform is successful, it will change the beneficiaries of the system, empowering those who benefit while neutralizing those sectors that are hurt by the reforms. To the extent that political reform is successful, it will change the initial conditions of the liberalization process. But, while economic and political reforms are different, they impact on one another (Rogowski, 1990). As Anne Krueger has argued, economic programs influence the political status quo. Economic policy choices have political consequences that typically result in "winners" and "losers." Political choices have economic consequences that change the political equilibrium that initiated those policies, often distributing the benefits and assigning the pain associated with structural reform by specifying who is to come out ahead and who is to come out behind in the next round of winners and losers. Krueger argued that both economic and political reform should be viewed in terms of dynamic "policy cycles" (Krueger, 1993; Alesina, 1997). A policy cycle may be defined as the closed loop that is formed by the interaction of a specific policy step upon the subsequent policy environment in a way that affects the initial conditions that gave rise to the policy step. Once an economic policy step is taken – for instance, once a reform package for a country's central banking institutions is introduced – the initial conditions that gave rise to the policy change are altered. The political equilibrium is altered in ways that will have implications for the success of the reform package.

The recognition that any policy step introduces a dynamic process of change may seem so intuitive that it is easy to overlook the implications of policy cycles for reform. Reform packages are often thought of as discrete, concrete steps that must be adopted, rather than processes that must be initiated, monitored, and modified. Reforms should be seen not only in terms of policy prescriptions (i.e. as outputs) but also in terms of the feedback loop between outputs and outcomes. Bureaucracies naturally tend to gravitate toward measuring outputs rather than outcomes. Bureaucracies prefer to focus on outputs because bureaucracies can produce outputs. The real world, however, is a world of outcomes. Analyzing reform in terms of policy cycles suggests that structural reform packages have to be suitable for the country and that the effects upon the political constituencies – the elements of the society that will determine whether the economic reforms are sustainable – should be taken into account in the adoption and implementation of the reform.

The analysis presented in this book is based on the proposition that there are many incidental linkages between markets and politics that incline open market systems toward democratic politics. These incidental linkages do not constitute a sufficient basis for structuring reform programming. However, there is a necessary causal relationship between markets and politics that does constitute an adequate basis for programming. That relationship is this: economic reforms change political sectors in ways that produce political alignments between the interests of the government and the interests of an influential sector or influential sectors. The point is very simple and straightforward. Economic reform inevitably alters political alignments. All alignments are not alike from the point of view of their political consequences.

Economic reform

The goal of economic reform is to improve market conditions. Market conditions seem to be best when politics is open and competitive. While we can be confident that free markets are associated with democracy, we cannot be sure that free markets will lead automatically to democracy precisely because free markets depend upon the existence of political institutions that facilitate and protect free markets. If political institutions do not support markets, markets may fail to exist. Markets are elemental forms of human exchange. Markets have functioned as long as human beings have voluntarily entered into exchange relationships with one another. But while they are elemental, natural, and ancient institutions, markets are by no means self-establishing, self-regulating, and self-sustaining in all cases. Markets require compatible political institutions.

When open, competitive markets function effectively they lead to gains from trade. Parties that enter voluntarily into transparent exchanges out of self-interest find that they are better off by virtue of having engaged in the exchange. The value that is brought into the world by such exchanges is referred to as the gains from trade. These gains constitute the single most significant element in economic progress, far out distancing in significance the value that is brought into the world by labor, resources, technology, or other factors contributing to economic development. If people could not trade, they would be forced to do everything themselves. Living as hermits, all people would be limited by their immediate situation and their immediate skills and talents. No person's grasp would ever exceed that person's reach. But in a world enriched by trade and exchange, people may gain from others, magnifying by many times the fruit that can be drawn from one's labors.

Markets are forums of exchange. Competitive markets are simple and elegant. The theory of the market holds that the optimal exchange of goods and services takes place when the value of the goods and services is determined automatically by the interaction of supply and demand. Demand is expressed in terms of the aggregate effect of consumer behavior as rational, value-maximizing decision-making. Supply is expressed in terms of the aggregate effect of producer behavior and the theory of the firm. Under optimal market conditions, the value of a good is given by the market-clearing price, that is, the price at which the quantity supplied is equal to the quantity demanded. When priced above this point, the quantity of the good supplied exceeds demand – there is a glut which tends to drive price down. When priced below this point, the quantity of the good demanded exceeds the quantity supplied – there is a scarcity, which tends to drive prices up. The aggregate effect of the interaction of these forces is to propel individual decision makers toward an optimally efficient allocation of resources. No central, omniscient authority decides questions of allocation. The logic of the situation naturally produces efficient allocation based upon the preferences of the actors and the availability of resources.

The existence of free and open market relations requires that certain conditions be maintained (Williamson, 1975, 1998; Eggertsson, 1990). Buyers and sellers must be able to engage in voluntary exchanges, acting as price takers. The goods or services must be substitutable across sellers such that there is a possibility for the buyer to switch to an alternative seller. There must be relatively open entry into and exit from the market. Buyers and sellers must have access to sufficient information to enable them to make rational choices. Some institutions, formal or informal, must provide for contract compliance, sanctions against default, and orderly dispute resolution to make certain that agreements are honored. Some institutions, formal or informal, are necessary to reduce transaction costs and thereby prevent buyers and sellers from having to engage in continuous renegotiation of the terms of exchange (Coase, 1937). Rights to the enjoyment of the benefits that flow from the control of assets, must be recognized and enforced, generally through private property conventions (Demsetz, 1967; Ely, 1992).

When these conditions are not met, markets may fail to function as optimal forums of exchange. If buyers are told, by the state or some other organization, what they can and cannot purchase among available goods and services, the market may fail. If the government through monopoly or monopsony practices artificially restricts the range or quantity of goods and services available, the market may fail. If entry or exit is artificially controlled, the market may fail. If the division of common pool resources is left exclusively to the designs of a particular subset of the common pool's appropriators, the market may fail (Hardin, 1968). If no adequate institutions exist to resolve disputes, the market may fail. If property rights are not respected, the market may fail (Alchian and Demsetz, 1973).

If public, non-rivalrous, non-substitutable public goods are divided among interested parties acting solely out of self-interest, the market may fail (Olson, 1971; Ostrom, 1990; Bromley, 1992). If public resources are used for private gain through bureaucratic rent-seeking, the market may fail (Krueger, 1974). In sum, there are many circumstances and conditions in which government organizations are necessary to ensure that the rules, standards, norms, and procedures of openness are maintained and enforced if markets are to function effectively.

Markets typically require governments – or some alternative organizations that serves a public purpose – to maintain competition and to overcome collective action dilemmas by discouraging free riding, opportunism, and inappropriate rent-seeking behavior. This is indeed one of the most basic explanations for the social compact. It is one of the most important underlying rationales for the very existence of government as an institution. Individuals voluntarily cede some measure of control over their lives to an outside authority, namely government, in order to establish equitable limits on how any given individual may act with respect to the interests of the community as a whole. There is a fundamental paradox in the role of the state in maintaining markets: a state that is powerful enough to control the instruments and mechanisms of public affairs is also powerful enough to abuse those instruments and mechanisms. If the state fails in its responsibilities, market distortion, anti-competitive arrangements, and official corruption may follow. The state may fail by either playing a role in the market that magnifies distortions or by failing to take steps to prevent other agents, such as monopolists and monopsonists, from defeating the market (Friedman, 1963).

If government plays a key role in the arrangements relating to domestic markets, it plays an even greater role in the arrangements relating to trade with external partners. Theorists speculate that governments originally came into being in order to protect communities from external threats and to ensure equitable arrangements in markets. But it was the search for foreign markets that historically played the key role in the empowerment of the modern state.

Mercantilism, the trade strategy that emerged among the European powers in the period 1400–1800, was a system of intense competition among many states whose trade policies were guided by the view that wealth and power were associated with the acquisition and retention of bullion as a source of wealth. Mercantilist states adopted policies aimed at accumulating bullion through maintaining a favorable balance of trade, through exploitative relationships with colonies, and through plunder. Imports were regarded as bad because they had to be paid for, which would cause the nation to lose specie to foreigners. Imports were also frowned upon because foreign goods might not be available in time of war. Mercantilists believed that taxing imports was justified as a way of creating jobs and income for the national population. Following mercantilist policy prescriptions, governments used all the means at their disposal to enhance their foreign trade posture. In seventeenth-century France, for instance, foreign minister Jean Baptiste Colbert used subsidies and tariff protection to encourage industry, while simultaneously building a large navy in support of commerce and colonization. In seventeenth-century England, the House of Lords approved an elaborate system of taxes and prohibitions on imports. The British Navigation Act of 1651 forbade importation of many goods unless carried in British ships.

By the beginning of the eighteenth century, mercantilist arguments gave way to capitalist free trade doctrines of Adam Smith, David Ricardo, and later theorists of free trade liberalism. Arguing that states could be seen in macroeconomic terms much as households could be seen in microeconomic terms, Smith argued against economic self-sufficiency and argued in favor of open trade among states. Ricardo contributed the concept of comparative advantage, demonstrating that an open trade order would benefit even those countries that did not have an absolute advantage in any particular good (Bhagwati, 2002).

The vast expansion of international trade brought about by free trade doctrines, imperial expansion, and market competition in the nineteenth century created the first truly global markets. These changes also brought about unprecedented prosperity. The changes, however, did not produce prosperity at equal levels in all regions of the globe that were affected by expanding world markets. Nor did these changes lead to conditions in which all states had equivalent opportunities to purse their economic interests in newly emerging global markets (Lijpart, 1966). The inequities of nineteenth-century markets led to the Marxist critique of market capitalism. The Marxists called for intervention in the economy in order to mitigate the social consequences of swings in the business cycle. Marxist criticism remained theoretical throughout the nineteenth century. It was only at the beginning of the twentieth century, with Russia's Bolshevik experiment, that the Marxist model was applied in practice. But Marxist theoretics and Marxist practices never quite came to seeing eye to eye on the role of the state. Critical Marxists theory maintained that the state would recede in importance, eventually withering away completely. Practical Marxist political leaders, in contrast, adopted policies that vastly empowered the state as a manager of last resort of all economic activity on the territory of the country.

Later in the twentieth century more limited forms of state interventionism in markets were championed by theoretical approaches that presumed the autonomy of the private sector but argued in favor of a more paternalistic posture on the part of the state. John Maynard Keynes argued in favor of enlightened intervention to fine-tune the economy with specific social and economic goals in mind. Keynes wanted to ameliorate unacceptable consequences of market failure, regardless of the causes of the failure.

By the late twentieth century, neo-mercantilist versions of state interventionism emerged that put the state in a leading position as a catalytic agent to leverage change in specific directions. Relying on export-led development strategies, the success of the "Asian Tigers" demonstrated that the state could play a role as the organizer of purposive economic development. By identifying preferred economic sectors, the state could be used to mobilize and concentrate resources in the form of directed educational programs, disguised subsidies, convenient banking practices, and other measures to magnify a comparative advantage for the purpose of capturing a specific market or market sectors.

Export-led neo-mercantilist strategies produced remarkable success in some cases. These hybrid economic development strategies often took the framework of the liberal model as a given, but then took liberties with the model by modifying particular policies to disproportionately advantage the state in particular markets or niches. Frequently, this implied violating basic principles of competition policy and *laissez faire* conditions. As Hilton Root has observed, in his analysis of the East Asian economic success stories, "industrial policy was practiced by a number of the high performers and most made subsidized and directed finance available to promote investment and infant industries" (Root, 1996: 4). In many of these countries the governments even went to the extent of reconfiguring the ownership structure of private firms. "These familiar tactics to promote strategic industries – avenues for rent seeking and bribe taking in most developing countries – were often effectively implemented in most of East Asia" (Root, 1996: 4).

Governments that relied upon state intervention found that there were trade-offs in the level and scope of state intervention. For instance, populist governments in Latin America stressed social stability and employment through subsidies, protectionist trade policies, and import substitution (Dornbush and Edwards, 1991). Yet in the 1970s and 1980s, many populist governments acquired insupportable debt as a result of trying to buy the political support of narrow urban coalitions by subsidizing consumption.

In the mid-1990s the luster of the Asian success stories faded following the Asian financial market crises. Such experiences called into question the paternalistic role of state interventionism. While the assumption had frequently been made that authoritarian forms of government are more efficient, empirical analysis showed that authoritarian systems were not more capable of achieving their economic goals than were democratic, participatory systems (Remmer, 1990). This led many analysts to the conclusion that economic interventionist strategies are a double-edged sword, cutting both ways. On the one hand, a capable state economic apparatus can serve as a catalytic lever for economic development. On the other hand, a capable state economic apparatus can turn its capacity toward self-service rather than toward public service. It is this ambivalence that led Root, in his analysis of East Asian success stories, to identify curbing the "predatory behavior of autocratic states" as "one of the major conundrums of political development" (Root, 1996: 4).

Today's globalization, characterized by instantaneous communication, highly mobile capital, and a well-developed infrastructure for transportation and movement of people, has created a qualitatively new environment for the relationship between markets and politics. On the one hand, globalization appears to diminish some traditional prerogatives of the state. An increasing proportion of most state economies is oriented toward foreign trade. Governments cannot, in most cases, exercise a controlling effect on foreign prices, suppliers, and relationships even if they desire to do this. So governments sometimes see globalization as eroding the traditional instruments of state power. On the other hand, it is clear that a globalized world does not imply a border-less and state-less world. The governments that have most enthusiastically and most successfully embraced changes in policy to integrate into world markets are those like China that tend see globalization as "state-enhancing" (Kim, 1999: 26). Successful globalization may hinge upon the state's ability to carry out key tasks. In other words, the state's role in the economy after globalization may be more narrowly defined than in the past, but it also may be more critical (Hirschman, 1972; Weber, 1979; Strange, 1988; Brada and Claudon, 1991; Dornbush, 1991; Przeworksi, 1991; Przeworski and Limongi, 1993; Diamond and Plattner, 1995; McFaul, 1995, 2001; Stiglitz, 1997, 2002; Haynes and Husan, 1998; Duquette, 1999; Olson, 2000; Glasser, 2001).

How are markets and politics related in the circumstances of globalization? We know that when markets are fully competitive, prices guide resource allocation. In such circumstances, free and open trade allows participating countries to benefit because trade leads them to specialize in activities that can be carried out comparatively efficiently. But many markets, particularly markets that extend by their nature over national borders, are highly structured and have disproportionately significant political effects. For instance, regional electric grids that span several national borders but are supplied from a power source in one country may link the consumers in several countries in mutual dependency in ways that create sensitive political relationships. Electric power consumers often cannot easily or costlessly choose alternative suppliers. They must rely on suppliers at least in the short run to bear in mind the public interest. When the supplier is located on the territory of a different sovereign state, public responsiveness can quickly become an issue of complicated international diplomacy.

In such circumstances, governments that otherwise would subscribe to free trade principles often point to the imperfections of markets to justify policies designed to shield the country from the consequences of market imperfections. Drawing attention to trade-related problems of severe unemployment, rigid wages, monopoly and oligopoly, or environmental pollution and other externalities, governments may propose modifications of trade policy to address difficulties. Rigid wages and high unemployment may fuel appeals for protectionism from foreign competition. Monopolies and oligarchies that control production may be offered as a rationale for establishing price controls and quota systems. Environmental pollution that imposes social costs not easily recoverable in the price of products may be offered as a rationale for introducing tariffs used to recapture revenue to offset the losses associated with social costs. In countries that have underdeveloped capital markets, protectionism may be promoted as a means to protect infant industries. The culturally homogenizing effects of global markets may be offered as a reason for restricting trade seen as disadvantageous to a country's culture or values. States that find themselves in trade arrears may seek to reduce imports through import substitution. If prices are distorted through past subsidies or protection, removing trade barriers may be offered as a means to bring prices back into equilibrium.

Seeking to avoid politically unpopular or at least highly visible actions, insecure political leaders without sound economic advice may seek to improve their situation through currency manipulation. For instance, a state may seek to finance a government deficit through currency overvaluation. An overvalued currency makes imports less attractive to domestic consumers. An overvalued currency tends to channel trade into narrow and more easily managed sectors.

It thus may appear to offer a solution to capital flight. However, there are great efficiency losses associated with currency overvaluation. The bureaucratic burden of maintaining strict currency controls can be expensive. It unavoidably creates an unfavorable climate for trade. Currency controls require strict regulation of financial transactions, imposing a heavy burden of monitoring and sanctioning. Well-connected parties with access to cheap, government-financed foreign exchange and import licenses may benefit greatly from this situation. These parties can be expected to lobby to maintain the situation despite great efficiency losses and the corresponding damage to the public interest. A policy of overvaluation creates a rationale for extending police sanctions even to the extent of replacing the goal of public safety with that of regulating private behavior. It can give rise to an incentive structure in which private parties have an interest in avoiding or evading the legal framework through various forms of side-payments and quasi-legal inducements. An overvalued currency also can be expected to lead to the depletion of foreign reserves that, in turn, can bring about pressures for severe import restrictions and, eventually, the collapse of the free trade policy.

Globalization implies achieving conformance with international standards and norms. This in turn means not only strengthening domestic market conditions but also conditions for foreign trade. Thus, in the context of globalization the goal of economic reform is simple: economic reform is designed to improve market conditions with respect to both domestic and external economic activity. Economic reform may seem like a technical and non-political undertaking. But economic reform hinges upon the will and capacity of the political system to carry out policy correctives.

Political reform

The goal of political reform is to improve the quality of political life. Political conditions seem to be best when markets are open and competitive. The insight that free market relationships are associated with democratic political practice is the cornerstone of traditional liberal democratic theory. Democracy is not possible without the fundamental freedom of individual choice. The freedom to choose in the private marketplace of goods in services is part and parcel of the freedom of choice in the public sphere of collective life (Hayek, 1960, 1972; Locke, 1690; Popper, 1971). Free market relationships create an environment for the competition of ideas by freeing the range of alternatives from the monopolistic control of entrenched interests, bureaucratic constituencies, and privileged interest groups. In an open political environment, policies gravitate not toward the protection of individual interests but rather toward the promotion of opportunities. Administrative bulwarks may emerge out of the defense of vested interests, but the aggregate effect of the process is to support general goals of fairness, openness, equality, and competition (Colomer, 2000).

The culture of open politics is a culture of fair play, stability, and tolerance. It is a culture of fair play because parties in transactions are viewed as equals. It is a culture of stability because people enter into exchanges with stable expectations about how their counterparts calculate and act. It is a culture of tolerance because differences of race, origin, language, and social station are unimportant to the success of the transaction. The parties enter into exchanges with their own benefit in mind. Ascribed qualities such as race, nationality, ethnicity, clan, color religion, or cosmetic features interfere with the search for benefit. Because ascriptive qualities play little role in the satisfaction of the individual's goals, people tend gradually to marginalize these qualities. Equal opportunity emerges naturally not because it is right, but because it is rational.

Liberalization is the transformation of authoritarian, oppressive, and exploitative political contexts into contexts of greater liberty and freedom of action. People around the world seek liberalization because it is intrinsically valuable and rewarding. Intelligent people want to make their own choices, chart their own destinies, and right their own wrongs. Freedom is a chance to be better, to be happier, to discover the limits of the human condition and, perhaps, to challenge whether those limits are fixed or malleable. From de Toqueville to Dahl, theorists have focused on the conditions and institutions of functioning democracy to discern the essential elements of liberal practice. Centuries of analysis, debate, dialogue, and dispute have compiled a rich analytical literature. Courts and legislatures have established a massive foundation of legislation and case law. Within the developed, Anglo-Saxon world, democratic institutions are well understood.

Democratic practice in the developed countries exhibits considerable institutional variety, but dissimilarities overshadow similarities (Haggard and Kaufman, 1975; Huntington, 1993; Hollifield and Jillson, 1999). In developed democracies the fundamental law of a society is its constitution. Many modern democracies have evolved with a three-branched government with a separation of powers among executive, legislative, and judicial powers, balanced through formal legal constraints stipulated in a written constitution and buttressed by widespread public support for the underlying principles and objectives of government (Almond and Powell, 1966). Limited government protects the competitive process through a separation of powers and through the countervailing influence of competing political parties, political constituencies, and interests groups (Dahl, 1989; de Tocqueville, 2000). Representative government reflects the popular will through a competitive electoral process. The rule of law subsumes all the participants under a single set of operating rules. Civil rights, including freedom of speech, assembly, association, and petition provide for the sanctity of individual thought and action and serve to strengthen the social compact. Civil control of the military, a free press and media, labor unions with the rights of collective bargaining, and free political association serve to strengthen civil initiative. Libraries have been written to chronicle and analyze how liberal institutions function in the advanced countries. These researches have led to a good comparative understanding of how these political institutions function in advanced countries around the world (Lijphart, 1984).

The uniformity of democratic practice in the developed world can easily lead us to expect that democratization in the underdeveloped world merely amount to adopting the institutions and practices so familiar from the developed world. Success in democratization, we might suppose, means progress along the lines of the historical development of Western, Anglo-Saxon democracies. Accordingly, democratization is equivalent to transplanting the successful political institutions of the developed world in the circumstances of the underdeveloped world. Moreover, the prevailing standards of democratic functioning may be used, according to this supposition, to determine to what extent a country has succeeded in the path toward democracy. A country's progress then can be gauged with respect to standard tests for democracy (Lijpart, 1984). Has a situation developed in which "the government can be changed by elections as opposed to one where elections are changed by the government?" (Lewis, 1996: 53). Has a situation developed in which "none of the major political actors, parties, or organized interests, forces, or institutions consider that there is any alternative to democratic processes to gain power, and ... no political institution or group has a claim to veto the action of democratically elected decision makers?" (Linz, 1990: 156). Has the country's civil society matured to the extent that civil initiative and civil development take place independently of the government's role within the society?[5] (Putnam, 1993).

When measured by these yardsticks, many developing countries fail to pass the key tests of democratic development. This may lead us to seek the explanation for these failures in the way in which the developing countries function. But there is another possibility. The failure of the developing countries to pass these tests also might lead us to ask whether these are the right tests of democratic development in the conditions of the developing world. All the advanced democracies share important institutional similarities, but this may not necessarily imply that liberal democratic development in the context of stable societies is the same process as democratization in the underdeveloped world. Moreover, democratization in the underdeveloped world may not be the same process as democratization in the post-communist world of sweeping institutional transformation and ideological revaluation.

There is a great deal of evidence to suggest that democratization in the developing world has unique features that cannot be ignored (Moore, 1966; Skocpol, 1979; Schumpeter, 1984; Pye, 1985; O'Donnell, Schmitter, and Whitehead, 1986; Migdal, 1988; Anspanger, 1989; Kohli, 1990; Sorensen, 1993; Smith, Acuna, and Gamarra, 1994; Young, 1994; Crawford, 1995; Ghadbian, Suleiman, and Entelis, 1997; Kim, 1999; Oh, 1999; Robinson *et al.*, 1999; Chao, 2000; Compton, 2000; Kienle, 2001; Lewis, 2001). Not all societies are alike. Not all societies share the cultural compatibility between abstract, impersonal Anglo-Saxon procedural formalism and the society's prevailing habits of thought and practise. In some societies political constituencies emerge from inter-group bargaining (Fox, 1993; Geddes, 1994; Glasser, 2001). In some societies the industrial sectors play a key role. In some societies the interests of agriculturalists play a key role in government policy (Moore, 1966; Huntington, 1969; Skocpol, 1979; Bates, 1981; Ranis and Mahmood, 1992; Van Atta, 1993). In some societies the constituencies internal to the government itself play a key role in the political process (LaPalombara, 1974; O'Donnell and Schmitter, 1986). In some societies the effect of deeply rooted cultural features tend to predominate over the influence of formal political institutions. Habits of thought and practice in Asia differ significantly from those of Europe and North America (McChesney, 1991, 1996; Wittfogel, 1957). A structural institution that functions in one way in Europe may function in very different ways in Asia (Pye, 1985; Kohli, 1990; Craumer, 1994; Maravall, 1997; Oh, 1999; Compton, 2000; Kienle, 2001; Lewis, 2001). These differences in circumstance exert important influences on the process of democratization.

Most liberal democracies emerged as a result of internal dynamics and compromises. But many democratizing societies, in contrast, are propelled toward political reform by forces outside themselves such as the demands of participation in international organizations. Many democratizing societies are undergoing changes by virtue of the circumstances in which they find themselves, not by choice. Those countries least likely to desire political reform, the most authoritarian and rigid countries, are those most likely to need it. Countries around the world have discovered, as Wayne Norman has put it, that despotism is "no longer acceptable even if democracy is not yet attainable" (Norman, 1993: 268). So these countries adopt political reform as inevitable even if it is not desirable from their point of view. Globalization is pressing upon societies the need to change rapidly to conform to the demands of a world that requires many qualities that are found only in democratic societies (O'Donnel *et al.*, 1986; Schmitter and Whitehead, 1986; Haggard, 1990; Helliwell, 1994; Diamond and Plattner, 1995; Haggard and Kaufman, 1995; Duquette, 1999; Glenn, 2001).

Political reform can emerge as a result of a variety of different motivations. Reform can be a response to widespread, popular pressures for change in the form of greater voice and participation. Such cases of bottom-up political reform have distinctive mechanisms. Reform may also be initiated and sustained from with the government itself. The dynamics of top-down political reforms are very different that grass roots reform movements. Finally reform may be initiated from the outside, either through the imposition of conditions from international organizations or other actors that sponsor the reform. Here too, the dynamics of democratization differ substantially from the other kinds of reform.

In cases of externally induced democratization, the state is likely to have an ambivalent relationship to political reform (Rodrik and Fernandez, 1991). Heads of state and government officials in most emerging countries embrace economic reform as offering economic liberation, but they share no such enthusiasm for political reform. State leaders and government officials endorse political reform, if they endorse it all, only with strong reservations. Reform is supported to the extent that it promises simplification of complex circumstances, but not to the extent that it diminishes the legitimacy of the standing government. Political reform programs, therefore, tend not to be pursued by governments simply because the reforms are desired, but only because it becomes apparent that conformance with international standards of political practice is a requirement of full participation in the international community. Reforms that originate outside the country may give rise to questions regarding the motives of the reform agenda. In assessing the reasons for the failure of foreign initiated reform programs William Easterly has argued that the failure of reform is often a failure of implementation. The most common recipes for economic growth – providing foreign aid, investing in technology, promoting technical capacity of government officials, fostering education, controlling population growth, and making aid loans and then forgiving those loans on the condition that the reforms were adopted – require host country ownership of the reforms in order for implementation to be successful. Easterly argues that the economic principles that lie at the basis of the economic reforms are frequently not implemented in the practice of the reforms (Easterly, 2001).

Governments have even fewer incentives to take ownership of reforms that are designed to transform the government itself. For this reason, implementation of technical assistance in externally induced political reforms has been very limited. Structural economic reforms often are large in scale, take place over a long period of time, and have substantial effects. Externally induced political reforms, in contrast, in the areas of government reform, political party development, legislative reform, judicial independence, human rights programming, media and labor union independence, and civic organizations tend to be small in scale and take place in limited time frames. It is extremely rare for the large multilateral international donors directly to support such political reforms. These political reform programs are typically supported by national foreign aid agencies, by philanthropic organizations, or by non-governmental organizations that receive pass-through financial support from the major donors.

In the post-communist world, democratization takes place at a rate of institutional change significantly greater than that characteristic of democratic development in the established liberal democracies (Bunce, 1995; L. Anderson, 1999; R. Anderson *et al.*, 2000). To a much greater extent than in typical authoritarian transitions, post-communist "reform from scratch" involves wholesale redefinition of the formal institutions of the society (Fish, 1996). A transformation on this scale inevitably involves severe systemic shocks (Murrell, 1993; Aslund, 1995; Elster, 1998). Such vast political and economic transformation, institutionalist theories would suggest, could not take place without disruption and disarray (Coase, 1937, 1960; March, 1989; Ostrom, 1990; Bromley, 1992; Wade, 1992).

In post-communist societies ample empirical evidence suggests that the tempo, mechanisms, values, and goals of post-communist transition are different than those of the more common cases of democratization (Rogowski, 1987; Bova, 1991; Roeder, 1993; Terry, 1993; Eckstein *et al.*, 1998; Bunce, 1999a,b; Colton, 2000; Easter, 2000; Gill, 2000; Sperling, 2000; Glenn, 2001; Reddaway and Glinski, 2001; Fish, 1998). There is ample empirical evidence that the interplay between social forces such as ethnicity and ethnic-based nationalism (Beissinger, 2002) or religious sectarianism are different than those of the more common cases of democratization (Bennigsen and Wimbush, 1986; Carrère D'Encausse, 1989; Esposito, 1992; Dawisha and Parrott, 1997b). Recent research points to the importance of rules and institutions in structuring post-communist outcomes. For instance, Steven Fish has argued that the most robust explanation or relationship between economic and political change is the outcome of the first competitive election (Fish, 1998). Pauline Jones Luong has shown how differences in electoral rules in Central Asian countries can explain differences in electoral outcomes. Luong's analysis shows that the jockeying for position of different constituencies in specific conditions resulted in quite dissimilar electoral outcomes in countries that are quite similar in other respects (Luong, 2002).

Some have argued that the tempo of reform has to be rapid to assure that the changes are institutionalized before opponents succeed in undercutting the reforms (Balcerowicz, 1995). But post-communist political reform has taken place in the context of an extraordinary level of structural adjustment. Price liberalization and privatization, for instance, have had the effect of disenfranchising large sectors of a country economically and socially, at the same time that political liberalization offered these same disenfranchised the ballot box to express their resentment at the cause of their immiseration (Przeworski, 1991). In these circumstances, political reforms are often apt to lead to conflicting tendencies, at least for a period of time (Blanchard, 1997; Aslund, 2000; Brada, 1996). Economic change has often empowered constituencies or otherwise strengthened political processes that have often been at odds with democratization (Bova, 1991; Hellman, 1998; Sperling, 2000; Hough and Armacost, 2001; McFaul, 2001; Reddaway and Glinski, 2001). In her work *Balkan Tragedy*, Susan Woodward argued that the IMF's stress on liberalization programs in Yugoslavia in the 1980s and early 1990s had the effect of rewarding the country's more advanced regions and punishing the more backward regions, thereby driving a wedge between the more and the less successful regions of the country at the same time that the IMF's support for government decentralization weakened the cohesion of state (Woodward, 1995). The failure of reforms in post-communist societies has led some to conclude that top-down economic reforms may not be sustainable without broader, supporting political reforms (Gill, 2000).

A last caveat. It should also be noted that democratization in the post-communist should not be expected to follow a course identical to democratization in authoritarian countries of the underdeveloped world. It is not realistic to define democratization in the turbulent circumstances of post-communist disintegration, as merely "a matter of progressive recognition and inclusion of different groups in the political life of society" (Dryzek, 1996: 486). Such a definition of democratization reflects more about the societal assumptions of the researcher and the convenience of measuring available data than about the process of democratization in transitional societies. Nor is it realistic to propose that post-communist democratization simply equals greater political institutionalization, or higher levels of political participation (Huntington, 1969).

Separating cause and effect in the policy cycle of economic and political reform requires some way of determining at any given point in time the status of structural reform with respect to political reform. Economists have developed highly sophisticated tools for measuring economic output and, to a lesser extent, for measuring economic functioning. Students of political reform have fewer clear indicators. By and large, measuring success at political reform efforts is still highly inexact, qualitative, and dependent upon the type of observation and attention to institutional detail that case studies provide.

The argument of the book

This book addresses a question of both practical and theoretical importance: what effect have economic reform efforts had on political liberalization in the countries of Central Asia? To answer this question, we need a means of assessing progress in economic reform and political reform. While the concepts of structural reform and political change have played key roles in analysis for many years, analysts have only recently attempted to standardize measurement of these phenomena. Most structural reforms involve changing agencies, changing their powers and authorities, changing their practices and tendencies, and making sure that they do what they are intended to do and not other things. Counting the number of changes in names of offices, the number of laws adopted, the number of new standard operating procedures established, and so on, is not likely to get to the core of structural reform. At the same time, simple, formalistic qualitative descriptions of governance reforms are also not adequate to provide measurements of the actual extent to which reforms have been undertaken. Thus, standard quantitative measures may not be fully appropriate for assessing the status of reforms across differing political systems and political cultures. Spurred on by the recognition in the international donor community that "governance matters," scholars and policy analysts have recently put substantial effort into developing comparable and replicable measures of governance involving both quantitative and qualitative dimensions. For quantitative measures this book relies heavily on the Governance Matters Database compiled by the World Bank's Development Research Group.[6]

The logic of the argument presented in this book is straightforward. Chapter 2 describes the general context of Central Asia in terms of the administrative, economic, and political legacy of the Soviet period. If one conceives of post-communist reform as a "transition" from point A to point B, the Soviet system represents the departure point A. Chapter 2 also outlines the post-communist reform agenda and broadly defines the qualitative and quantitative measures used for purposes of comparison and analysis. Chapters 3–7 present detailed case studies of the five Central Asian countries. Each case study addresses the simple question: what effect has economic reform had on political change? The case studies start with a country profile, that is, with a description of the broad features of the country. Each case study has a section that describes the country's policies of economic and political reform, analyzing the structural reform policies that were implemented, and evaluating the political impact these policies had. The analysis in all cases makes reference to the effects of reform in terms of statistical data describing outcomes. The data is included in the form of an appendix to each chapter. Chapter 8 summarizes the case studies in terms of the effects of market reform on politics and the effects of politics on market reform.

2 Post-communist structural reform

Structural reform, in the broadest sense, is anything that happens within a country that allows the country to participate more effectively in the global economy. Structural reform entails a process by which a country's institutions, policies, and practices are brought into line with prevailing international standards. The purpose of structural reform is to create a favorable policy environment for accountable, transparent economic policy with well-defined public and private sectors working in mutually reinforcing ways to promote prosperity and sustainable development. Countries undertake structural reform programs because they realize that full participation in the global economy requires policy conformance with international standards.

Structural reform is a change in structures that is designed to bring about a change in functions (North, 1981). Some structural reform measures are narrowly economic in their purpose; others are more broadly oriented at improving governance, that is, oriented at improving the policy environment to facilitate economic activity. Some structural reform measures are intended to change the nature of the government itself in ways that will bring about desired economic policy changes. Policy changes alter the status quo, producing winners and losers. As a consequence, all policy changes influence the balance of constituencies in a society. Moreover, economically oriented structural changes and politically oriented structural changes are linked in terms of reciprocal effects. These reciprocal relations constitute policy cycles.

Policy reform packages include economic and political measures. These can be analytically separated and usefully analyzed in isolation from one another, but their broad social and developmental impact is not ordered chronologically. Implementation of reform packages may in some cases involve sequencing, but in general economic and political reform policies are adopted simultaneously. Policy cycles are loops of reciprocal influences. When legislatures adopt privatization laws they affect incomes of certain individuals and groups. Individuals and groups lobby to influence legislatures to adopt, change, or alter the implementation of privatization laws. Separating cause from effect, input from output is often difficult. But to understand the policy cycle, it is necessary to start somewhere. No social setting is ever without institutional context. Understanding the institutional context is the departure point for any analysis of policy cycles. We begin the analysis of policy cycles in the post-communist world by analyzing the initial conditions of the post-communist transition.

Communist management legacy

The "Great Soviet experiment" was the most sweeping attempt in history to create a utopian, rationally organized, teleological, state-less, classless, laterally organized, color-blind, internationalist, collectivist society. It was based on principles of an official ideology that specified society's goals, emphasized the primacy of production for use rather than profit, sought the equitable distribution of income, and implemented the collective ownership of property. The Soviet experiment, its early proponents maintained, would free society from the vicissitudes of the business cycle by creating cooperative production. It would free society from bureaucracy and from all forms of organizational formalism. It would free society from economic exploitation by removing the profit motive. It would free society from the sources of ethnic enmity by doing away with socio-economic disparities that gave rise to ethnic competition.

In practice, the Soviet experiment worked out differently than its designers intended and expected. The official Soviet ideology became an intellectual straitjacket. The individual became the ward of the state and the state became the ward of the communist party. Incomes were broadly equalized but at low levels. The management of all the society's resources was placed in the hands of the state. Industrial production came to be driven by the iron law of incremental increases, seemingly creating a system of production for production's sake rather than for either use or profit. Ethnic animosity was diminished but primarily through suppression. The fusion of political and economic control led to mismanagement of resources on a historically unprecedented level. The Soviet economy was endemically involved in inefficient use of resources and even, in its later years, systematically promoted wealth-destroying activities. But what was perhaps most striking about the experiment was that the bureaucracy that was possibly created during Soviet socialism was probably the most extensive Leviathan yet devised by mankind. The entire society was conceived of as one vast bureaucratic organism with Moscow – the "center" – at its core.

The Soviet economy was referred to as a "command economy." This concept was suggested by the importance of central planning, centralized decision-making, and the "top-down" quality of the economic control that was exerted. This description was probably useful for those who thought of central planning as a control-optimization process that began at the center and radiated outward. From the perspective on those who were situated on the radians, however, the command aspect of the system was much less salient that the requisition aspect. In order to draw attention to their needs, managers developed an array of stratagems and mechanisms that could direct the allocative priorities of the system in their direction. From this point of view, it is better to think of this system as a "requisition economy."

Property held in the hands of the state did not become everyone's property – as the Marxist theoreticians said it would – it became no one's property (Schroeder, 1988). As the countries of Eastern Europe bolted the Soviet bloc in the late 1980s, criticism of the formal ideology within the USSR mounted. The principle of state ownership and management, at least in theory, was abandoned in favor of the market. All goods and services, previously treated in terms of distribution and allocation procedures as "public goods," were reclassified. This posed a vexing practical question: "what services and goods could be quickly privatized and what would remain in the hands of the government?" (Shliefer and Vishny, 1995).

It has long been apparent that the centralized Soviet system involved inner compromises and agreements that permitted the system to function. As Merle Fainsod research on the Smolensk archives illustrated, the Soviet system created patron and client relations that were relatively resilient to change (Fainsod, 1958). Jerry Hough's research on industrial managers in the Soviet system illustrated the circularity of power that reinforced the system (Hough, 1969, 2001). With the passage of years, the Soviet system became less capable of delivering sufficient benefits through the patron–client relations and grew increasingly inflexible. Donna Bahry analyzed this evolution, showing how the hyper-centralized economic planning system eventually resulted in bureaucratic compartmentalization, ossification, and an inability to respond to the challenges of change (Bahry, 1987). At the system's center, Moscow, a fixation with control eventually developed: there was a sense that "if control is relaxed, the situation will deteriorate" (Pchelintsev, 1989: 2). This stimulated a counterproductive search for absolute control. As Bahry summarized it, "the proliferation of central controls led to an erosion of control" (Bahry, 1987: 163) and eventually resulted in what Gorbachev referred to as "impotent centralism" (Gorbachev, 1988: 1). To the extent that this description was true in the Russian areas of the USSR, it was even more so in many of the outlying areas. As Gorbachev opined toward the end of the USSR, "for years individuals and even whole territories" in Central Asia "were outside government control" (Gorbachev, 1988: 1).

As Mikhail Gorbachev's effort to introduce reforms gathered steam in the late 1980s, it became clear that the Soviet system was resistant to incremental change. Janos Kornai described the Soviet model as being a self-contained system of ideas, resistant to criticism through continual self-vindication and, therefore, resistant to reform based upon that criticism. Like a house built of bricks, reform removes the bricks from this structure. In such circumstances, Kornai argued, "reform destroys the coherence of the classical system and proves incapable of establishing a new order in its place." Kornai spoke of reforms as unleashing elements that had no natural affinity. "The Party proclaims 'glasnost' but instead of showing gratitude," Kornai argued, "people dig up all the tragedy and injury they have undergone, for which they hold the party and system responsible" (Kornai, 1992: 571).

Dissatisfaction with the Soviet system led to economic crisis within the USSR. The crisis discredited the Marxist model. Moreover, it reinforced widespread dissatisfaction among policy analysts and political leaders of what came to be viewed as excessive state controls over markets. The Soviet collapse took place at a time when many critics of the state's role in national economies were already arguing for scaling back the bureaucratic reach of the state in order to unleash fundamental economic forces. In an effort to discourage economic abuses of power by the state, many critics of state-led economies argued for a state reduced in size and capacity. A minimalist state, in the view of supporters of this approach, would be less likely to abuse its powers in the markets precisely because its capacity to exercise influence in markets would be limited. Downsizing the state, the minimalists argued, could create or restore competition, prevent abuse of public office, and reduce the risk of the appropriation of public goods for private gain (Savas, 1987).

The Soviet economic crisis culminated in the collapse of the USSR. During autumn 1991 waves of escalating political crises engulfed the country. By early December 1991, following independence votes in Ukraine and Kazakhstan, the top leaders of the three western Slavic republics signed an agreement that claimed to abolish the USSR. A short time later, on December 21, 1991, former communist part chiefs of eleven of the fifteen republics of the USSR gathered in the Kazakhstan capital of Almaty, then still known as Alma-Ata, in a dramatic meeting to decide what to do about the collapsing Soviet Union.[1] The outcome of this meeting was the "Alma-Ata Declaration." The Alma-Ata Declaration announced that the Union of Soviet Socialist Republics would "henceforth cease to exist." The Alma-Ata Declaration also established a loose coordinating structure called the "Commonwealth of Independent States" (CIS) (Gleason, 1992).

At the time of the breakup of the USSR, the five states of Central Asia shared many cultural, structural, and institutional similarities (Schuyler, 1876; Park, 1957; Wheeler, 1964; Allworth, 1967, 1973; Becker, 1968; Rywkin, 1974; Bacon, 1980; Lubin, 1984; Akiner, 1986, 1992; Wimbush, 1986; Rumer, 1989, 2000; Fierman, 1991; Akchurin, 1992; Gleason and Buck, 1993; Banuazizi and Weiner, 1994; Hiro, 1994; Hopkirk, 1994; Massell, 1994; Haghayeghi, 1995; Kubicek, 1995; Pomfret, 1995; Sagdeev and Eisenhower, 1995; Hunter and Broxup, 1996; McChesney, 1996; Dawisha and Parrott, 1997a; Gleason, 1997b; Kaser, 1997; Jonson, 1998; Kasenov, 1998; Solnick, 1998; Roy, 2000; Rashid, 2001; Weinthal, 2002). The states had similar and in some cases common cultural traditions and shared a common *lingua franca*, the Russian language. All the states had the same communist management legacy. All the states had specialists trained in similar intellectual traditions and bureaucracies accustomed to working in similar ways. All the states had economies specialized to the production of primary commodities. All the five states underwent a wrenching withdrawal from the Soviet system of trade and commerce. All the Central Asian states pursued liberalization following the path taken by Russia and were highly conscious of the Russian liberalization experience, both good and bad (Brada *et al.*, 1989; Pryor, 1991; Schmitter and Karl, 1994; Åslund, 1995, 2001; Boycko, Shleifer, and Vishny, 1995; Lavigne, 1995; Leitzel, 1995; Brady, 1999; Braguinsky and Yavlinsky, 2000).

While there were important similarities among the states, there were also important differences. The states were quite different in terms of their national resource endowments, connections to foreign markets, and government strategies. For instance, agriculture makes up a large proportion of employment in all the Central Asian states but makes a strikingly different contribution to the overall gross domestic product in the states. In Kazakhstan, Turkmenistan, and Tajikistan, for instance, agriculture was responsible for less than 10 percent of the country's GDP. Yet in Kyrgyzstan agriculture made up more half of the country's GDP. In Uzbekistan agriculture made up 31 percent of the country's GDP and farm employment played a major role in the economy.

Another important factor differentiating the countries was their export dependencies. All the countries had substantial dependence on a particular commodity or group of commodities; gas in Turkmenistan, oil and metals in Kazakhstan, cotton in Uzbekistan and Tajikistan. Commodity-dependent export economies are quite common in the developing world. There are many examples of oil-exporting and monocrop economies that reflect the dominance of a particular sector or cluster of sectors. Yet in Central Asia there were many cases in which the country's dependence was upon a small cluster of producers. For instance, nearly 40 percent of Tajikistan's GDP came from a single factory, the Tursunzade aluminum factory. The effects of such a concentration of potential revenue upon the country's decision-making with respect to foreign policy were immediately apparent.

Wide agreement existed on the necessity of post-communist governments to undertake domestic structural reform and liberalization as key elements in the transition to international standards. But not everyone agreed on the best mix of foreign and domestic policies for attaining these objectives. Two contrasting approaches dominated the debate; what might be called the open competition approach and what might be called the guiding-state approach. The open competition approach was often referred to as the "Washington consensus," reflecting that fact that the approach was widely supported by the analysts and policy makers associated with the international financial institutions, most of which were headquartered in Washington. The open market approach dominated the structural reform programs developed for and adopted in most developing countries in recent years. The guiding-state approach was more varied. This approach was championed by those who favored state intervention in the economy on theoretical grounds, as well as those who favored liberalization at a tempo that was determined by the success of reforms in terms of output criteria (Haynes and Husan, 1998).

The open competition approach argued that the best structural reforms are those that most rapidly and effectively free fundamental economic forces to play their natural roles in an economy. The open competition approach argued that a rapid shift to privately owned assets, monetarization of the economy, trade liberalization, currency convertibility, and government structural reforms were necessary preconditions to establishing rational market incentives (Guerrieri, 1995). The set of policies associated with this approach typically involved cutting government budgets and subsidies, privatizing some previously public operations, raising interest rates, opening national economies to foreign imports, corporations and capital, and increasing exports of raw materials or goods produced with labor made relatively cheap by these policies.

The guiding-state approach differed in maintaining that incremental reform measures were viewed as more likely to lead to rational industrial and agricultural restructuring than would an allocation of resources that was structured by forces operating in the existing imperfect markets. The guiding-state approach argued in favor of a phased and gradual introduction of reform-oriented measures, emphasizing incentive selectivity, dynamic technical efficiency, and government guidance throughout the process of change. In many respects, the open competition and guiding-state prescriptions sought to arrive at the same destination. Both approaches ultimately sought to develop government fiscal responsibility and encourage disinflationary policies, price liberalization, trade liberalization, currency stabilization, and foreign investment attraction. But the respective recommendations of these two approaches differed regarding the style and speed of transition.

Variations of these two approaches are illustrated by the national macroeconomic development policies that emerged in Central Asia in the period 1991–2001. Prominent political leaders of all the countries of Central Asia identified market-based economies and democratic governments as their desired goals in the post-communist transition process. Yet the development paths adopted by the countries were significantly different. Kazakhstan's and Kyrgyzstan's foreign policy postures illustrate a version of the open competition approach. Kazakhstan was an early supporter of the transition to international standards. Kazakhstan's President Nursultan Nazarbaev was among the most articulate of post-Soviet leaders in explaining that the rejection of communism and the adoption of international standards was "simply common sense" (Nazarbaev, 1996: 19). In contrast, Uzbekistan's and Turkmenistan's foreign policy postures illustrate exaggerated forms of a guiding-state approach. Tajikistan's approach lies somewhere between these two. Judging from Tajikistan government statements, the desire to reform and accommodate to international standards has been strong and continuous, but the capacity to implement these goals has been largely absent.[2]

The governments of developing countries broadly have accepted the proposition that domestic policy reform and the transition to a liberal trade order offer great benefits (North, 1981; Onuf, 1989). But some governments in developing countries have sought to manage structural reform to avoid what they saw as unsatisfactory elements (Krasner, 1985; Strange, 1988; Tilly, 1992). Even governments that have enthusiastically attempted to carry out structural reform programs have often found it difficult to initiate and sustain reform.

There are many reasons why governments retreat from a commitment to an open trade environment. The most common is the tendency for governments to live beyond their means (Rogowski, 1987; Thomas and Nash *et al.*, 1991). Poor capacity to control expenditure, collect revenue, and manage debt can lead to fiscal deficits. Large fiscal deficits imply an increase in the tax burden. Tax increases are highly visible and frequently unpopular. Given these considerations, governments may chose to surreptitiously address deficits through policies that are not as visible and not as unpopular as fiscal austerity. Some governments have sought to give the appearance of adopting reforms when actually avoiding genuine structural changes. It is just this kind of concern that moved Clifford Gaddy to question whether earlier stages of Russia's transition constituted an institutional transformation – and thus a permanent change – or whether there was only a superficial form of "virtual transition" in which the true underlying principles and values were significantly different than those of most capitalist societies (Gaddy and Ickes, 1998; Breslauer *et al.*, 2001).

It is also important to note that the states of Central Asia exist in a security environment as well as in a development environment. Security considerations often took precedence in decisions regarding development strategies. Kazakhstan, as heir to a substantial portion of the USSR nuclear weapons capability at the time of independence, had certain advantages in its diplomatic interactions with European and North American countries. Uzbekistan and Tajikistan, however, inherited the legacies of lawlessness and underdevelopment that resulted from a decade long civil war in Afghanistan. As the Central Asian states began to respond to the conditions and constraints of transition, reflecting their leadership priorities and cultural priorities, exploiting their comparative economic advantages, and conscious of guarding their newfound independence in an insecure regional context, they adopted significantly different development strategies.

Anatomy of structural reform

The ways in which countries come to the realization that they need to adopt structural reforms differ (Vagel, 1998; Van Bergeij and Sinderen, 1999). Some countries realize that success in economic development requires that their policy framework be compatible with the prevailing policy framework in the international community, even if differences exist on particular policies. Even those countries that recognize they need to undertake reforms are frequently not aware of the specific steps that they need to take or, even if they are aware, they are usually not prepared for a variety of reasons to take those steps without external assistance. The realization that a country needs to adopt a structural reform program may be one in which, as Joseph Stiglitz has argued, "a few players – the finance, commerce and trade ministries, closely linked to certain financial and commercial interests – dominate the scene" (Stiglitz, 2002: 21–2).

In practice, structural reform programs are usually undertaken with the help of – and sometimes at the not so diplomatically disguised insistence of – the world's major international financial institutions, or IFIs. In the case of countries in financial crisis, the decision to adopt a structural reform program may be forced upon it by circumstances far beyond its control. But even in these cases, the structural reform program continues to be the property of the country itself.

While it may be the case that the elements of a country's structural reform program may be imported, or even imposed, from an IFI, the program is implemented within the country and by the country itself. The impact of the program will be felt locally.[3]

The world's major IFIs include the International Monetary Fund (IMF), the World Trade Organization, the World Bank, and the regional multilateral development banks such as the Asian Development Bank, the European Bank for Reconstruction and Development, the Inter-American Development Bank, and the African Development Bank[4] (Culpepper, 1997). The IMF plays a lead role among the IFIs. The IMF's mandate, while originally focused on currency stabilization, has extended over the years of its existence to general macroeconomic reform issues. The IMF's mission is typically seen as logically primitive to loan programs of multilateral institutions and to the provision of technical assistance through national foreign aid agencies with the exception of humanitarian aid and disaster relief. The IMF also plays a leading role in establishing the conventional wisdoms of development economics (Stiglitz, 1997, 2000). The professional ethic of the IMF has had a direct impact on that of the World Bank and other major multilateral donor institutions.

Other important IFIs play a supporting role in structural reform programs. This group includes such organizations as the UN Conference on Trade and Development (UNCTAD), the World Customs Union (WCU), the United Nations Drug Control Programme (UNDCP), and the United Nations Environment Programme (UNEP). The IFIs are international public sector organizations owned and operated by nation-states for the collective benefit of the international community. The IFIs are sometimes collectively referred to as the international donor community, because their primary purpose is public assistance, not profit. The guiding objective of reform programs consists of making strategic changes to improve the country's ability to participate in the international market while protecting key social values. This general objective is transformed into action through the adoption of specific steps.

The international financial organizations have carried out many programs of reform. The research and project implementation experience of these organizations serves, therefore, in a *de facto* sense to provide the authoritative statement of reform program components. IFI sponsored structural reform programs usually consist of a number of elements, comprising phased recommendations and actions designed to bring about policy improvement.

A reform program typically begins with an assessment. The assessment is followed by analysis. The analysis prescribes a reform agenda. The IFI sponsor then undertakes to negotiate an official reform agenda with the host country government. If this step is successful, an official reform program, in some form or another, will be adopted by the host country and approved by the IFI. The official reform program, usually formalized in a memorandum of understanding, will consist of a package of reform measures that the country agrees to undertake and a commitment on the part of the IFI sponsor to cooperate in the program, through providing technical assistance or material assistance or some combination of both. The agreement may include other parties, either other IFIs or other non-governmental organizations. If the parties agree, the IFI then undertakes to cooperate with the host country and the other program partners in the process of implementation of the program. At some point in the process of implementation, the program will be evaluated. The cycle of interaction among the IFI, the host country, and the other partners is ongoing. Structural reform is not a discrete event or series of acts; it is a dynamic process of learning and change that can be time consuming and can require flexibility on the part of all parties as situations evolve.

The first step in implementing an official structural reform program begins with an assessment of the country's internal and external sectors. This assessment may be carried out by the government itself or by an IFI, but it is usually best done as a collaborative effort on the part of both the government and a major IFI. Following the assessment, the IFI staff analysts, working in conjunction with the country staff analysts, will generate initial proposals for institutional and policy reform. Macroeconomic functioning is considered to be at the core of the IFI package of proposed changes, but microeconomic, local governance, and even non-economic factors that might impact substantially on the success of the proposed policies also may be included.

The product of the assessment is usually a package of interrelated policy correctives designed to improve both the external and internal policy environment. Improvements in the external policy environment are designed to enhance the country's ability to reap the gains of trade and enable access to foreign capital. Policies may be proposed to improve the country's fiscal situation, reduce poverty, steward natural resources, and to widen access to public services. Improvements in the internal policy environment may be included to improve the efficiency and equity of government functioning and to improve regulatory and oversight capacities with respect to the maintenance of a policy environment for private economic activity. Measures may be included to increase the predictability of government policies, strengthen the protection of property rights, establish fairness in tax administration, reduce the presence of corruption, and increase access to finance. Measures may be included to encourage the government to live within its means by avoiding unfunded fiscal deficits that encourage irresponsible borrowing. Measures may be included to stabilize the banking system and the currency. Measures may be included to protect the mobility of capital while creating conditions to prevent capital flight. Measures may be included to minimize distortions in markets by eliminating unnecessary regulation that protects particularlist interest rather than the public interest.

In practice the typical sequence of events in the implementation of a structural reform program goes as follows. An IFI assessment mission will visit the host country, conduct courtesy meetings with political officials and identify country staff counterparts. Then the IFI country team, working in close collaboration with the host government staff counterparts, will draw up a draft memorandum based on the assessment and on proposed recommendations. The proposals will be discussed with both the government and the other members of the international donor community. A policy memorandum will then be prepared. The government will then review the policy memorandum. If the government accepts the policy memorandum, the government will then submit this memorandum to the IFI as the basis of the government's official reform program. The policy memorandum will typically reflect an assessment of the current situation, a set of priorities for policy reform, and requests with respect to specific forms and levels of IFI assistance. The government's reform program will typically be stated in the forms a policy matrix with an implementation timetable complete with benchmarks that will be used to gauge progress toward the achievement of the program's goals. If the government agrees to undertake the reform, the program is then handed over to the government and it is henceforth referred to as the "government's reform program."

The reform agenda

When structural reform programs are implemented they introduce changes to the rules, policies, procedures, enforcement mechanisms, and other public institutions that support market transactions. How do these reforms impact on the broader political system outside the sphere of market-oriented institutions?[5] For the purposes of this analysis, we analyze structural reform programs in terms of three broad arenas of activity: (1) core fiscal and monetary reform programs; (2) programs designed to improve capacity through policy correctives and capacity building in governance and administration; and (3) the broader elements of governmental and democratic reform (see Figure 2.1).

Elements of fiscal and monetary policy reform
- Fiscal and monetary policy
- Privatization and price liberalization
- Trade and investment
- Banking, finance, and financial markets

Elements of governance and administrative policy reform
- Constitutional, legal, and regulatory policy
- Legislative, executive, and judicial policies
- Transparency and integrity policy
- Regional administrative policy

Elements of governmental reform
- Public participation and openness
- Election policy
- Civil and human rights
- Political stability and support

Figure 2.1 Arenas of structural reform.

These three arenas are not necessarily ordered chronologically, although there is normally some sequencing of specific reform activities. A national currency may be introduced, for instance, prior to banking reform legislation. The banking reform may be introduced prior to the financial markets legislation. In specific reform activities, sequencing may be crucial, but in broad compass, activities within the three broad arenas take place simultaneously. There cannot be banking reform if the constitution prohibits it. There cannot be a constitution supporting banking reform if there is no legislature that can legitimately adopt a constitution. There cannot be a legislature unless there is some mechanism for selecting representatives, and so on. Thus for our purposes, all structural reform activities are conceptualized not in terms of "phases" or "stages" – which would suggest a chronological ordering – but rather in terms of "arenas." Constitutional change, something that we identify as in the second arena, must take place in ways that are consistent with the financial regulatory change in the first arena. At the same time, changes in legislative and electoral practice, something we identify as in the third arena, must take place at the same time as financial regulatory change within the first arena.

A country's economic development hinges above all on the financial circulatory system of the society. Successful structural reform frees the financial resources of the society, allowing financial resources to flow from areas of lesser importance to areas of higher importance. It is natural, therefore, that in order to spur a moribund economy into action, structural reform packages start with the goal of kick-starting the country's financial circulatory system. The immediate primary arena of any structural reform package is directed specifically toward financial rejuvenation. The second arena of structural reform is focused on improving the quality of the country's public administration and public management in order to ensure that the circulation of financial resources continues to benefit the public interest. The third arena focuses on what may be referred to broadly as democratization, that is, those changes that are designed to bring about desired levels of public participation, openness, and political satisfaction.

The first major arena is fiscal and monetary reform. The key elements of fiscal and monetary policy include fiscal and monetary policy, price liberalization and privatization, trade and investment measures, and banking and financial markets. Macroeconomic institutional reform affecting foreign policies usually involves the adoption of institutions, policies, and practices that will support currency operations, financial operations, customs operations, and policy improvement that will support foreign trade and improve the domestic business environment for both domestic and foreign enterprises.[6] Governance measures often also include reform of the treasury system; the establishment of a single independent auditing agency to control the efficiency of public finances and eliminate redundant inspection rights; establishment of control over quasi-fiscal operations of the central bank; prevention of unjustified intervention by public officials in the operation of private enterprises; and public procurement reform.

The purpose of a national currency is to allow the central economic planners and bank managers a measure of control over the economic activity of the country and to provide a medium of exchange to promote domestic commerce and foreign trade. To be an effective medium for commerce, the currency must be tradable so that buyers and sellers can exchange their goods and services with knowledge that the currency is a reliable medium for exchanging things of value. The marketability of the currency depends upon a system that allows purchasers of the currency to buy it and sell it in accordance with their currency needs. This, in turn, requires that the banking system is arranged in such a way that banks may settle their accounts among themselves and foreign banks on a regular basis, moving the currency of the country and of other countries in response to the demands of the currency users. Governments can spend more than they bring in only if they operate in deficit, borrow, or influence the value of their currency. Borrowing is expensive. Altering the value of currency is risky. So estimation of future revenue is a key function in the effort to operate a responsibly financed government.

One of the most important elements in the transition is the transfer of property rights from the government to the private sector. If property belongs to everyone – as is the case under communism – it is often treated as if it belongs to no one. Establishing private property rights is therefore a first step in the transition to the economically rational use of resources.

The advantages of an open trade order are widely recognized among countries undergoing transition from state socialism to new forms of economic organization. Yet developing a policy framework that establishes national sovereignty while at the same time promotes international integration has proved challenging. A liberal or open trade order is characterized by an absence of non-economic factors influencing trade. Non-economic factors include any governmental or non-governmental policies or actions that inhibit the ability of individuals or firms to pursue mutually advantageous transactions as defined by their individual preference and interests.

An efficient, transparent, and equitable banking and financial system is a precondition of an efficient market economy. Financial markets play a key role in the development of a modern market economy. The goal of bank restructuring is to increase the stability of the banking system. Reform of the banking and financial system may discourage governments from risky fiscal policies such as printing money to cover government debt. A sound banking system is necessary to create and maintain stable expectations among investors and consumers. The goal of these measures is to keep capital control barriers low enough to enable needed investment while keeping the incentives stable enough to prevent sudden reversals of investment that may spark panics that could lead to massive capital flight.

Efficiently functioning financial markets facilitate capital formation for government and businesses. They serve to rationally allocate resources in the economy by making it possible for financial resources to flow from areas of low priority to areas of high priority. They act to transform public savings into investment as the best projects bid for the available capital in the market place. An efficiently regulated capital market invites crucially needed foreign investment, the key to economic transformation in today's globalized economy. Capital markets also play a role in civil development. Active circulation of financial resources allows for a more equitable distribution of the gains of prosperity. For instance, pension fund investments capture the rising tide of prosperity for pensioners, encouraging them to become shareholders in the market transition rather than see themselves as victims of structural adjustment. Financial markets are those in which stocks, bonds, and other forms of investment and savings can be bought and sold. In the transition from a planned economy to a market economy, the growth of financial markets is critical to success. Financial markets facilitate capital formation for businesses and governments and provide a means of profitable utilization of assets for investors. Efficient markets make it possible for people to know what lowest prices the market will offer, that is, what economists call "price discovery." Efficient markets also encourage a lot of otherwise idle financial resources to circulate more freely in the economy, what economists refer to as high "liquidity." A well functioning financial market is an engine of savings and investment for any free-market economy.

A second major arena of reform is governance and administrative reform. The foundation of governance and administrative reform is the adoption of the principle of the rule of law under a body of laws beginning, in most cases, with a national constitution. The constitutional body of law is drawn into greater detail in the form of a legal, regulatory, policy, and administrative framework. A third key element is the set of policies that maintain arms-length relationships between and among the various institutional actors in a civil society, namely transparency and integrity policies.

A structural reform program usually assumes that the country has a constitutional basis for government authority and a legal and regulatory framework in place. If this is not the case, the reform program may address establishing the rule of law as a first priority program goal. The rule of law means that all components of society, including the public bureaucracy, operate under the same legal constraints and with the same legal rights, thus enabling peaceful and predictable political and economic participation. Strengthening the rule of law requires that the legal system exist not only on paper, but also in practice. Written laws must also be implemented, enforced, understood, accepted, and used. Strengthening the rule of law, therefore, requires the development of independent and professional judicial and legal institutions. In societies moving from authoritarianism to greater levels of public participation, the stability of the legal system plays a key role in establishing the foundations of sound government.

Governmental and political reform is a third major arena of reform. According to communist theory, government's function is twofold; first to provide public goods and, second, to carry out production and distribution of goods and services. The Soviet government evolved with respect to this broad definition of the public mandate. The Soviet system created "ministries," that is, implementing agencies to carry out these broadly defined functions of government. The list of

Soviet ministries, consequently, included agencies defined in terms of public service delivery, such as public health, public safety, and education, as well as sectors of the economy such as agriculture, machine building, and fishing. As the Central Asian states became independent, the Soviet ministerial organizations were simply grandfathered into new, national ministerial organizations. Often this transformation initially amounted to little more than changing the names on the doors of offices. That is not to say that there were not intense conflicts over bureaucratic scope and jurisdiction during this period, but only that the public mandate of government agencies was not in essence changed during the early period of independence.

The existence of laws, rules, and procedures on the books does not necessarily imply that procedures will be followed, rules will be obeyed, and that laws will not be circumvented. Thus enhancing the rule of law does not entail creating merely a more powerful government. In authoritarian systems, the executive branch is often excessively centralized, given to top-down policy making, and is rarely accountable to the public for its actions. Programs designed to facilitate the rule of law, consequently, should not be directed merely at increasing the capacity of government, but at increasing the quality of governance. Transparent, formal legal and regulatory systems exist in all developed societies and in many developing societies. But in developing countries, to a much greater degree than in developed countries, informal authority structures exist side by side with the transparent, public order. In developing societies these informal authority structures sometimes take precedence over the formally established procedures (Gleason, 1991).

A modern state is one with a robust distinction between the public and private sectors. A robust boundary is not necessarily a static boundary. In the modern world, there is a dynamic boundary between the public and private sectors. The public sector plays a key role in promoting the health of the private sector. Consequently, there must be provisions for the facilitation of private sector activity using public sector resources. The private sector should constitute a level playing field, allowing for normal entry and exit of enterprises and firms. In many emerging market countries, the most significant element in the balancing of the public and private sectors is the withdrawal of the government from the production and distribution of certain goods and services.[7] This may be accomplished either through divestiture or privatization. The goal of privatization is to raise productivity and support growth targets. Privatization may also aid in the achievement of fiscal goals by bolstering revenues and lowering direct or indirect subsidies. In post communist structural reform programs, particular emphasis is placed on measures that lead to a greater reliance on monetarized commercial transactions and a reduction in inefficient and non-transparent barter relations. One goal of these measures is to prevent biased and self-interested financial relationships between the public and private sectors, such as "crony capitalism," by making it less likely that government will yield to interest group pressure to offer sweetheart deals on the basis of insider information.

The Central Asian states relied heavily upon informal authority structures. An informal authority structure is any process of public governance that functions parallel to the constitutional provisions of the society without benefit of a formal public mandate. Typically, constitutionally mandated public decisions processes are transparent. Informal authority structures, in contrast, tend to exist on the basis of what legally resemble informal and *ad hoc* agreements and tacit understandings. In Central Asian circumstances, these informal agreements are often secured by bonds of blood or fealty that are far more secure than the overt legal and regulatory infrastructure of the society. Ethnic ties link communities in ways that transcend political boundaries (Huntington, 1997). The Turkic-speaking Uigur community, for instance, reach across virtually all the Central Asian states and beyond, linking Central Asian states with groups in China, Russia, and other Eurasian states. Uigur ethnic loyalties are sometimes more important that political loyalties (Roberts, 1992). Central Asian mutual protection societies are based upon personal credibility whose source is affinitive relationships instead of commercial and economic factors. These mutual protection triangles usually involve finance, industry, and government, but they are rooted and governed primarily by family relations.

These Central Asian policy networks resemble the traditional Japanese *zaibatsu* family owned conglomerate and its more contemporary Korean variant, the *chaebol*. They form an interlocking directorship of vertically integrated industries, closely controlled in tandem by the government apparatus and family relationships. This model of relationships between market and politics comes into sharp contrast with the Anglo-Saxon model of independent, profit-maximizing enterprises relying on impersonal, abstract Anglo-Saxon legal rules to ensure freewheeling competition. The Central Asian business networks rely on personal relationships and social obligations. The former stresses *laissez-faire*, open economics; the latter relies on national strategies for industrial development and actively supervises, monitors, and even regiments the competitors in the market place. The cornerstone of one is individualism; the cornerstone of the other is loyalty. As long as Suharto style family relationships dominate the political life of the Central Asian countries, the relationship between markets and politics will continue to be shaped by forces that are subterranean to official political reforms.

Economic and administrative compromise, or what is widely and often inaccurately regarded as "corruption," takes place when administrative systems fail to function for their intended purpose because the public interest is not adequately separated from private interests. Public officials or individuals with monopolistic access to resources can extract benefits from scarce public goods by seeking out rents. Rent-seeking, of course, is a natural tendency related to people's rational, self-interested tendency to attempt to improve their position. Economic compromise, that is, the tendency to use available collective resources for personal gain is also a natural tendency. To a certain extent it is inevitable. Good governance does not eliminate natural tendencies. But good governance does limit situations in which rent-seeking individuals can employ the coercive powers of government to extract unfair benefits by artificially limiting the market for public services.

Government plays a leading role in structuring market arrangements. Economic corruption is not the illegal act itself, but rather the abuse of the policy environment that makes it possible and sometimes even permissable for public officials to use the coercive powers of government for improper personal gain. The overall effect of economic corruption is to impose a form of tax on the economy. It reduces efficiency. It undermines the rule of law. Corruption exists on may levels, from the situation of "grand corruption" in which powerful and resourceful private vested interests "capture the state" in order to use their power to preserve monopolies, hinder competition, and inhibit reform, to the level of local *baksheesh* style side payments of petty officialdom. The consequence of grand corruption is a social contract built on oligarchy. In circumstances of oligarchy, the public interest becomes identified with that of the oligarchs rather than the population as a whole. The solution to corruption in general is transparency and dialogue. Anti-corruption campaigns include a free and independent press, civic initiative that respects rights, the development and protection of a transparent legal and regulatory framework, an independent judiciary, trustworthy law enforcement agencies, and better trained, properly paid civil servants and judges. Democracy is the most auspicious environment for this kind of openness.

For most of the period of the Soviet Union (1917–91) there was only one political party, the Communist party. The Communist Party fulfilled roles relating specifically to the direction and management of the society and economic relations within the society. Although the Communist Party was not actually referenced in the Constitutions of the USSR, the Soviet Union maintained a one-party system with the Communist Party at the center of all political and economic activity. The Communist Party served, in the words of political slogan of the time, as the "mind, the honor, and the conscience of the society." It did not serve as a competitor in a competition of ideas. Competition of ideas existed, but the party's job was to direct and implement rather than to debate and deliberate.

The Central Asian states began the transition by departing from these assumptions of the communist model. In terms of internationally accepted assessments of democratic development, the Central Asian societies have not realized their full potential. The benchmark criteria for measuring democratic progress used by Freedom House rank the Central Asian countries as the lowest of the transition countries.[8] The annual Human Rights reports of the US State Department underscore the authoritarian nature of government in all the societies. The opening lines of the Human Rights Reports on the Central Asian countries suggest the overall character of the appraisal. Kazakhstan: "The Constitution of Kazakhstan concentrates power in the presidency. President Nursultan Nazarbayev is the dominant political figure." Kyrgyzstan: "Although the 1993 Constitution defines the form of government as a democratic republic, President

Askar Akayev dominates the Government." Tajikistan: "Tajikistan is ruled by an authoritarian regime that has established some nominally democratic institutions." Turkmenistan: "Turkmenistan, a one-party state dominated by its president and his closest advisers, continues to exercise power in a Soviet-era authoritarian style despite Constitutional provisions nominally establishing a democratic system." Uzbekistan: "Uzbekistan is an authoritarian state with limited civil rights."[9]

3 Kazakhstan and globalization

How have Kazakhstan's economic policy choices since independence affected the country's political development? The data and analysis presented in this chapter offers a portrait of Kazakhstan as the most successful Central Asian country in terms of measures of both economic and political reform. But to what extent has Kazakhstan's progress in political development been specifically a product of economic policy? This chapter argues that three factors should be borne in mind as particularly significant in answering this question. First, Kazakhstan is a Eurasian country, simultaneously manifesting cultural features of both Asia and Europe. Kazakhstan's cultural traditions are more consonant with economic and political institutions of European design than is the case with the other Central Asian countries. Second, Kazakhstan's close physical, economic, and cultural linkages with Russia tie its development path to that of Russia. Most key industries in Kazakhstan have economic ties to suppliers and consumers in Russia. Kazakhstan's population, while predominantly ethnic Kazakh, continues to be strongly influenced by Russian traditions and continues to rely heavily on the Russian language for purposes of commerce, science, industry, and culture. Third, Kazakhstan's natural resource endowment, particularly its oil and mineral wealth, distinguish it from its neighbors by offering great opportunities for economic and political development.

The following profile of Kazakhstan surveys some distinguishing features of the economic and political development of the country. The section on "Kazakhstan profile" section describes in detail the economic policies adopted during the first decade of independence. The section on "Transition of the state in Kazakhstan" describes administrative end political development and analyzes the effect of economic policy choices on government and politics. Throughout the analysis, we emphasize the dominant feature of Kazakhstan's post-independence experience – the role of export-oriented economic sectors.

Kazakhstan profile

Kazakhstan is a country of superlatives. It is a large, sparsely populated country, exceptionally rich in resources, and situated in a geographic position which affords special opportunities and poses unique challenges. In terms of territory, Kazakhstan is the world's ninth largest country, more than five times the size of

Table 3.1a Kazakhstan key indices: production

	1991	*1992*	*1993*	*1994*	*1995*	*1996*	*1997*	*1998*	*1999*	*2000*
Population (million; as of 1 July)	16.45	16.52	16.48	16.30	15.80	15.58	15.33	15.07	14.93	14.87
Labor force (million; calendar year)	7.72	7.57	6.96	7.12	7.36	7.49	7.44	7.05	7.06	7.07
Employed	6.49	6.58	5.67	5.42	5.21	4.92	4.27	3.78	3.35	3.35
Agriculture and forestry	1.21	1.18	1.13	1.21	1.08	1.08	0.90	0.71	0.53	0.33
Industry	1.39	1.42	1.21	1.12	1.08	1.28	1.08	1.01	0.91	1.04
Production (thousand metric tons; calendar year)										
Agriculture (crop year)										
Wheat	6889	18,285	11,585	9052	6490	7678	8955	4746	11,242	9073
Barley	3085	8511	7149	5497	2208	2696	2583	1093	2265	1664
Potatoes	2143	2570	2296	2040	1720	1656	1472	1263	1695	1693
Sugar beets	674	1160	843	433	371	341	128	225	294	273
Vegetables	955	985	808	781	780	778	880	1079	1287	1544
Mining										
Iron ore	21,993	17,671	13,129	10,521	14,902	12,975	13,133	9336	9617	16,161
Manufacturing										
Steel	6355	6063	4558	2969	3027	3217	3880	3116	4105	4797
Rolled steel	4700	4400	—	—	—	2288	3030	2585	3186	3691
Sulphuric acid	2815	2349	1179	681	695	653	635	605	685	634
Sugar	307	213	164	97	97	143	148	230	228	271

Production indexes period averages										
Agriculture, 1989–91 = 100	—	108.7	96.4	80.7	63.5	61.2	60.4	49.5	67.4	59.9
Mining, 1980 = 100	119.2	110.2	90.8	78.3	74.2	67.1	69.1	68.0	74.6	90.6
Manufacturing, 1980 = 100	138.8	117.7	99.6	71.6	65.7	57.8	59.2	56.9	58.0	67.0
Energy (annual values)										
Crude petroleum ('000 m. t.)										
Production	22,036	21,934	19,572	18,544	18,123	21,050	23,409	23,819	26,736	30,612
Exports	20,800	18,174	13,697	9445	11,307	14,503	16,382	20,429	23,674	29,349
Imports	12,500	11,400	8684	1836	692	340	1726	2074	714	1010
Consumption	18,300	17,100	14,600	11,785	10,858	10,925	9758	8791	7294	6725
Coal ('000 m. t.)										
Production	1,26,463	1,22,384	1,11,880	1,04,625	83,355	76,831	72,647	69,773	58,377	74,790
Exports	51,200	43,553	34,483	22,481	20,768	20,840	24,857	23,578	16,175	25,679
Imports	5600	1000	4748	193	1209	1060	975	1211	1121	689
Consumption	84,800	83,200	7750	68,303	65,116	55,801	50,025	47,155	40,106	43,876
Natural gas (Mn cu. m.)										
Production	7885	8113	6685	4488	5916	6524	8114	7948	9946	11,500
Exports	4200	3915	3451	1636	2566	2342	2432	2306	4245	5221
Imports	12,800	13,400	9772	7173	9121	5495	3004	3052	2783	4218
Consumption	16,500	17,600	14,700	10,155	11,513	11,581	11,016	4772	5155	5525
Electricity (Mn kWh)										
Production	85,984	82,700	77,444	66,397	66,651	59,038	52,000	49,145	47,498	51,444
Exports	12,700	15,447	—	—	—	26	1	133	85	38
Imports	28,200	29,619	11,706	13,031	7395	6615	4704	3992	3256	3102
Consumption	1,01,200	96,500	88,900	74,428	73,945	64,602	56,700	53,004	50,669	37,126

Source: Asian Development Bank. *Key Indicators 2001: Growth and Change in Asia and the Pacific*. New York: Oxford University Press, 2001.

Table 3.1b Kazakhstan key indices: foreign trade

	1991	*1992*	*1993*	*1994*	*1995*	*1996*	*1997*	*1998*	*1999*	*2000*
External trade (r/ Mn)	16.45	16.52	16.48	16.30	15.80	15.58	15.33	15.07	14.93	14.87
(US dollars; calendar year)										
Exports, fob	928.0	1451.0	1486.0	3542.5	5912.7	6720.4	6497.0	5435.8	5592.2	9139.5
Imports, cif	584.0	566.0	472.0	5284.7	6891.1	7123.7	4300.8	4349.6	3686.5	5052.1
Trade balance	344.0	885.0	1014.0	−1742.2	−978.4	−403.3	2196.2	1086.2	1905.7	4087.4
Direction of trade (Mn US dollars; calendar year)										
Total exports	—	244.4	1088.0	3355.6	5250.2	5931.4	6366.3	5403.8	5282.1	7734.8
1 Russia	—	—	—	1438.3	2365.8	2484.4	2157.1	1542.7	1265.0	1997.4
2 China, People's Republic of	—	128.1	239.1	148.9	297.0	458.9	442.2	381.1	585.8	800.2
3 Germany	—	37.4	89.4	73.2	171.1	183.0	353.0	281.4	539.0	923.6
4 Italy	—	13.4	54.1	42.3	142.5	197.1	357.3	492.6	470.3	516.8
5 United Kingdom	—	—	75.8	64.9	111.5	230.8	548.7	478.8	75.1	82.3
6 Ukraine	—	—	—	128.0	121.5	212.5	303.5	262.2	149.9	149.9
7 Turkey	—	—	39.1	49.1	70.4	51.7	102.2	94.3	269.0	443.7
8 Netherlands	—	2.1	24.2	247.8	511.5	303.0	203.6	274.9	70.0	67.6
9 United States	—	21.7	37.1	75.1	43.6	59.7	139.2	76.0	209.0	382.0
10 Switzerland	—	4.6	2.6	138.0	203.5	213.4	286.0	330.5	7.6	9.9
Total imports	—	459.5	1687.6	3561.2	3806.7	4279.5	4275.1	4256.6	4213.1	5914.1
1 Russia	—	—	—	1292.8	1899.7	2324.6	1965.7	1670.8	1343.7	2470.9
2 Germany	—	96.2	488.0	293.6	196.7	197.7	367.7	365.0	292.8	374.2
3 China, People's Republic of	—	244.7	188.9	69.8	34.7	35.8	46.6	50.6	543.8	919.6
4 United States	—	16.2	74.5	109.3	64.7	66.3	201.7	264.9	202.4	140.0
5 Italy	—	15.7	101.9	60.7	30.2	42.3	84.7	88.9	444.3	176.8
6 Turkey	—	—	73.7	87.2	123.5	151.2	177.0	202.1	106.3	106.3
7 United Kingdom	—	—	24.6	66.4	83.6	76.5	141.4	213.8	117.0	126.2
8 France	—	15.9	72.3	30.7	48.6	34.1	61.6	80.3	63.1	302.6
9 Uzbekistan	—	—	—	—	269.5	89.3	65.6	96.3	127.5	158.7
10 Korea, Republic of	—	—	44.9	67.0	43.2	87.8	129.5	−86.0	−12	62.0

Source: Asian Development Bank. *Key Indicators 2001: Growth and Change in Asia and the Pacific*. New York: Oxford University Press, 2001.

France yet with a population less than one-third the size of France's. Kazakhstan is a landlocked country, and given its enormous size and continental location, has some of the longest borders in the world. Its northern neighbor, Russia, has long been and continues to be Kazakhstan's largest trading partner. Russia shares with Kazakhstan a naturally integrated infrastructure of rail, road, energy, and telecommunication linkages. Caspian seaports in Kazakhstan's far west connect the country with the Caucasus and the Middle East. Kazakhstan shares a coastline on the Aral Sea with Uzbekistan and Kazakhstan shares land borders with Turkmenistan, Uzbekistan, Kyrgyzstan, and China.

Kazakhstan had an estimated population of 14.8 million people in mid-2001.[1] Kazakhstan's population has been declining since independence, in part from migration to other countries and in part from increased mortality. Kazakhstan's workforce has historically been distributed about evenly between agriculture and industry, with the small service sector accounting for only a minor share of overall employment. Since independence in 1991, Kazakhstan's agricultural workforce has declined sharply in size while industrial employment has declined modestly. Service sector employment has grown.

Since independence, agricultural output declined substantially with great annual variation (Table 3.1(a)). For instance, wheat production during the decade varied on an annual basis by nearly as much as a factor of four. Industrial output for most categories during the period also declined. Iron ore and coal output declined by more than half between 1991 and 1999. Natural gas and electricity production declined substantially during the period. As these declines were taking place, petroleum production increased substantially. A growing share of Kazakhstan's oil production was exported. The foreign exchange earned from Kazakhstan's oil exports contributed to improvements in the country's foreign trade balance. Kazakhstan had a modest trade surplus until 1993. A trade deficit arose in 1994 and continued until 1997. After 1997 Kazakhstan's oil exports increased rapidly, leading to a strong trade surplus by the late 1990s. Kazakhstan's export trade partners were primarily Russia, China, Germany, Italy, and Turkey, with imports coming from Russia, China, and France. Exports and imports from other Central Asian countries contributed only marginally to Kazakhstan's overall foreign trade (Table 3.1(b)).

Kazakhstan is widely regarded to be comparatively successful among the Central Asian states in terms of measures of economic and political reform (Cummings, 2000). Some areas of macro-economic reform in Kazakhstan have been so successful that Kazakhstan is often singled out as a model for other post-communist countries. The government introduced a national currency, the *Tenge*, in November 1993. The *Tenge* became and has remained fully convertible. The government introduced privatization legislation in late 1993. Kazakhstan proceeded to move most major state-owned assets through the privatization process by the end of 1996, including assets in the key sectors of industry, telecommunications, and energy. Kazakhstan lifted virtually all subsidies on consumer goods in September 1994 and phased out many industrial subsidies before the end of that year. Kazakhstan commenced the process of balancing the public and private sectors with a series of major reductions in force of public employees and privatization of state-owned public service facilities.

The Kazakhstan government put great effort into establishing a legal foundation and regulatory system for a private economy (Nazarbaev, 1997). The government established sound monetary and fiscal policies including revenue, spending, and borrowing policies. The government actively encouraged international trade and foreign investment. The government established a regulatory structure for the private banking and financial sector. The government passed environmentally sound, oil and gas legislation meeting international standards. Kazakhstan became a regional leader in the efforts to spur Eurasian economic integration and policy harmonization in accordance with international standards. In May 2000 Kazakhstan won praise from the International Monetary Fund for its decision to repay $385 million in IMF credits prior to the due date. In March 2002 Kazakhstan was classified by the US Department of Commerce as a market economy, the first post-Soviet country to be so classified.

Kazakhstan also made steps in the direction of political liberalization (Table 3.2). In relative, terms, that is to say, if Kazakhstan's progress is compared with that of its Central Asian neighbors, Kazakhstan's record is highly positive. If evaluated in absolute terms, however, the progress appears less significant. Kazakhstan has a "presidential system," a system that was formally introduced with the 1995 constitution. The primary feature of the system is a strong and independent executive branch. Kazakhstan's judicial and legislative branches are subordinate to the executive branch. The president, as the head of state and chief executive officer of the government, has the authority to create legislation by decree, disband the parliament, and appoint and remove most important state officers. The legislature cannot appropriate state funds without presidential approval. National elections in Kazakhstan have been regarded by leading monitoring organizations as less than free and fair. Nongovernmental organizations are given the opportunity to form and operate in Kazakhstan, but media organizations and human rights organizations have faced harassment from the government. Unlike its neighbors to the south, Kazakhstan does not have any significant insurgency movement. While the government has political opponents who could constitute threats, even violent threats to the stability of the state, there is no appreciable threat from militant Muslim groups. Kazakhstan's human rights record is regarded as poor by leading human rights organizations. Governance indicators

Table 3.2 Kazakhstan: political freedoms

	Nations in transit 2001 political indicators								
	1991–92	*1992–93*	*1993–94*	*1994–95*	*1995–96*	*1996–97*	*1997–98*	*1998–99*	*1999–2000*
Political rights	5	5	6	6	6	6	6	6	6
Civil liberties	4 PF	5 PF	4 PF	5 NF	5 NF	5 NF	5 NF	5 NF	5 NF

Source: *Nations in Transit*, 2001. New York: Freedom House.

Table 3.3 World Bank Institute governance indicators for Kazakhstan

Governance indicator	*Year*	*Percentile rank (0–100) in %*	*Estimate (−2.5 to +2.5)*	*Standard deviation*	*Number of surveys/ polls*
Voice and accountability	2000/01	24.1	−0.80	0.16	7
Political stability/no violence	2000/01	59.3	+0.29	0.25	7
Government effectiveness	2000/01	31.9	−0.61	0.19	8
Regulatory quality	2000/01	23.7	−0.51	0.35	5
Rule of law	2000/01	31.8	−0.60	0.18	9
Control of corruption	2000/01	23.0	−0.83	0.18	8

Source: Kaufmann, Kraay, and Zoido (KKZ), 2002. *Governance Matters II: Updated Governance Indicators for 2000–01*. World Bank Institute.

used by the World Bank ranked Kazakhstan in 2001 in the bottom third percentile in five key governance measures (Table 3.3). In a sixth key measure, "political stability," Kazakhstan ranked in the fifty-ninth percentile. In other words, Kazakhstan ranked low in most governance measures but relatively high in political stability.

Transition of the state in Kazakhstan

Kazakhstan's economic reform measures began with a deliberate goal of transforming the socialist state[2] (Nazarbaev, 1995). Significant progress toward establishing a policy environment conducive to globalization and integration in world markets was made by Kazakhstan in the early years of independence. Kazakhstan was host to the December 1991 conference of former communist party officials that produced the "Alma-Ata Declaration," the legal instrument that brought about the end of the USSR (Gleason, 1992). The Alma-Ata Declaration also established the loose coordinating community called the "Commonwealth of Independent States" (CIS). Kazakhstan was thus symbolically the resting place of communism and the birthplace of the post-communist order. Kazakhstan's president, Nursultan Nazarbaev, had previously been a promoter of democratic change within the former USSR and, when the transition came, identified the new Kazakhstan government with the pro-market, democratic reform at an early point. At the Coordinating Conference on Assistance to the New Independent States that took place in Washington in January 1992, US President George Bush noted that "in Central Asia, President Nazarbaev ... [is] ... leading the fight for reform" (Dispatch, 1992: 57). Early in 1992 the US extended diplomatic recognition to Kazakhstan. Scores of other countries soon followed suit. Major international organizations, multinational corporations, and dozens of non-governmental assistance and humanitarian organizations established offices in Kazakhstan's physically remote but dramatically beautiful capital, Almaty.[3] Soon Almaty became the preferred Central Asian headquarters for legions of diplomats, international consultants, and business people. Almaty became home for the largest international diplomatic community in Eurasia, east of Moscow, and west of Beijing.

Kazakhstan took steps to integrate into the international community of nations, joining the United Nations in March 1992. Kazakhstan joined the World Bank, the International Monetary Fund (IMF), the Asian Development Bank (ADB) and the European Bank for Reconstruction and Development (EBRD). Kazakhstan started the process of accession to the World Trade Organization (WTO). Kazakhstan initiated a diplomatic dialogue that resulted in a series of bilateral and regional trade agreements and border normalization agreements. Kazakhstan was the initiator of the "CIS Customs Union," an organization that attempted to implement the goals of the CIS founding documents by maintaining a "common economic space" throughout the former USSR. Kazakhstan was the initiator of the discussions that led to the Cholpon–Ata Regional Cooperation Agreement of April 1994 at which Kazakhstan, Kyrgyzstan, and Uzbekistan pledged to observe the principle of maintaining transparent, open borders to facilitate trade and cooperation. Kazakhstan was the initiator of the agreement to establish the Eurasian Economic Community in October 2000. Nazarbaev's government remained steadfast in the commitment to bring about post-communist reform. At the critical juncture following the collapse of financial markets in Russia, when some Central Asian politicians were arguing for the adoption of a neo-mercantilist "Asian path," Nazarbaev held firm to the reform programs, pledging "to continue the promising advances toward an independent, open and free market economy" (Nazarbaev, 1998).

Fiscal and monetary policy

At the time the USSR came to an end, none of the Central Asian states was in a good position to rapidly introduce its own currency, yet none of the countries wanted to be dependent upon fiscal and monetary decisions taken by Russia. Each of the post-Soviet states considered the idea of introducing separate currencies during the first months of independence. Early in 1992, just months after independence, Ukraine began issuing state ration coupons. Estonia, not a member of the CIS, introduced the first post-Soviet currency, the *Kroon*, in June 1992. Russia announced that it would make the *Rubles* a fully convertible currency by July 1, 1992, and then changed the date to August 1, 1992. As soon as the Russian *Rubles* became tradable, its value immediately plunged, falling from 130 to over 450 *Rubles* to the American dollar. Russia began printing post-Soviet *Rubles*, creating a two-tier system of "new *Rubles*" and "old *Rubles*." Huge amounts of old *Rubles* moved into the former Soviet countries, particularly to Kazakhstan. The Kazakhstan money supply grew from a trillion *Rubles* in September to between 3.5 and 4.5 trillion in November 1992.

On advice from international financial consultants, the Kazakhstan government had initially intended to remain in the *Ruble* zone. At the CIS summit in Bishkek in October 1992 the Central Asian states agreed to maintain the *Ruble* zone. Soon thereafter, however, Kyrgyzstan was the first CIS state to opt out of the *Ruble* zone by introducing the Kyrgyz *Som* in March 1993. After Russian central bank officials demonstrated unwillingness in late 1992 and early 1993 to adopt measures to stabilize the Russian currency, Kazakhstan shifted its position, withdrawing from the *Ruble* zone in November 1993 by the introduction of the Kazakhstan *Tenge*. At the time the *Tenge* was introduced the value was set at 4T to one US dollar. The *Tenge* was tradable but state-issued licenses were required to conduct currency exchange. Following the introduction of the national currency, the Kazakhstan government sharply restricted the money supply. Billions of Russian *Rubles* were frozen in accounts while government commissions ruled on the legitimacy of their origin. The Kazakhstan government took steps to assure that the *Tenge* remained a tradable currency by establishing provisions for clearing and settlements among banking institutions.

During 1994 Kazakhstan experienced very high inflation rates, although this stabilized in 1995. The 1995–96 the "expansion program" under Kazakhstan Prime Minister Akezhan Kazhegeldin was produced good economic results, but Kazakhstan's trading position deteriorated when the Asian crisis shook commodity prices, forcing the price of oil down by nearly 40 percent and non-ferrous metal prices down by margins as high as 40 percent. Inflation rose again in 1998 in association with the Russian financial collapse. Kazakhstan's high degree of reliance on Russian Federation buyers for oil, gas, and metals meant that the 1998 financial crisis in Russia had immediate impact on Kazakhstan's exports. Given that oil and metals constitute roughly 60 percent of Kazakhstan's exports, the country's terms of trade deteriorated substantially and quickly. In response, Kazakhstan authorities initially tightened fiscal policies in mid-1998, restraining government spending and borrowing, but they relaxed these policies again as presidential elections approached in January 1999. In the wake of the Russian financial crisis, the Kazakhstan National Bank increased interest rates to avert hyperinflation.

The Kazakhstan National Bank, the government agency responsible for maintaining the stability of the currency, sought to maintain a stable but flexible exchange rate for the *Tenge*. In April 1999, Kazakhstan shifted from a monetary policy that allowed the government to peg the currency to the US dollar in order to restrain wide fluctuations to a policy of a true floating exchange rate. The value of the *Tenge* fluctuated in a narrow band at about T 138–43 per US dollar in late 1999 and early 2000, settling at about T 142.5 per US dollar in late 2000. Given the strong growth in bank deposits and the confidence of market participants in a stable exchange rate, interest rates thereafter declined. Rates on three-month treasury bills (government controlled investments) declined by about one-half in late 2000, reaching about 8 percent per annum. In sum, it is accurate to say that Kazakhstan's fiscal and monetary policy successfully moved from a communist system to a true market orientation in the first decade of independence.

Privatization and price liberalization

The Kazakhstan government identified price liberalization and asset privatization as two key economic reform tasks. The first step in liberalization was freeing prices for retail goods and services. Most consumer goods price subsidies were eliminated in 1992. But many government officials were reluctant to push Kazakhstan's large enterprises into the free market too swiftly for fear of unemployment and bankruptcy. Subsidies on wholesale prices continued to exist despite mounting criticism from Nazarbaev and his closely associated reformers that the Kazakhstan government was moving too slowly toward full reform. By mid-1994 Kazakhstan newspapers were filled with discussion of the country's "economic crisis." In September 1994, Nazarbaev appointed one of the architects of the economic reform program, Akezhan Kazhegeldin, as Prime Minister. Kazhegeldin immediately took bold and decisive steps in the direction of reform, adopting some politically unpopular measures. The remaining governmental controls on prices were eliminated in October 1994. The price of bread increased overnight by a factor of eight as a result. By 1995 most prices had been decontrolled and most product subsidies had been eliminated.

Price liberalization was relatively swift in Kazakhstan but it did not take place in one step; rather a series of steps introduced decontrolled prices. Although it was brief, this interim period created opportunities for great transfers of wealth. No reliable estimates exist for the amount of the country's wealth that shifted hands as a result of the sequencing in price liberalization. Many long-term purchase and supply contracts that had been established prior to the price decontrol continued to be honored. Many factories continued to function, paying some of their bills in decontrolled currency and paying others in controlled currency. Massive inter-enterprise arrears built up until the Kazakhstan government prohibited factories from these practices in early 1995.

The second major plank of Kazkhastan's market reform was asset privatization, that is, the transfer to private hands of state-owned enterprises and assets. In mid-1993 the Kazakhstan government, with assistance from bilateral assistance agencies and from international organizations, began to develop a program for divestiture of state-owned properties and enterprises. The government began the task of developing the legal and institutional infrastructure of a market economy. The formal documents outlining the legal and regulatory framework for privatization were made public in late 1993. The privatization program officially began in March 1994. It was a period of intense and conflicting political pressures in Kazakhstan. Privatization was already complete in several central European countries and well underway in Russia and Ukraine. Some critics charged that Kazakhstan was lagging behind. On the other hand, other critics noted that the Russian privatization program was turning into a heartless political free for all, abandoning any semblance of social justice and that, accordingly, Kazakhstan's privatization program should go slow to avoid Russia's travail.

The Kazakhstan government vacillated in 1994 as a new parliament was formed and priorities were established and reestablished. In early 1994 privatization coupons were distributed to the population. Mass privatization and small-scale privatization auctions began amid much fanfare in March 1995 and continued on a regular basis at locations around the country until September 1996. Sales and public auctions were held to distribute the country's four main categories of properties. The "case-by-case privatization program" sold the country's largest and most unique major factories, mines, and assets. The "mass privatization program" held auctions for most of the country's large factories. Most small shops and stores were sold in the country's "small scale privatization program." The Agricultural privatization program privatized agricultural assets, although agricultural land itself was not privatized. Residents were allowed to privatize the apartments and houses in which they were living at the time. Residents were required to pay a nominal sum for their property, but there were few cases of people who were left without hearth and home by the privatization program. Foreign participants took part in the privatization, but there were legal constraints on the rights of foreigners to own Kazakhstan assets.

By the end of 1996, price liberalization was accomplished and the country's privatization program was officially complete. To be sure, large amounts of the country's assets remained under state control. The privatization of many factories only affected a portion of the shares of the joint stock company. Large and in many cases majority portions of the shares remained in the hands of the State Property Committee. But the fact remains that goal of price liberalization – to attain true scarcity values of goods and services – and the goal of privatization – to establish private property incentives for management – were attained in Kazakhstan's first decade of independence.

Trade and investment

Since independence Kazakhstan has become a relatively open economy, oriented toward export of primary commodities. Kazakhstan is landlocked, with long, inaccessible borders and an inadequate but developing infrastructure for trade and communication.[4] In 2000 the shares of export and imports in terms of GDP stood at 38 percent and 35 percent, reflecting a favorable trade balance. Trade is concentrated in the oil and gas, and minerals and mining sectors. Together these have accounted for about 80 percent of Kazakhstan exports while consumer products dominated imports. Kazakhstan's long-standing largest trading partner is Russia. For instance, in 1999 Kazakhstan exports to Russia accounted for 20 percent of all exports, followed by China accounting for 8 percent, Italy for 7 percent, Germany for 6 percent, and Switzerland for 6 percent. The US accounted for less than 2 percent of Kazakhstan's exports. Russia was also the largest importer to Kazakhstan, accounting for 37 percent of total imports. The US accounted for 9 percent of imports followed by the UK accounting for about 6 percent, and Italy for about 3 percent. Other trading partners accounted for less than 2 percent each.

Kazakhstan has substantial untapped agricultural potential, yet Kazakhstan's agricultural sector is underdeveloped and under-financed. The country's capital, Astana (previously was known as Tselinograd) was the epicenter of a major Soviet agricultural expansion program – the "Virgin Lands" program – of the 1950s and 1960s. During this period, tens of thousands of households moved to central Kazakhstan to assist in the expansion of agriculture. During the first decade of independence agriculture remained the country's major employer.

Yet agriculture plays a distant second to the mining and metals sector in attracting government attention for investment and support.

Kazakhstan is a world leader in minerals and mining, having about one-third of the world's chromium and manganese deposits as well as substantial reserves of tungsten, lead, zinc, copper, bauxite, silver, and phosphorus. Kazakhstan is a major producer of beryllium, tantalum, barite, uranium, cadmium, and arsenic. Major iron mines are located in the north of the country. Large coal reserves are found in the central and northern parts of the country and large reserves of phosphorus ores in the southern parts of the country. Kazakhstan has major aluminum, copper, steel, uranium, and zinc factories. The country's major steel producer, the Karaganda Metals, or Karmet, was privatized in 1994 and sold to the foreign steel firm, Ispat. Production at Karmet dropped for several years but in 2000 began to increase, reaching 300,000 tons. The major aluminum producer, Aluminum of Kazakhstan, is engaged in a major expansion of output. The country's chief zinc complex, Kazzinc, announced in 2000 that it would expand production to 250,000 tons. Kazakhstan also has a growing precious metals sector, with production increases in recent years in gold and silver production in particular. The majority of gold and silver output comes as a by-product from base metal production, but there are also deposits that stand on their own. There are twenty-three gold-bearing regions in Kazakhstan. The Vasilkovskoye mine in north Kazakhstan is considered to be the fourth largest gold mine in the world.

All the Central Asian countries are highly interdependent with respect to energy resources, transportation infrastructure, and markets. The greatest source of wealth in the region is natural resources, particularly gas and oil. The Caspian region's major rich oil and gas reserves are located in Azerbaijan, Kazakhstan, Turkmenistan, and Uzbekistan. Much of the oil wealth is located in the shallow coastal regions of the Caspian Sea or in the remote regions of western Kazakhstan. Oil industry analysts expect that the greater Caspian region could be exporting as much as two million barrels a day by 2010. But because all the region's oil-producing countries are landlocked, routes to the market invariably involve shipment through third party countries. As a consequence, the complexities of the region's geography and the differing national interests of the countries make access to market a matter of mutual agreement, or at least mutual negotiation (Dorian, 1994).

The Kazakhstan government relies heavily on oil and mineral exports for state revenues and for financing social programs. Kazakhstan oil production rose to over 800,000 barrels per day in 2001, with nearly 70 percent of production bound for export. Major new oil fields will be brought on line in the years ahead, including the giant Kashagan oil field that represents the world's largest new find in the past forty years. The Kazakhstan government is aware that too swift a course toward an oil-based economy may carry risks. Too heavy a reliance on primary commodity exports can lead to the so-called "Dutch disease" – situation in which oil-rich countries draw in large amounts of foreign capital for needed oil industry development but find that the resulting strong exchange rates hinder the country's ability to competitively price its other goods and services. An overdeveloped energy sector ends up dominating other branches of the economy, both economically and politically. As powerful constituencies become ensconced in key decision making positions, Big Oil's influence over national policy making can then self-perpetuating.

In 1991, the Kazakhstan government began negotiating what the Kazakhstan press referred to at the time as the "the deal of the century" to develop Kazakhstan's "Tengiz" oil fields. The Kazakhstan government joined the large multinational oil firm Chevron to form a joint venture, "Tengizchevroil." The agreement committed Chevron to spend about $20 billion over twenty years to develop the Tengiz field's six billion barrels of proven reserves. Other firms, including Birlesmis Muhendisler Burosu, British Gas, and Agip also committed investment in the country's oil fields. Russia first sought to impose high taxes and surcharges on the movement of gas and oil and then, in order to block economic development that might run contrary to the interest of Russian energy firms, sought to blockade its southern neighbors by cutting off access to foreign markets entirely. Chevron's returns from the Tengizchevroil joint venture, falling far short of expectations because of bureaucratic red tape, were threatened by Russia's intransigence. When the Tengizchevoil agreement was first reached, it was anticipated that eventually Kazakhstan would be exporting as much as 700,000 barrels a day. Yet as late as October 1995 the Tengiz field was producing only 50,000 barrels a day, about half pumping capacity.

Beginning in 1992, Kazakhstan's northern neighbor, Russia, restructured the management of the Russian state-owned oil and gas companies. Private, but nevertheless large, powerful, and politically well-connected oil companies emerged from the reorganization in Russia. These new Russian firms and the Russian government cooperated to restrict the access of the Caspian states to the Russian pipeline system and its connections to Western markets. Russia first sought to impose high taxes and surcharges on the movement of gas and oil and then, in order to block economic development that might run contrary to the interests of Russian energy firms, sought to blockade its southern neighbors by cutting off access to foreign markets entirely.

In response to the Russian measures, the Caspian oil and gas producing countries (principally Kazakhstan, Azerbaijan, and Turkmenistan) began seeking ways to bring energy supplies to market without having to pass through Russian territory. Russia lobbied for a continued reliance on the Soviet-era pipeline system, the so-called "northern option." European and North American countries favored the idea of shipment across the Caucasus and on to world markets through the Bosporos, the narrow straights that lead from the Black Sea to the Mediterranean Sea. The Economic Cooperation Organization (ECO), based in the countries of the Middle East, urged pursuit of a "southern option." Four routes for the Caspian oil eventually gained attention. One of these was a pipeline from Baku (Azerbaijan) to Ceyhan (Turkey), the Baku–Ceyhan line. Another was a pipeline that originated in Kazakhstan, went through Turkmenistan, and Afghanistan, before going to Pakistan to the Indian Ocean. Yet another pipeline discussed was one going from Turkmenistan through Iran,

Turkey and then onward toward Europe. Finally there was a discussion of a pipeline that would supply Uzbek and Turkmen gas to Pakistan through Afghanistan.

In 1995, negotiations among the oil and gas producing countries resulted in the "Caspian Littoral Agreement" and led to the creation of the "Caspian Pipeline Consortium" (CPC), founded by Russia, Kazakhstan, and Oman in 1995. The goal of the consortium was to deliver oil from the Tengiz field in Kazakhstan to a Russian port on the Black Sea for shipment to Western markets. In the summer of 1997, Kazakhstan and China concluded an over $10 billion agreement for the extraction and transportation of Kazakhstan oil. In 1998 the two countries began to develop and operate the Uzen oil field and the Aktyubinsk oil and gas field in northwestern Kazakhstan. The Chinese National Petroleum Corporation (CNPC) bought a 60 percent stake in Kazakhstan's large Aktobemunaigaz oil field for $325 million and pledged to invest another $4 billion in it over the next twenty years. Kazakhstan and China began exploring the possibility of jointly laying an oil pipeline from western Kazakhstan to China.

Kazakhstan's high degree of reliance on Russian Federation buyers for oil, gas, metals, meant that the 1998 financial crisis in Russia had immediate impact on Kazakhstan's foreign sales. Given that oil and metals constitute roughly 60 percent of Kazakhstan's exports, the country's terms of trade deteriorated substantially and quickly. In response, Kazakhstan authorities initially tightened fiscal policies in mid-1998, restraining government spending and borrowing but relaxing these policies again as presidential elections approached in January 1999. In the wake of the 1998 Russian financial crisis, the Kazakhstan National Bank increased interest rates to avert hyperinflation. In April 1999, the government shifted from the existing monetary policy that allowed the government to peg the currency to the US dollar to restrain wide fluctuations to a floating exchange rate. This allowed the currency markets to equilibrate more quickly. Kazakhstan's economic performance in 2000 exceeded expectations of the IFIs. In sum, it is accurate to conclude that, led by the successes of the gas, oil, minerals, and metals industries, Kazakhstan has made significant headway in transforming itself into an open, export-oriented country.

Banking, finance, and financial markets

At the time of independence, Kazakhstan's minerals, mineral related industries, and oil and gas sector were already functioning effectively. Kazakhstan's banking and financial sectors strike a sharp contrast; at independence there were no independent financial and banking institutions at all. The rapid development of Kazakhstan's banking sector during the first decade of independence is one of the significant success stories of the transition. With the lifting of restrictions on the financial industry, hundreds of new banks and financial institutions appeared in the first half of the 1990s. Privatization, currency operations, and small enterprise development spurred the growth of these new financial institutions. Overexpansion, however, led to a shakeout in the period between 1997 and 2001, when the number of banks in Kazakhstan fell from 129 to forty-eight as many small and non-competitive banks went out of business, merged or were acquired by larger banks.

Kazakhstan's banking sector has won high marks from international institutions for its rapid adoption of international standards of policy and practice. But these standards have not yet succeeded in convincing international investors and Kazakhstan's citizens that the financial services that are offered by Kazakhstan's major banks are critical to business success and personal finance. Kazakhstan's major banks have still not managed to attract major foreign investment. A very small percentage of Kazakhstan citizens after ten years of independence regularly used personal banking services such as checking and consumer credit cards. As a result, most small business transactions in Kazakhstan continued to be cash transactions.

Kazakhstan's central bank has sought to avoid many of the problems associated with the "boom and bust" syndrome of economies that are dependent upon the sale of natural resources, minerals, and other primary commodities. During 2000 the fiscal balance of the government recorded a substantial surplus. Exports grew strongly, resulting in a current account surplus as a percentage of GDP. During 2000 the Kazakhstan government borrowed money on the international market by issuing "Eurobonds" of $350 million. These bonds were Kazakhstan treasury bills that the government issued with a promise to pay at a later date. They are called "Eurobonds" simply because they could be purchased by investors in European markets.

With the success of the banking sector, there was also an expectation that Kazakhstan's national financial markets would grow rapidly and attract the attention of foreign investors. However, a decade after independence, Kazakhstan's capital markets and stock markets had still not developed sufficiently to attract significant foreign investment. Investors have not found Kazakhstan stocks and bonds in general to be attractive investments. Most foreign investment has been concentrated in a few sectors, particularly oil, gas, and minerals development. While the Kazakhstan's offering of government bonds has met with interest from investors, this is primarily because investors have confidence that the Kazakhstan government, with its long-term expected revenues from the oil, gas, and mineral sectors, would continue to make good on its promise to pay off its state debt.

One of the steps the Kazakhstan government has taken to address this situation is the strengthening of the funded pension system that was introduced January 1, 1998. This fully funded pension system was designed to help the government improving the marketability of financial assets held by the pension funds, to compel pension funds to use internationally accepted accounting and valuation standards; and to make it possible for pension funds to exercise greater freedom to invest in high-quality foreign assets, subject to financial safeguards. Kazakhstan's new pension system is based on sound actuarial and accounting principles. In the long run, workers in Kazakhstan can be assured that their earnings over their productive years will grow and pay them dividends in retirement.

However, the new system amasses money as new entrants into the work force begin regularly paying a portion of their incomes into the pension funds. Those workers already on pension or close to pension will receive little benefit from the funds. One of the great social injustices of the transition period is the large number of pensioners who worked their entire productive live and now receive monthly pensions amounting to no more than $15 per month.

Kazakhstan enacted its first post-communist Tax Code in April 1995. The Kazakhstan Tax Code is based on international standards and stresses equity, economic neutrality, and simplicity. Taxation takes place at the three levels of government: central, province, and local. The three most important taxes in the Code are: the enterprise profits tax; the individual income tax; and the VAT, or Value Added Tax. Enterprise profits for most private firms are taxed at a rate of 30 percent. Most business expenses are deductible, including wages. The individual income tax ranges from 5 to 30 percent. Tax is typically withheld at the source of payment. Accordingly, businesses withhold tax for their employees. The VAT is a tax on the difference between the purchase price of a good and its resale price. The VAT is applicable to all goods, work, and services, including imports into Kazakhstan. The VAT on imports is usually 20 percent of the value added, or the difference between the purchase and resale price. In addition to these basic taxes, there are a number of other, less common taxes such as the Natural Resource tax paid for the right to explore for oil and other mineral resources. Land is taxed annually. Business assets are taxed at one half of 1 percent yearly. And individually owned landed is taxes at one-tenth of 1 percent of the assessed value. Automobiles and trucks are taxed on their value.

In sum, Kazakhstan during the first decade of the country's independence adopted reforms that provided for the development of the financial, banking, and taxation systems of a modern economy. Kazakhstan's financial institution reforms compare well with those of the most successful transition and developing countries in the world.

The politics of export-led development

At the same time as economic reform measures were taken, the Kazakhstan government undertook institutional reforms designed to improve administration and government effectiveness. The government of Kazakhstan has its roots in the communist party of the former Soviet Union (Olcott, 1995). The head of the Kazakhstan Communist Party (KCP) prior to independence, Nursultan Nazarbaev, was a party-activist who entered high-level industrial management in 1977 when he was assigned responsibility for communist party management of major industry in Kazakhstan. Nazarbaev was appointed head of the KCP in 1989 and soon thereafter became a highly visible politician in the USSR. By 1990 Nazarbaev was probably second only to Mikhail Gorbachev in nation wide visibility. Nazarbaev was often identified in the Soviet press at the time as a possible successor to Gorbachev. Nazarbaev was elected chairman of the Kazakhstan parliament, the Kazakhstan Supreme Soviet, in February 1990. The following month, Kazakhstan's first open parliamentary elections took place, the result of Gorbachev's efforts at political reform. In one of its first actions, the new Kazakhstan parliament elected Nazarbaev President of the Soviet Republic of Kazakhstan in April 1990.

The disintegration of the USSR that proceeded incrementally through 1990 and 1991 and culminated in the August 1991 coup attempt against Gorbachev, hastened the growing pressures for national independence in Kazakhstan. Nazarbaev's previous elections had been through parliaments. In the turbulent autumn of 1991, Nazarbaev scheduled a nation-wide plebiscite for the post of presidency. Shortly after Nazarbaev's election on December 1, 1991, as president of Kazakhstan, he outlined the new independent Kazakhstan government's reform agenda.[5] Nazarbaev said that the goal was clear – it was the establishment of a free, sovereign, democratic Kazakhstan. He said that the means to achieve this goal were also clear – the establishment of a system of government with clearly defined separation of powers, creation of an effective executive branch, and transformation of the Soviet-era parliament into a professional parliament. Nazarbaev underscored support for the principle of political pluralism. He urged freedom for differing parties and political movements but also warned that there should be an absolute prohibition against ethnic extremism and hatred, separatism, and treason against the new Kazakhstan state. Nazarbaev spoke of the need to maintain public order through respect for the law. Nazarbaev pledged the new government would protect equality of the rights of all Kazakhstan citizens regardless of ethnic heritage. Nazarbaev spoke at length of the importance of ending isolation and backwardness in the country, through returning Kazakhstan to the standards of contemporary civilization by integrating fully into the international community. Nazarbaev won high marks from world political leaders and from the world's major international organizations for his commitment to market oriented, democratically directed change.

On rhetorical and formal levels at least, steps the Kazakhstan government has taken over these years of independence follow a textbook description for the establishment of a modern government and free society – a constitutionally organized, secular, civil society based on the rule of law, the protection of human and civil rights, and the limited role of popularly elected, accountable government. The Kazakhstan government established the fundamental institutions of civil development – a constitutional form of limited government based on a separation of powers, open electoral process, a professional judiciary, a deliberative parliament, free press, and rights of speech, assembly, and religion. But formal institutions of democratic rule do not necessarily equate with democratic process. Kazakhstan's formal steps have indeed been significant, but have not been followed by significant political change.

Constitutional, legal, and regulatory policy

Kazakhstan is a constitutional republic with a strong presidency. The constitution offers protection for fundamental human rights as well as the fundamental economic rights of a civil society. The constitution describes a democratic, representative, limited, secular government with checks and balances among the three separated branches of executive, legislative, and judicial power. In practice, however, most decision-making authority and most moral authority in the country is concentrated in the office and the person of the presidency.

Kazakhstan's government reform proceeded in a number of clearly delineated stages. The first stage was the unpredictable period of 1990–92. During the period the country's political leadership abandoned communist ideology and the social, political, and economic institutions of Soviet socialism and developed a vision of an independent, democratic, secular state, based on market economic relations and recognizing conventional principles of international law. A second stage, beginning in 1993 and extending to the end of 1994, was consumed with designing the outline for a new form of government and preparing for the creation of a private sector. This was the period in which Kazakhstan carried out major macroeconomic reforms such as price liberalization and the introduction of a national currency. During this period the size of the public sector contracted as state revenues shrank with the slowdown in economic production and the shift to a new foundation for public finance. Many public employees in health, education, and science simply ceased to carry out their job functions because work conditions deteriorated, benefits disappeared and often salaries were not paid or not paid on a regular basis.

The period between 1995 and the end of 1998 may be thought of as the third stage. During this period the government adopted the legal and regulatory framework of a civil society, completed the privatization of state-owned property, and entered the world marketplace. Prime Minister Akezhan Kazhegeldin resigned under pressure in October 1997 and was replaced by Nurlan Balgimbaev, a former oil industry executive. This was the stage in which government reform began to decelerate. The capital was moved to Astana, closer to the geographic center of the country. The country's technocratic–managerial elite was also called upon to relocate from Almaty. The reelection of Nazarbaev in January 1999 marked the end of the innovative period of reform. In a fourth stage, Kasymzhomart Tokayev replaced Balgimbaev as Prime Minister in October 1999. Government scandals relating to the conflicts of interest among the Astana administrative elite led to the resignation of Tokaev in favor of another oil industry insider, Imangali Tasmagambetov, in January 2002.

Legislative, executive, and judicial policies

In theory Kazakhstan's constitution 1992 described a constitutional republic. It described a representative government with separation of powers among three co-equal branches of government based upon popular sovereignty through free elections. The reality, however, was somewhat different. The president exercised a decisive voice in agenda setting, policy, budgeting, and dispute resolution. This became clear in 1993 as disputes over economic policy emerged in the Kazakhstan legislature. The legislature was internally divided but intent on exercising greater control over economic issues, particularly over privatization. The parliament eventually became deadlocked in a competition between those who supported Nazarbaev's market reforms and those who favored a partial restoration of the economic machinery of the Soviet period. A pro-reform contingent of parliamentarians in December 1993 voted to disband the deadlocked parliament. Nazarbaev recognized the vote immediately and, acting as head of state, closed the parliament and ordered that the legislative chambers be locked. With this act, Kazakhstan's Soviet-era parliament came to an end.

Elections for a new parliament were held in March 1994. This new, more openly experimental deliberative body first met in April 1994. The new parliament quickly asserted its constitutional mandate to exercise legislative control and the powers of the purse. A number of parliamentary committees began to exert direct influence over legislation related to privatization. Several visible parliamentary politicians assumed a watchdog function over the privatization process. The March 1994 parliamentary election had been a carefully structured process, with the most important decisions being made during the nomination process rather than the election itself. For these and other reasons, the election was criticized as flawed by international observers, particularly the Conference on Security and Cooperation in Europe (CSCE, now known as the Organization for Security and Cooperation in Europe, OSCE). Several unsuccessful candidates filed Court challenges to the election. A challenge lodged by one unsuccessful candidate resulted in a Constitutional Court ruling in March 1995. The court issued the surprising ruling that the entire parliamentary election was invalid. Nazarbaev vetoed this Constitutional Court decision but the Court then overruled his veto. Nazarbaev then dismissed the parliament.

Nazarbaev then called for a referendum to extend his own term of office. He easily won a five-year extension of his mandate in an April 29, 1995 referendum. A new Kazakhstan constitution, drafted at the direction of the executive branch, was drawn up and also won popular approval by nearly 90 percent of the voters in a referendum in August 1995. This new constitution granted greatly expanded powers to the executive branch, established a bicameral parliament, and did away with the Constitutional Court in favor of a Constitutional Council. It gave the president an unambiguous mandate to issue decrees "with the force of constitutional law." New parliamentary elections for the Kazakhstan Senate took place on December 5, 1995 and were followed by elections to the National Assembly, the Majlis, on December 9, 1995. Following the constitutional amendments of October 1998, the Kazakhstan parliament was bicameral, consisting of the upper house, the Senate, and the lower house, the Majlis. The Senate had forty-seven seats, forty of which are elected from districts and seven of which were appointed by the president. The Majlis had seventy-seven seats, sixty-seven of which were elected from districts and ten of which are elected from party lists. Senators served six-year terms and Majlis Deputies served five-year terms.[6]

The April 1995 referendum that extended Nazarbaev's tenure as president until 2000 was expected to result in new presidential elections in 2000. Instead, the Kazakhstan parliament voted to move the date of the presidential elections forward. The presidential election was held in January 1999. His leading rival, former Prime Minister Akezhan Kazhegeldin, attempted to enter the presidential race but was denied registration on the grounds that he had participated in an unsanctioned political meeting. The elections took place in January 1999. Nazarbaev won easily, but international observers criticized the election as less than free and fair.

Transparency and integrity policy

There is a consensus that one of the weakest elements of Kazakhstan's reform program is the effort to develop a competitive, fair, and transparent government system. There is wide agreement that the Kazakhstan government has made substantial progress in developing a market-based policy framework that is "on the books". But making this framework function in practice is the real challenge facing the country's economic managers. The Kazakhstan government also has been criticized for failing to curb rent-seeking behavior of minor officials. In 1999 Kazakhstan ranked 86 on the Transparency International Corruption Perception Index, a ranking better than that of neighboring Uzbekistan but not far removed from countries with notorious level of corruption such as Uganda and Pakistan (TI, 2000). One of the most frequent explanations for the failure of Kazakhstan's framework to function in practice is that the abstract, external rules of Anglo-Saxon accounting, competition, and integrity institutions simply do not grow and develop on the soil of Kazakhstan's "Eastern" cultural traditions.

The importance of family and clan relations is very real in Kazakhstan. Kazakhstan's political culture is a heterogeneous mix of traditions, values, institutions, and influences. Kazakhstan culture may be described as open, friendly, and cooperative. But, when discussion concerns the bottom line, family connections stands out as the most important single element in any interpersonal transaction. It is not considered to be acceptable for an ethnic Kazakh to prosper without including members of his or her family in that prosperity. The pressures, therefore, to make special arrangements for family members are quite intense in Kazakhstan. These family traditions are rooted in Kazakhstan's past. Located in the center of the Eurasian landmass, the territory of Kazakhstan has long served as a meeting ground of various cultures. Mongol influences from the East brought the Kazakh language, Persian and Islamic influences from the South brought many cultural and social institutions, and Slavic influence from the North brought the political institutions of the twentieth century. Although the metaphor should not be pushed too far, there is an obvious relationship between the openness and indefensibility of the broad Kazakh steppes and the openness and friendliness of Kazakh political culture. Traditionally a nomadic, herding people, the original Kazakh political institutions were loosely structured, almost confederal in design (Masanov, 1995). Nomadic peoples, whose livelihoods are closely connected to the seasonal migration of game, are inclined to develop political institutions that reflect the autonomy of independent movement and decision-making. Plains peoples, living in a single, uninterrupted field and whose livelihoods are easily interrupted by influences flowing in from outside the cultural unit, are inclined to confederal political institutions such as the Kazakh *juz*, or tribe.

This may explain to some extent why Kazakhstan, which in some ways has such an open economy, is so closely controlled in other ways. Some observers attribute this to an effort to re-establish the dominant role of Kazakh people in the wake of the collapse of the multi-nationalism of the Soviet period. To be sure, the past several years have witnessed a determined effort in the country to restore the primacy of the national traditions of the ethnic Kazakhs. The Kazakh language, while not the dominant language in written and spoken communication, was re-established as the official state language. Legislation was passed to require that all government documents be written in the Kazakh language. The Kazakhstan Ministry of Justice was charged with developing programs such that all elements of the justice system would eventually function in the Kazakh language. Ethnic Kazakh business people, government officials, and cultural figures assumed a visibly dominant role in Kazakhstan society. The country's privatization program was carried out in such a way that, in the eyes of some of its critics, inordinately benefited citizens of Kazakh ethnic background. The capital of the government was moved from the city of Almaty northward to the city of Astana to consolidate, in the eyes of many observers, the position of ethnic Kazakhs in the historically Russian dominated north-central regions of the country. The government's main statistical reporting agency has ceased to provide detailed statistical reporting on ethnic composition – a fact interpreted by some as a suggestion of the sensitivity of the ethnic question.

On the other hand, there is also evidence to suggest that the changing cultural features of contemporary Kazakhstan society do not reflect anything like a "nationalist conspiracy." The promotion of racial antagonism in Kazakhstan is a violation of the constitution. There are no official Kazakh clan-based political organizations of any kind. All Kazakhstan citizens talk openly and frequently about the various Kazakh tribes, the *juz*, but this is no more than a cultural construct; one looks in vain, for instance, through the phone books to find the phone number of the senior tribe. The Russian language is widely spoken. Kazakhstan citizens of Russian ethnicity have occupied some of the highest government posts, for instance, the Minister of Finance and the Ministry of Labor and Social Protection. Many of the most prominent social and business figures in the country are of non-Kazakh ethnic origin.

The cultural arguments are overshadowed by the fact that so much of the revenue generating capacity of Kazakhstan is cloistered in narrow and hard to monitor sectors, the oil, gas, and minerals industries. The oil, gas, and minerals sectors, in Kazakhstan as in other countries, give rise to special opportunities for insider arrangements.[7] The intrigues of financing "Big Oil" may be likely to be the source of constraints on transparency and openness that Kazakh nomadic traditions.

Regional administrative policy

Kazakhstan is physically an exceptional country. Kazakhstan is a large, sparsely populated country with a large percentage of the country's population concentrated in a small number of large cities. Given the size of the country and the country's historical traditions, one might conclude that a federal principle of organization would be appropriate. But the Constitution and the political leadership have maintained that the integrity of the Kazakhstan state is best served through a unitary principle of organization. In a unitary system, all jurisdictions are located within a single national jurisdiction. Administrative divisions are subordinate to the national level. Kazakhstan has four levels of administrative divisions: national, province, district, and municipality (Table 3.4). In 1997 a territorial reform consolidated the provinces, reducing their number from nineteen to fourteen.[8]

In the Kazakhstan system of public finance, revenue and budget functions are separated. The collection of taxes is assigned to the various levels of government organizations and the collected taxes are then submitted to the central government. Spending decisions are made at the central level and funds are then allocated to the various levels as earmarked allocations. Local provincial assemblies have no independent taxation or revenue functions and no source of independent revenue generation other than local service fees, which themselves are subject to central approval. One of the most hotly debated political questions in Kazakhstan is the selection of province governors through province election. At present, governors are appointed by the president and serve at the pleasure of the president. While the president has repeatedly identified this as a natural element

Table 3.4 Administrative divisions

	Kazakhstan administrative divisions (2002)		
	Territory ($1000\,km^2$)	*Districts*	*Regional center*
Kazakhstan province	2724.9	162	Astana (national capital)
Akmola region	121.7	16	Astana
Aktiubinsk	300.6	12	Aktiubinsk
Almaty	224.2	16	Almaty
Atyrau	118.6	7	Atyrau
East-Kazakhstan	283.3	15	Ust-Kamenogorsk
Zhambyl	144.3	10	Taraz
West-Kazakhstan	151.3	12	Uralsk
Karaganda	428.0	9	Karaganda
Kyzylorda	226.0	7	Kyzylorda
Kostanai	196.0	16	Kostanai
Mangistau	165.6	4	Aktau
Pavlodar	124.8	10	Pavlodar
North-Kazakhstan	123.2	16	Petropavlovsk
South-Kazakhstan	117.3	12	Shymkent
Almaty city			Almaty

of the transition to democratic rule and to be expected in Kazakhstan in the future, no date has been set for these elections.

Kazakhstan's population is multinational. Soviet demographic practice was to record the ethnic balance of general population based on criteria of ethnic identification that many sociologists regarded as suspect. Nevertheless, according to Soviet era data, ethnic Kazakhs comprised plurality of the population, but did not form a majority. These data reflected a population composition of roughly 40 percent Kazakhs, 40 percent Russians, and 20 percent other nationalities. Some current semi-official sources report that Kazakhs are in the majority, making up just slightly over 50 percent of the population. However, official government sources no longer report figures on ethnicity.[9] Given the paucity of reliably reported official data, misconceptions about the ethnic make-up of Kazakhstan are common. One important misconception is that that the Kazakhs are concentrated in the southern regions while the Russians occupy the northern tier oblasts. In fact, the ethnic composition is variegated, with nationality and ethnic groups concentrated in pockets but scattered in no simple pattern.

One argument frequently heard for moving the country's capital from Almaty to Aqmola (which in April 1998 was renamed Astana) was that it would place the dominant Kazakh ethnic group closer to the geographic center of gravity of the country. According to this view, this would have the effect of reducing the likelihood of separatist sentiment among the northern Slavic population. But given the fact that ethnic populations are widely distributed, it is hard to see how a move of the administrative apparatus of the state could have any discernible effect upon the balance of ethnic group power in the country. The more likely explanation for the expensive and involved movement of the capital is that it represents an effort to transplant the capital in a way that would reorganize the state both in terms of territory and in terms of administrative structure.

Public participation and openness

The most important avenue of political participation is participation in political parties. In the USSR, the period of *perestroika* and political reform in Kazakhstan inaugurated a period of experimentation with social and political movements. As the USSR came to a close, alternative political parties in Kazakhstan were legalized. Kazakhstan may be described as having a multiparty system. The Kazakhstan Constitution (1995) specifically legalized political parties acting within the confines of the law. However, the registration of parties is complex and does not lend itself to the formation of new parties. Between five and ten major political parties have been active during the first decade of Kazakhstan's independence. The parties serve to mobilize and spur public opinion in the public marketplace of discussion.

During the 1999 presidential elections there were nine political parties registered in Kazakhstan with the Kazakhstan Ministry of Justice. Some of the most important political parties included the KCP. The KCP was formed in September 1991, the successor to the Bolshevik Party. The KCP platform called for the return of the socialist development model in the republic, review of privatization, restoration of state property, and the restoration of social guarantees. The KCP leader was Serikbolsyn Abdilidin. The Kazakhstan Social Party was also formed in September 1991, following the reformation of the KCP. The platform of the Kazakhstan Socialist Party emphasized radical reforms directed at increasing social welfare, and the maintenance of human rights and freedoms.

The "*Otan*" [Fatherland] party was formed March 1999 as a result of the combination of the "Kazakhstan Liberal Movement," the "Kazakhstan People's Unity Party," the "Democratic Party," and the "For Kazakhstan – 2030" movement. *Otan*'s platform emphasized strengthening the state through democracy, prosperity, social partnership, and popular participation. The chairman of the party was Sergei Tereshenko, a former Prime Minister.

The "Kazakhstan People's Congress" party was formed in October 1991. The founders were the "Nevada–Semipalatinsk" movement and "Aral–Asia–Kazakhstan" movement, the Union of Kazakhstan Women, the "Birlesu" independent trade union, the "Kazakh Tili" society, the Association of Young Builders and several national cultural centers. The platform of the People's Congress stressed efforts to maintain a democratic society in an independent, legal, unitary state. The leader of the party and honorary chairman of the Central Coordinating Committee was Olzhas Suleimenov.

The Kazakhstan Republican People's Party was formed in December 1998. The goal of the party was the promotion of a democratic state with socially oriented market economy. The chairman of the party was Akezhan Kazhegeldin, the former Prime Minister. Kazhegeldin was not registered as a candidate in the presidential election due to the government's finding that he had violated the law by participating in an unsanctioned meeting.

The "Azamat" Democratic movement was formed in 1996 and was reformed as a party in March 1999. The platform of Azamat stressed alternative economic and political policies including local self-administration, changes in the tax system, and increased social benefits. The leaders were Galym Abilsitov, Murat Auezov, and Petr Svoik.

A second major pillar of civil society is openness in press and electronic media. The Kazakhstan constitution and Kazakhstan legislation relating to the media rhetorically provide for freedom of speech and freedom of the press. Yet the Kazakhstan government has engaged in close monitoring and, at times, harassment of independent media. There have been reports of intimidation and retaliation against editorial office and journalists. In critical circumstances, the government has frequently invoked Kazakhstan laws and policies that conflicted with editorial and journalistic independence. For instance, the Kazakhstan law on national security allowed the police to suspend the activities of news organizations that were regarded as endangering state security. A 1999 Kazakhstan state secrets law specified a list of government secrets. Release of these secrets was punishable under the criminal code. The list of secrets included information about the amount of government debt owed to foreign creditors, and certain kinds of data regarding the country's mineral reserves. The law also made illegal disseminating information about the health, financial circumstances, or the private affairs of the country's president and members of his family. This law has been used in conjunction with Article 46 of the Kazakhstan Constitution that maintains that the honor and dignity of the President "shall be inviolable."

The new March 2000 Kazakhstan media law reasserted the requirement that news organizations could only function if registered by the government. The law contained libel provisions that limited editorial autonomy as well as requiring journalists under some conditions to receive permission prior to taping interviews of news subjects. The law also limited the re-broadcast of some programming, particularly news programs of Russian origin. Many news organizations are owned by holding companies, the ownership of which is not required under Kazakhstan law to be made public. Government opponents frequently claim that the media organizations are in this way secretly controlled by the government or by family members of government leaders.

Civil and human rights

Section II of the Kazakhstan Constitution specifies basic freedoms of thought, speech, religion, privacy, integrity, and association. Freedom of assembly is restricted in part by the Kazakhstan law on national security. The law specifies that unsanctioned gatherings, public meetings, marches, demonstrations, picketing, and disruptive labor strikes are a threat to national security. Under the law, organizations must apply for a permit to hold a demonstration or public meeting ten days in advance of the gathering. The government authorities are under no constraint to issue the permits, however, and have frequently failed or refused to issue them. In some cases, as in the case of Akezhan Kazhegeldin the former Prime Minister, participation in an unsanctioned meeting has been prosecuted as a criminal violation.

Freedom of association is protected by the Constitution. However, the government imposes stiff registration requirements on organizations that act as a corporate entity, conduct meetings or joint activities, and maintain independent financial accounts and resources. Those organizations that have a membership base, such as unions or associations, are required to register with the government in their locality. Non-membership organizations, for instance, civic groups or special purpose nongovernmental organizations such as human rights organizations, are required to register with the central governmental authorities. The registration process gives the government a measure of control over the organization's activities.

Kazakhstan's Constitution and other legal and regulatory acts affirm basic standards of human and civil rights. Yet Kazakhstan's human rights record is relatively poor. There have been reports of arbitrary arrest and detention and prolonged detention. There have been reports of police brutality, mistreatment of detainees, torture, and a few reports of extra-judicial killings. Inhumane prison conditions existed in some cases. There were cases of trials *in absentia*, in particular of the former Prime Minister, Akezhan Kazhegeldin. The government has violated citizens' basic rights to privacy. Trafficking in human beings is widespread in Kazakhstan, although the Kazakhstan government has taken steps to combat this. On the plus side, there were no bona fide cases of imprisonment on purely political grounds. And the Kazakhstan government has made a good faith commitment to combating drug trafficking.

Political stability and support

There is widespread public support for certain policies of the Kazakhstan government as reflected in public opinion polls. There is also widespread criticism of certain aspects of political practice in Kazakhstan that could lead to political instability in the event of a critical juncture in governmental functioning. The Kazakhstan government has been accused of giving in to clanism and family relations that could lead to consequences similar to those experienced by the Suharto regime in Indonesia (Masanov *et al.*, 2002). Political opposition accuses Nazarbaev himself of monopolizing political power for persona benefit (Kazhegeldin, 2000).

The most dramatic illustrations of potential instability, however, are visible from the infighting and recrimination of Kazakhstan's elite politics. The cross-cutting cleavages resulting from the compromises between Kazakhstan's powerful Astana-based families and the large and powerful financial interests of oil and major industries came to the fore in the autumn of 2001. Since the mid-1990s, the rise of Rakhat Aliev, Nazarbaev's son-in-law, in gaining financial control over key privatized industries and in eventually gaining the position of Deputy Chairman of the Kazakhstan National Security Committee was bitterly contested by many Kazakhstan officials. Accusations of influence peddling plagued Aliev. When relations between Aliev and his wife, Nazarbaev's well-placed daughter became strained in 2000, the family crisis acquired the features of a political crisis. Responding to criticism of favortism, on November 14, 2001, Aliyev, resigned as deputy chairman of the National Security Committee. He was given a face-saving ceremonial post in the President's personal guard. But the Aliev scandal focused attention on the close relations between power and influence in Kazakhstan's narrow circle of insiders. Pro-reform business and political leaders stepped forward to urge government reforms. Announcing the intention to register a new party called "Democratic Choice of Kazakhstan," a number of political leaders appealed for the election of province governors and greater legislative and judicial independence. On November 21, 2002, then Prime Minister Toqaev announced the firing of Deputy Prime Minister Uraz Djandosov and Deputy Defense Minister Zhannat Ertlesova. Toqaev also offered to resign as Prime Minister, but President Nazarbaev declined to accept the offer.

The prospect of a change of government came at an inopportune time for Nazarbaev. Nazarbaev, in the midst of preparations for a planned trip to Washington, DC in the near aftermath of the September 11 terrorist attack, was anxious to find a resolution to the scandals and divisiveness that would not diminish his ability to take credit for Kazakhstan's booming economic growth, rapidly developing energy sector, and support for international anti-terrorism. Nazarbaev's trip to Washington was a public relations success. A joint statement adopted by President George W. Bush and Nazarbaev in December 2001 emphasized the importance of international standards of governance. The statement reaffirmed Kazakhstan's and Nazarbaev's commitment to promoting the rule of law, freedom of religion, human rights, and strengthening democratic institutions and processes, such as independent media, local government, pluralism, and free and fair elections.

At this point the reformists and opposition parties in Kazakhstan regrouped. Early in 2002 the Republican People's Party of Kazakhstan leader Akezhan Kazhegeldin, executive committee Chairman Amirzhan Qosanov, Azamat Party Co-Chairman Petr Svojk, and Gulzhan Ergalieva of the People's Congress of Kazakhstan signed an agreement to merge three groups to form a new United Democratic Party (UDP). At a press conference in Almaty on January 14, representatives of the National Congress, Azamat, and the Republican People's Party of Kazakhstan endorsed the program of the UDP. UDP supporters favor transforming Kazakhstan's presidential system into a parliamentary republic. They advocate abolishing the present bicameral parliament in favor of unicameral body and reforming the country's administrative-territorial structure to reduce the number of provinces to seven with popularly elected leaders. Democratic Choice (DCK) regrouped as well. DCK leaders Uras Zhandosov and Bulat Abilov recently announced plans to register the "Ak Zhol" party to pursue a pro-business political agenda. The announcement of Imangali Tasmagambetov as Kazakhstan's New Prime Minister made by President Nazarbaev at an afternoon legislative session in Astana on Monday, January 28, 2002 came as little surprise in the country's capital. The appointment of Imangali Tasmagambetov, a conservative and trusted Nazarbaev ally, as Kazakhstan's new Prime Minister reflected a defensive response to increasingly open challenges to Kazakhstan's key policies.

Summary

Many areas of Kazakhstan's macro-economic reform have been highly successful, even providing a model for other post-communist countries to follow. The Kazakhstan government established a legal foundation and regulatory system for a private economy. The government introduced a national currency, the *Tenge*, which became and has remained convertible. The government moved quickly to establish sound monetary and fiscal policies, including establishing a modern civil code and tax code, and banking and investment laws that accorded with international standards. The government carried out macro-economic reforms including true price liberalization, freeing the markets from government controls. The government turned major enterprises over to the private sector, including the majority of power generation facilities and coalmines. The government actively encouraged international trade and foreign investment.

The government passed environmentally sound, oil and gas legislation meeting international standards.

In contrast with these economic policy successes, Kazakhstan's reform has made less headway in other areas (Olcott, 2002). Kazakhstan's foreign policies did not create a level of prosperity sufficient to enable a broad distribution of the economic benefits of the transition. The country continued to rely upon oil sector revenues, fiscal redistribution, and foreign donor assistance to finance the alleviation of the social consequences of the more difficult aspects of structural reform. Further development of Kazakhstan's oil and mineral sectors cannot be expected to lead to a wide redistribution of income unless exceptional steps are taken to ensure that this is the case. Kazakhstan's agriculture remained without adequate investment in infrastructure such as roads, processing equipment, and farm inputs. Moreover, the banking reforms virtually ignored agriculture, failing to provide much needed credit for farm expansion. Kazakhstan adopted a private pension system, moving ahead of other former communist countries, but the social safety net has worn thin in many areas. With a per capita income of $1,300 in 2000, most citizens of Kazakhstan did not receive the benefits of macroeconomic reform and the resurgence of world prices for the country's significant oil, gas, and gold deposits. The social safety net has been weakened with declines in health status, benefits for senior citizens, and education opportunities. Dramatic increases in infectious diseases such as drug-resistant tuberculosis posed serious social threats.

As one moves further along the spectrum from purely economic reforms to governance reforms, to administrative reforms, and then on to political reforms, the indicators of success grow less impressive. Kazakhstan stands out as the most democratic country of the region – in no other Central Asian country is there such open debate and contestation over policy alternatives. But in absolute respects much of the expected spillover from the free choice of market economics has not materialized in the political sphere. There is little collateral effect of market improvements on the political marketplace of ideas. The most important explanation for this is the dominating influence of the oil and minerals sectors. Revenue from these sectors sustains the Kazakhstan government and is offered as a palliative to the political opposition as a source of revenue that will eventually reduce social competition and lead to "oil prosperity" thereby enabling less competitive politics. But it is a mistake to assume that oil revenues will ever be sufficiently redistributed to create the basis for social justice. Kazakhstan's oil constituencies can be expected to continue to reinforce the strong state in Kazakhstan. The more direct route to political liberalization would be to promote economic reform measures that lead to the growth of democratically oriented constituencies. Auspicious reform measures are specifically those that would promote diversification, trade, small enterprises, and other broadly distributed constituencies.

4 Kyrgyzstan and the reform path

How have Kyrgyzstan's economic policy choices since independence affected the country's political development? The data and analysis presented in this chapter offers a portrait of Kyrygzstan as the Central Asian country initially most dedicated to economic reform. Kyrgyzstan's enthusiasm for the reform path early on earned Kyrgyzstan an early reputation as the "democratic showcase of the former Soviet Union." Soon after independence, the Kyrgyzstan government embraced the policy prescriptions of the "Washington consensus." Kyrygzstan attempted to implement the policy prescriptions of the Washington consensus in good faith. At the same time, Kyrgyzstan was a Central Asian country that faced substantial natural obstacles to successful economic reform. Kyrgyzstan's economic reform measures did result in rapid and significant advances in state capacity. However, Kyrgyzstan's economic reform did not lead to the expected growth in economic output, did not result in the expected improvements in social welfare, did little to improve the government's capacity to protect civil rights, and had negligible effects on the process of political liberalization.

The following profile of Kyrgyzstan surveys the distinguishing features of the economic and political development of the country. The transition of the Kyrgyzstan state carried out through structural reform is described in next section. The succeeding section analyzes the effect of economic policy choices on government and politics, emphasizing the dominant feature of Kyrgyzstan's political development – the inextricable cultural and economic links with Kyrgyzstan's neighbor to the south, Uzbekistan.

Kyrgyzstan profile

Nestled between China and Kazakhstan, Uzbekistan and Tajikistan, Kyrgyzstan is a country of rare natural beauty, sometimes referred to as the "Switzerland of Asia." (Brantsen, 1977; J. Anderson, 1999) During the period of the USSR (1917–91), Kyrgyzstan had a highly specialized economic niche in the communist economic system. Kyrgyzstan served primarily as a provider of primary commodities for industries located in the European parts of the USSR. Cut off from Soviet era suppliers and customers immediately after the collapse of the USSR, Kyrgyzstan's small and uncompetitive industrial enterprises quickly became insolvent and many closed entirely. Kyrygzstan's agricultural sector was blocked from access to farm inputs and also quickly slipped back toward subsistence farming. The transition to an open economy was difficult for this small country with few manufactured goods. Between 1991 and 1994 farm and industrial output fell, trade dropped, inflation soared, and the government ran a large fiscal deficit. The Kyrgyzstan economy reached a nadir in 1994, at about the time that substantial official foreign development assistance began to arrive.

The Kyrgyzstan economy began to rebound in 1996 from the post-collapse contraction. Inflation was reduced. The budget deficit as a proportion of GDP was cut in half during the period 1995 through 1997. With international donor assistance, the Kyrgyzstan government made good headway in establishing the legal and regulatory foundation for a market economy. Kyrgyzstan carried out privatization of small enterprises and overhauled the country's banking and financial systems. In 1998, the Kyrgyzstan constitution was amended to allow for private ownership of land. Also in 1998, Kyrgyzstan became the first post-Soviet country to join the World Trade Organization. The Kyrgyzstan government eliminated export registration in 1998 and eliminated export duties in 1999. Kyrgyzstan essentially eliminated quantitative tariff restrictions (Gürgen *et al.*, 1999).

Kyrgyzstan had an estimated population of 5 million people in mid-2001.[1] Its population has been growing modestly since independence, despite out migration, and its workforce was previously spread about evenly among agriculture, industry, and service. In the past decade industrial employment dropped to less than half its 1991 level. At the same time, agricultural employment grew by 50 percent. Agricultural output, which dropped initially after independence, increased overall by the end of the decade. But industrial production saw steep declines in the early years of independence and, with the exception of a few mining sectors, has not rebounded. Coal production in 2000 was less than one-quarter of its 1991 level. Hydroelectric production increased, however (Table 4.1(a)). During the first years of independence, Kyrgyzstan ran a persistent balance of payments deficit. Russia, historically Kyrgyzstan's largest destination for exports, was overtaken by Germany for first place among Kyrgyzstan's export partners after the 1998 Russian financial crisis. Russia continued to be the largest source of imports for Kyrgyzstan, followed by imports from neighboring Uzbekistan and Kazakhstan (Table 4.1(b)).

Kyrgyzstan in absolute terms has made the most visible progress toward democratic institution of the Central Asian states. While Kyrgyzstan retained a "presidential" form of government, Krygyzstan's parliament has grown relatively independent, often challenging presidential authority on key issues. Opposition political figures were often visibly subject to harassment and intimidation, but the very fact that this was taking place so often is an indication that Kyrgyzstan's political context is one of competing views and constituencies (Table 4.2). Nongovernmental civic organizations were relatively widespread and influential in public affairs. Heads of local administrations were elected in 2000 for the first time rather than appointed, as they had been previously in Kyrgyzstan,

Table 4.1a Kyrgyzstan key indices: production

Item	*1991*	*1992*	*1993*	*1994*	*1995*	*1996*	*1997*	*1998*	*1999*	*2000*
Population (million; as of July 1)	4.39	4.49	4.48	4.47	4.62	4.69	4.76	4.83	4.90	4.97
Labor force (thousand; calendar year)	—	—	1710	1716	1741	1791	1792	1811	1901	1911
Employed	1754	1836	1681	1645	1641	1651	1689	1705	1764	1767
Agriculture	623	700	669	686	771	778	816	837	924	938
Manufacturing	466	414	359	318	271	241	228	219	204	202
Others	665	722	653	641	599	632	645	649	636	627
Unemployed	—	—	29	71	100	140	103	106	137	144
Unemployment rate (%)	—	—	1.7	4.1	5.7	7.8	5.7	5.9	7.2	7.5
Production (thousand metric tons; calendar year)										
Agriculture, crop year										
1 Wheat	434	634	831	566	625	964	1274	1204	1109	1039
2 Barley	557	582	477	288	159	166	152	162	180	150
3 Potatoes	326	362	308	311	432	562	678	774	957	1046
4 Maize	365	281	184	129	116	182	171	228	308	338
5 Vegetables (fresh, frozen, etc.)	399	404	259	266	318	369	479	556	719	747
6 Meat	230	228	214	197	180	186	186	191	196	196
7 Milk	1131	961	946	872	864	885	912	973	1064	1105
Production indexes period averages										
Agriculture (1985 I 1989–91 = 100)	107.0	100.6	97.0	88.0	81.2	89.8	97.9	100.8	106.3	107.7
Industry (1985 I 1995 = 100)	118.0	87.0	65.0	47.0	100.0	108.8	163.6	178.0	170.5	185.7
Energy (annual values)										
Coal ('000 m.t.)										
Production	—	2151	1721	848	463	410	522	432	417	419
Exports	—	1024	531	171	171	100	78	23	11	22
Imports	—	1339	1028	1355	500	844	290	806	764	726
Consumption	—	2465	2218	2032	792	1154	734	1215	1170	1123
Electricity (Mn kWh)										
Production	14,171	11,892	11,091	12,932	12,349	13,758	12,637	11,618	13,119	14,886
Exports	—	—	—	—	1622	2881	2417	998	2011	3153
Imports	—	—	—	—	254	815	715	394	184	321
Consumption	8814	8616	8467	8189	10,981	11,678	10,854	10,893	11,262	12,054

Source: Asian Development Bank. *Key Indicators 2001: Growth and Change in Asia and the Pacific* (New York: Oxford University Press, 2001).

Table 4.1b Kyrgyzstan key indices: foreign trade

Item	*1991*	*1992*	*1993*	*1994*	*1995*	*1996*	*1997*	*1998*	*1999*	*2000*
External trade (Mn US dollars; calendar year)										
Exports, fob	—	317.0	339.6	340.0	408.9	505.4	603.8	513.6	453.8	504.5
Imports, cif	—	420.7	447.8	317.0	522.3	837.7	709.3	841.5	599.7	554.1
Trade balance	—	−103.7	−108.2	23.0	−113.4	−332.3	−105.5	−327.9	−145.9	−49.6
Direction of trade (Mn US dollars; calendar year)										
Total exports	—	314.9	360.1	339.2	483.3	505.9	609.5	513.4	454.0	527.3
1 Germany	—	6.0	5.4	6.6	7.2	2.8	18.0	196.8	148.2	115.7
2 Russia	—	94.0	113.6	58.5	114.3	134.3	98.9	83.8	70.7	67.6
3 Uzbekistan	—	24.9	23.8	43.6	88.9	115.2	101.5	38.6	46.5	87.5
4 Kazakhstan	—	53.8	71.9	95.2	112.5	111.9	87.1	85.5	44.9	38.0
5 Switzerland	—	4.1	0.7	0.3	—	0.9	162.3	0.9	18.0	68.1
6 China, People's Republic of	—	28.0	59.2	56.1	3.0	35.8	31.6	15.6	25.3	50.0
7 United States	—	—	—	0.6	2.3	17.4	18.2	7.6	11.3	2.7
8 United Kingdom	—	11.6	30.0	29.5	6.0	5.2	1.4	1.6	12.5	36.1
9 Tajikistan	—	3.4	6.2	3.0	4.8	12.1	12.6	8.4	9.5	7.3
10 Czech Republic	—	—	—	—	—	8.1	15.3	8.7	6.9	4.6
Total imports	—	418.4	447.1	316.4	391.5	795.2	709.4	841.1	610.5	572.9
1 Russia	—	171.7	158.3	69.3	104.8	174.5	190.8	204.1	109.3	129.5
2 Uzbekistan	—	31.9	58.2	63.7	70.0	131.5	128.6	122.2	50.6	47.3
3 Kazakhstan	—	81.4	97.0	58.3	66.8	139.5	69.6	75.3	72.6	84.3
4 United States	—	23.2	54.6	35.0	3.2	35.7	39.7	40.8	54.3	42.4
5 Germany	—	6.3	3.0	6.8	2.3	31.8	38.4	53.0	47.3	30.1
6 Turkey	—	3.4	8.8	15.0	3.6	47.6	43.8	37.3	23.0	25.4
7 China, People's Republic of	—	16.3	18.6	10.6	27.4	7.8	32.4	44.4	36.8	37.5
8 Canada	—	2.7	—	1.6	2.9	42.5	5.2	14.4	25.4	8.9
9 Korea, Republic of	—	0.7	0.2	3.6	—	5.1	5.3	26.3	27.1	7.1
10 Turkmenistan	—	21.3	7.2	10.4	2.2	13.6	15.5	8.2	7.8	21.0

Source: Asian Development Bank. *Key Indicators 2001: Growth and Change in Asia and the Pacific*. New York: Oxford University Press, 2001.

Table 4.2 Kyrgyzstan: political freedoms

	Nations in transit 2000 political indicators								
	1991–92	*1992–93*	*1993–94*	*1994–95*	*1995–96*	*1996–97*	*1997–98*	*1998–99*	*1999–2000*
Political rights	5	4	5	4	4	4	4	5	5
Civil liberties	4 PF	2 PF	3 PF	3 PF	4 PF	4 PF	4 PF	5 PF	5 PF

Source: *Nations in Transit*, 2000, New York: Freedom House.

Table 4.3 World Bank Institute governance indicators for Kyrgyzstan

Governance indicator	*Year*	*Percentile rank (0–100) in %*	*Estimate (−2.5 to +2.5)*	*Standard deviation*	*Number of surveys/polls*
Voice and accountability	2000/01	31.6	−0.57	0.19	3
Political stability/No violence	2000/01	39.5	−0.32	0.48	2
Government effectiveness	2000/01	31.9	−0.61	0.31	3
Regulatory quality	2000/01	20.7	−0.63	0.37	4
Rule of law	2000/01	26.5	−0.72	0.22	4
Control of corruption	2000/01	20.5	−0.85	0.23	4

Source: Kaufmann, Kraay, and Zoido (KKZ), 2002: *Governance Matters II: Updated Governance Indicators for 2000–01*. World Bank Institute.

and as they continued to be in other Central Asian states. While Kyrgyzstan's human rights record received criticism from international organizations, there was more open discussion and fewer instances of direct coercion and intimidation of human rights activists than in other Central Asian states. Petty crime and violent crime grew to be a problem in Kyrgyzstan. Freedom of the press suffered, in part aided by a growing government concern with terrorism and insurgency. The World Bank Institute governance indicators ranked Kyrygzstan in 2001 as below the fortieth percentile in all six key governance categories (Table 4.3).

Transition of the state in Kyrgyzstan

After national independence on August 31, 1991, the newly established Kyrgyzstan government quickly identified establishing a market-based economy and integrating into the world economy as one of the country's foremost goals. Kygyzstan began the transition period with a deliberate goal of transforming the nature of the post-socialist state.[2] Among the former communist countries, Kyrgyzstan became a leader in the movement of the post-Soviet states toward an open market economy. However, Kyrgyzstan's limited resource endowment and trade dependence constrained its real progress.[3] With assistance from international organizations such as the World Bank and the International Monetary Fund (IMF), the Kyrgyzstan government made good headway in establishing the legal and regulatory foundation for a market economy. Kyrgyzstan carried out privatization of small enterprises and overhauled the country's banking and financial systems.

Soon after independence, the Kyrgyzstan government went through functional reorganization and staff reduction. Shortly thereafter, the size of the government increased as the new demands of meeting international standards called for greater state capacity. Criticized for overexpansion, the government again entered into a reduction in function and staff size. In turn, pressing social problems called forth another wave of government expansion. Under pressure again from international donors, the Kyrgyzstan government reduced the public sector in 2001, cutting the number of government ministries from seventeen to twelve and reducing the number of government agencies and committees from forty-two to twenty-nine. But even given these efforts at downsizing the public sector, the public share of overall employment remained exceptionally high, estimated to account for nearly one-quarter of all employment in the country.[4]

Fiscal and monetary policy

The Central Asian states disagreed with one another over monetary policy soon after independence. All the Central Asian states were concerned about the implications of Russian hyperinflation for their economies. But the Central Asian states drew differing conclusions regarding the speed and depth of the structural reforms that were called for. Kyrgyzstan was cautioned by its southern neighbor Uzbekistan to act within the context of Central Asian cooperation. Kyrgyzstan, however, decided to move quickly toward liberalizing prices. Kyrgyzstan broke with the go-slow, coordinated approach by introducing its national currency, the Kyrgyz *Som*, in March 1993. In response to the adoption of the Kyrgyzstan currency, Uzbekistan acted in the spring of 1993 to establish border and customs inspection posts along the many thoroughfares linking the two countries. Trucks, busses, and passenger traffic piled up in long lines as customs officials and citizens on both sides of the borders attempted to sort out arrangements with respect to transit, payments, and currencies.

Between 1995 and 1997, positive developments in the economy reinforced the Kyrgyzstan government's intention to restrict the supply of money. A scarce currency will tend to be valuable. Conversely, as the currency becomes more available, its value will tend to decline. Inflation soared in the period 1993–95 and was then brought under control. Following the 1997 "Asian Flu" economic disruptions and, in particular, following the collapse of financial markets in Russia in August 1998, the Kyrgyz economy again suffered dramatically. Kyrgyzstan's money supply rose in 1998 and 1999. During this period inflation rebounded, reaching nearly 40 percent in 1999. During 1999, the *Som* lost 35 percent of its value to the US dollar. Public confidence in the currency was further shaken by press coverage of major financial fraud scandals involving some of the country's largest commercial banks.

The responsible agency for currency arrangements was the National Bank of the Kyrgyz Republic (NBKR). By 1998, the NBKR had separated its functions from the government and discontinued providing deficit financing to the government or other quasi-fiscal government lending. The NBKR is the country's account holder for the national treasury.

Privatization and liberalization

To promote foreign invest the Kyrgyzstan government established the Committee on Foreign Investments (Goskominvest). The Committee served as an ombudsman to assist foreign investors by providing information and business assistance, simplifying visas and permits, and helping with registration, licensing, and customs procedures. A comprehensive foreign investment law was adopted in September 1997. The law broke new ground in the CIS in serving as regulatory foundation for creating an attractive policy environment for foreign investment in the country. Reflecting its enthusiasm for entering the international trading system, Kyrgystan in December 1998 became the first CIS country to join the World Trade Organization.

In the late 1990s agriculture reported good performance, growing by almost 9 percent over the previous year. The service sector grew by about 3 percent. Industrial production, following a long-term trend, continued to decline. Kyrgyzstan produces cotton, tobacco, fruits and berries, grain, wool, and meat. Agriculture is the dominant sector of the Kyrgyz economy, accounting for about 45 percent of GDP, for about half of total employment, and for 22 percent of exports in 1999. Agricultural production dropped in 1992 from earlier levels and then began to rise. Production began to increase after 1996. At the same time, livestock and wool production, two of the traditional mainstays of the rural economy, continued to decline. In connection with the Kyrgyzstan government's goal of maintaining a liberal economic order, the government has avoided intervention in the agricultural economy through price supports and targeted subsidies. This policy contrasts sharply with that of neighboring Uzbekistan, where the government has continued to maintain a major presence in the agricultural economy. During the 1990s, despite substantial recovery in agricultural production, rural incomes per capita fell substantially. Kyrgyzstan instituted a land reform program. Over 90 percent of farms are in private hands. Farmland may be bought and sold. The Kyrgyzstan government recognizes that agriculture is the most promising sector for solving the country's economic and social problems. The agricultural and food processing sector is a high priority sector. The Kyrgyzstan government is targeting creameries, food packaging, breweries, and other forms of agriculturally based enterprises as promising areas for future investment.

Mountainous Kyrgyzstan has abundant low-cost hydropower but only very limited amounts of oil, gas, and coal. Consequently, Kyrgyzstan is dependent upon the other Central Asian countries for much of its gas and petroleum.

Kyrgyzstan trades hydroelectric energy for natural gas with both Uzbekistan and Kazakhstan. With the urging of international donors, Kyrgyzstan is seeking to adopt an energy policy that will reduce the role of the state, increase private sector involvement, and explore the potential for energy exports, particularly to China. China's recently adopted "Go West" policy has opened a potentially rich market for hydroelectric energy in the adjoining Xinjiang-Uigur Autonomous Province of China.

The most important assets pending the privatization process were Kyrgyz Telcom, Kyrgyz Energo, Kyrgyz Gas, and Kyrgyz Airlines. These state-managed entities have been slated for privatization throughout the late 1990s but the government has moved reluctantly for fear of potentially disruptive consequences in consumer access to energy, communication, and transportation.

Trade and investment

The three most important sectors of Kyrgyzstan's economy are: agriculture, accounting for about 45 percent of the GDP; industry, accounting for about 20 percent of the GDP; and services accounting for the remaining 35 percent in 1999. The most significant economic sector is agriculture. Agriculture is the largest employer in the country. Other important sectors are hydroelectric energy production, mining, particularly gold mining, and service. Small industries and processing plants are located in Kyrgyzstan's larger cities, particularly Jalalabod, Osh, and Talas in addition to the capital, Bishkek. After the USSR collapsed, Kyrgyzstan's mining and industrial enterprises underwent rapid contraction due to the loss of orders from northern buyers and the inability of the existing transportation infrastructure to make possible a rapid entrance into other markets. Kyrgyzstan's military industrial enterprises soon lost their financing. Production at Kyrgyzstan's gold, mercury, and uranium mines fell sharply.

The only industrial sectors that experienced growth in recent years was engineering and metalworking and gold mining. With the interruption of supplies of small-scale electrical equipment and components from suppliers in Russia, new demands have arisen for the production of these manufactured goods locally. Production has thus begun to rebound. The other main contributor to Kyrgyzstan's industrial production was caused by the expansion of production at the country's largest gold mine, the Kumtor gold mine. It is the largest single enterprise in the country, described as a $500 million development project and one of the world's largest gold fields. The only industrial sector that experienced significant growth was gold mining. In May 1997, the Kumtor Operating Company, which is two-thirds owned by the Kyrgyzstan Republic and one-third by a Canadian company, began gold mining operations. The construction of the mine cost $450 million. The initial estimate of recoverable gold was 16.5 million troy ounces of gold and gold was expected to average around 485,000 ounces a year over the life of the project. In late 1999 the company revised its estimates of recoverable gold downward, taking into account the changes in the price of gold and a revision of the geological expectations of the mining work.

Accordingly, the amount of recoverable gold was revised downward to 4.27 million troy ounces. Company officials announced that the mine would be closed in 2008. This represents a major setback for the Kyrgyz government's development plans, given that revenue from the gold mine constituted a major portion of the government's income (40 percent in 1999).

The decline in Kyrgyzstan industrial sector has pushed many people out of technical and professional positions. Most of this movement has been in the direction of the service sector. A large proportion has also moved to agricultural employment. While the legal system and social security systems traditionally provide for fewer protections for these sectors, in fact working conditions in Kyrgyzstan's declining industry had deteriorated significantly in recent years. Workers unions and collective bargaining was unsuccessful in promoting the health and safety of working conditions in such declining industries. The international donor organizations and multilateral development banks have identified social protection as one of the highest priorities of future assistance to Kyrgyzstan.

Kyrgyzstan's largest trading partner is Russia, comprising almost 40 percent of foreign trade. Behind Russia is Ukraine, the US Uzbekistan, Turkey, the UK, Germany, South Korea, and other countries. Reverberations from the financial crisis in mid-1998 in Russia had a significant impact on Kyrgyzstan. Total external trade in 1999 declined by about 25 percent. Imports declined by nearly 30 percent and exports around 19 percent. Kyrgyzstan's main exports were processing industry products (67 percent) and agricultural goods (17 percent), while the main imports were machine-building products (21 percent), coal and petroleum products (11 percent), food and tobacco (7 percent) and textiles (6 percent). Very nearly half of Kyrgyzstan's foreign trade is with former Soviet countries.

Kyrgyzstan is a landlocked country with inadequate trade and transportation infrastructure. Kyrgyzstan producers of goods and services face high transport costs due to the country's landlocked location and mountainous terrain. The Kyrgyzstan government has undertaken the rehabilitation key roads including the Bishkek–Almaty road and the Bishkek–Osh road. The Bishkek airport recently underwent modernization. A regulatory framework for a modern telecommunications sector was adopted in April 1998. A National Communications Authority has been set up to serve as an independent regulatory agency, with the broadcasting service, Kyrgyz Telecom, functioning as a majority state-held operator. The Kyrgyzstan government has taken measures to improve the trade environment. Customs procedures and non-tariff barriers have been reduced in recent years. However, the trade situation is complicated by the fact that Kyrgyzstan is landlocked. Few goods and services move from Uzbekistan into Kyrgyzstan. The borders with Tajikistan and China have been subject to heavy regulation. Kyrgyzstan's border with Kazakhstan is a long and relatively open border. The Kazakh and Kyrgyz languages are closely related and mutually comprehensible. However, Kazakhstan produces few of the manufactured goods that Kyrgystan requires. Consequently, Kazakhstan serves mainly as a transhipment point for goods from outside Central Asia, particularly Russia and Europe.

The Kyrgystan government has taken steps to improve the foreign investment climate in the country (Butler, 1999). A new foreign investment law was adopted on September 4, 1997. The law was adopted to bring the country into conformance with the standards of the World Trade Organization and has the key provisions necessary from the point of view of promoting foreign direct investment. The law provides protection against expropriation. Under the law, foreign investors have the same legal status and conditions as Kyrgyz investors, and can do business as wholly owned foreign businesses in Kyrgyzstan, or as joint ventures either with Kyrgyz partners or other foreign partners. Foreigners can buy stocks and securities in Kyrgyz companies and participate in privatization programs. Foreign investors can repatriate capital, freely export profits as foreign currency, or as goods produced, or as commodities or services bought. Local currency is freely convertible into foreign currency, including for import purposes or payment against project expenses. Investors may retain earned foreign currency, without having to convert it into local currency.

Banking and financial markets

The Soviet-era banking system had been expanded and slightly modified during the period 1992–95, but had not adopted standards of bank operations in accordance with international practice. Kyrgyzstan banks made a large number of directed loans to loss-making state farms and state industrial enterprises. As a result, in 1995, according to a World Bank study, over half of the all the commercial banks had a negative net worth.[5] The study also concluded that 60 percent of all the banking sector's loans were considered unrecoverable, that is, these loans would never be paid back by the borrowers. A World Bank financial sector adjustment credit helped the government to reorganize the banking sector and make improvements in the legislative and regulatory framework. New laws were passed, including a central bank law, a banking law, a collateral law, a secured transactions law, a bankruptcy law, and the second part of the Civil Code was drafted and adopted by the legislature.

But these institutional changes came too late. A large number of non-performing loans led to a bank crisis. The public lost confidence in the banking system and many people withdrew their funds, leading many of the banks to go out of business. In 1998, in the wake of the Russian financial market collapse, the Kyryzstan banking system also suffered a major financial crisis that led to the closing of half of Kyrgyzstan's twenty-six commercial banks in 1999.

Liberal reform, democratization, and decline

The Republic of Kyrgyzstan was an early leader in the post-communist transition. The country's pro-reform leader, Askar Akaev, a scientist and former president of the republic's Academy of Sciences, quickly established an impressive record of encouraging political and economic liberalization. Akaev, born in 1944 in the Kyrgyz village of Kyzyl-Bairak, was trained as a physicist and graduated from Leningrad Institute of Mechanics and Optics. Akaev worked in Leningrad (now St Petersburg) before returning to the Kyrgyzstan capital of Bishkek (previously named "Frunze" in honor of a Bolshevik Red Army military commander). Akaev entered communist party work late, becoming a party member only in 1981 and serving as a minor party official in Kyrgyzstan. He rose through the scientific hierarchy in Kyrgyzstan, being elected vice president of the Kyrgyz Academy of Sciences in 1987 and, two years later, becoming president of the Academy.

In the passions of post-communist reorganization, the Kyrgyzstan parliament split on the selection of leading candidates for the republic's presidency. The deadlock resulted in reopening the nomination process and Askar Akaev emerged as the victorious compromise candidate in the fourth round of voting in October 1990. Akaev became pesident of the Soviet Socialist Republic of Kyrgyzstan. In January 1991, Akaev introduced new government structures and appointed a new government comprised of younger, reform-oriented technocrats. In October 1991, Akaev ran unopposed and was elected president of the new independent Kyrgyz Republic, which can also be called Kyrgyzstan, by direct ballot, receiving 95 percent of the votes.

Constitutional, legal, and regulatory policy

Kyrgyzstan's legal system is based on the Continental legal system. Kyrgyzstan's Constitution was adopted in 1993. The Constitution recognizes a separation of powers among three branches of government, an accountable executive, a deliberative legislative, and an independent judiciary. The Constitution has provisions to ensure checks and balances, competitive elections, and judicial independence. The judiciary consists of Constitutional Court (to decide issues of constitutional import), a Supreme Court, an arbitration court to resolve commercial disputes. There is a system of lower courts.

As in most countries with the Continental system of law, the core of law regulating commercial and economic activity is the country's civil code. The Kyrgyz Civil Code went into effect June 1, 1996. The Kyrgyz Civil Code is regarded by legal authorities to be one of the most advanced codes of the former communist countries. It sets forth the basic principles of the free market, guaranteeing equality of persons in their relationships under civil law. It provides protection for the rights of persons and their property from interference. It guarantees the rights of persons to use and transfer their property. It provides for the right of persons to conclude contracts with Kyrgyzstan citizens and with foreigners and foreign entities.

An accountable government is one in which the people have the right to exercise sovereignty. But public accountability also implies that the citizens are willing to pay costs of government through a system to raise revenue. The Kyrgyzstan government is financed through a variety of taxes and revenues. A comprehensive tax code went into effect in July 1996. The code provided for a uniform compilation of laws relating to taxes on income, profits, excise and sales, value-added, customs, land, vehicle use, and other public activities. The tax code specified the conditions of taxation of foreign entities.

The Kyrgyzstan government has sought to limit the size of the government sector to enable greater opportunities for the growth of private industry and services. Accordingly the government has sought to reduce the total government revenue as a percent of GDP. However, in recent years as a result of increased costs of social protection programs and government development programs, the proportion of total government revenue to GDOP has increased slightly to over 18 percent. In addition, tax collection has fallen behind anticipated levels. Tax revenue collection relies heavily on industry. Poor industrial performance contributed to the shortfall in tax revenue. Non-tax revenue and grants remained weak.

Total Kyrgyzstan government expenditures were higher than anticipated in recent years. International financial institutions have urged the Kyrgyzstan government to maintain a tight monetary policy, reduce government spending, and increase revenue collection. However, the Kyrgyzstan government is reluctant to adopt these politically unpopular measures. During the first decade of Kyrgyzstan's independence, official foreign financial assistance on a per capita basis in Kyrgyzstan far exceeded levels of other Eurasian former communist countries. However, Kyrgyzstan's limited resource endowment and trade dependence continued to constrain Kyrgyzstan's economic and social progress.

Legislative, executive, and judicial policy

In 1992 the Kyrgyzstan parliament, renamed the *Jogorku Kenesh*, began to debate the provision of a new Kyrgyzstan constitution. Debates centered on relations between executive and legislature, language policies, and privatization, particularly of land. The draft version of the constitution that was favored by Akaev provided for a presidential system with strong executive powers. The other version of the constitution, the one favored by Akaev's opponents, favored a strong legislature. Akaev argued that a parliamentary system would spell disaster for the country because it would encourage regional and clan divisions within the country. The new constitution, Akaev's preferred version, was adopted on May 5, 1993. The constitution expanded the president's powers.

Akaev's expanded powers, however, did not restrain the Kyrgyzstan political opposition. Throughout the difficult economic circumstances of 1994 the debates grew more acrimonious. Akaev circumvented his political opponents by enlisting his five appointed province governors in a complex political ploy that brought the parliament to a deadlock in September 1994, a situation that allowed the president to disband the parliament. Akaev then announced an October 1994 referendum to amend the constitution to establish a bicameral parliament.

The new Kyrgyzstan parliament, the *Jogorku Kenesh*, was bicameral, consisting of a sixty-member Legislative Assembly (*Myizam Chygaruu Jyiyny*) elected for five-year terms and a forty-five-member People's Representative Assembly (*El Okuldor Jyiyny*) also elected for a five-year term. A national referendum on February 10, 1996 – held apparently in violation of the Constitution and the law on referendums – amended the Constitution to again expand the powers of the president at the expense of the legislature. An October 1998 referendum approved constitutional changes that increased the number of deputies in the upper house, reduced the number of deputies in the lower house, rolled back Parliamentary immunity, reformed land tender rules, and reformed the state budget.

Transparency and integrity policy

The Kyrgyzstan government has made well-publicized, visible rhetorical commitments to curbing corruption, graft, and the use of public office for private gain. The Kyrgyzstan procurator general has investigated several cases of official corruption. Yet the government has prosecuted few senior officials, and many of those who have been convicted on corruption charges have received light sentences. Prosecution appears to be selective. The Kyrgyzstan government has made little headway in tighten the legal regime against corruption. Parliament has debated several draft laws on financial disclosure and conflict of interest, but has not adopted the laws. Many of those cases that have been prosecuted appear to have features of government vendettas against opposition figures. Real progress in the fight against corruption has been minimal.

In October 1997, the procurator published a list of parliamentary deputies allegedly involved in suspect business deals. The government suspended privatization measures enacted that year until late 1998 in an effort to reform practices in the Privatization Ministry. Former Vice-President Felix Kulov was arrested and charged with a range of offenses, including abuse of power and embezzlement of about $20,000 from government contracts. Kulov was acquitted of the charges in a criminal court, but a military court then took up the case and reversed the acquittal. Kulov's arrest on corruption charges coincided with a wave of public protests against the shortcomings in Kyrgyzstan's parliamentary elections. Kulov had planned to run against Akaev in the presidential election.

Regional administrative policy

Kyrgyzstan is a unitary political system, organized into seven provinces. Budget allocations are determined by the national government although the provincial governments do have access to some limited own-source revenues. The key dimension of regional relationships in Kyrgyzstan, however, is not provincial but geographical. The country's topography and ethnic distribution divides the northern provinces from the southern provinces in terms of economy, culture, and political orientation. The southern regions include the high mountain areas of Naryn as well as the foothill regions adjacent to Uzbekistan (Table 4.4).

Table 4.4 Administrative divisions

	Kyrgyzstan administrative divisions					
	Territory (1000 km²)	*Districts*	*Towns*	*Small towns*	*Villages*	*Administrative center*
Kyrgyzstan	199.9	39	21	29	430	Bishkek
Provinces						
Batken	17.0	3	3	5	29	Batken
Jalalabad	33.7	8	5	8	68	Jalalabad
Issyk-Kul	43.1	5	3	5	58	Karakol
Naryn	45.2	5	1	2	56	Naryn
Osh	29.2	7	3	2	79	Osh
Tallas	11.4	4	1	1	35	Tallas
Chui	20.2	7	4	5	105	Tokmok
Bishkek city	0.1			1		

Political participation and openness

There are many political parties active in Kyrgystan. In the 2000 parliamentary elections, fifteen parties were registered although the candidates of several of the opposition parties were disqualified by the electoral commission on technical grounds. Among the most important pro-government parties are the Social Democratic Party of Kyrgyzstan (SDPK) founded in July 1993; the Democratic Movement of Kyrgyzstan founded in May 1990; and the Republican Popular Party of Kyrgyzstan. The opposition parties include the Communist Party of Kyrgyzstan and the Democratic Party of Free Kyrgyzstan, or Erkin Kyrgyzstan was founded in October 1991. Erk was led by Topchubek Turganaliev and drew its support from businessmen and interested in speeding economic reforms. Turganaliev, arrested and accused of embezzlement in December 1996, has been a prominent critic of Akaev's reforms.

Election policy

Elections to the Kyrgyzstan parliamentary lower house, the Myizam Chygaruu Jyiyny, were held on February 20, 2000 and March 12, 2000. An OSCE report noted that the elections failed to comply with commitments to free and fair elections and were not in compliance with OSCE standards.[6] Questionable judicial proceedings against opposition candidates and parties limited the choice of candidates available to Kyrgyz voters, while state-controlled media reported favorably on official candidates only and government officials put pressure on independent media outlets that favored the opposition. The Kyrgyz Government was being urged to pursue more free, fair, and transparent elections in the future.

The most recent presidential election, on October 29, 2000, returned Askar Akaev to office for a five-year term with almost 75 percent of the vote based on 77 percent voter turnout. The candidate of the Socialist Party Ata Meken,

Omurbek Tekebayev, came in second with about 14 percent of the votes. The Organization for Security and Cooperation in Europe, OSCE, issued a report on the presidential election that concluded that the "October 2000 presidential election in the Kyrgyz Republic, despite some positive features, failed to comply with OSCE commitments for democratic elections and failed to reverse the negative trends identified during the parliamentary elections."[7]

Civil and human rights

Chapter II, Articles 13–20 of the Kyrgyzstan Constitution enumerate an extensive list of basic freedoms, including thought, speech, religion, privacy, integrity, association, and interpersonal communication. Kyrgyzstan's political sphere is active with citizens taking a substantial role in government. Nevertheless, the Kyrgyzstan government's human rights record was poor overall. It limited the ability of citizens to bring about change in their government even though non-governmental organizations and parliamentary deputies did on occasion succeed in blocking presidential initiatives through parliamentary action and grassroots campaigns.

The government routinely restricted constitutionally guaranteed rights to privacy, freedom of speech press, and political opposition. On notable occasions it restricted freedom of assembly and freedom of association.

Prison conditions were poor in Kyrgyzstan. There were many documented cases of arbitrary arrest and detention. Members of the Kyrgyzstan security forces at times unfairly detained, beat, tortured, and otherwise mistreated persons. Executive domination of the judiciary limited citizens' right to due process.

Executive branch interference affected verdicts involving prominent opposition figures. Violence and discrimination against women were continuing problems as was the persistent problem of trafficking in persons. The government harassed and pressured some political groups and carried out a systematic campaign against insurgency movements that extended to legitimate opponents of the regime.

In 2000 Kyrgyzstan ranked ninety-eight out of 174 countries listed on the UNDP Human Development Index. Income distribution and social indicators for Kyrgyzstan fell considerably behind other countries at comparable stages of development. For instance, nearly one-quarter of the population was not expected to reach age sixty. The proportion of young people enrolled in schools dropped. The rates of infectious diseases, particularly tuberculosis, increased. By 1997 an estimated half of the population had fallen below the official poverty line, living on the equivalent of less than $0.75 per day. The average monthly pension payment was among the lowest in the former Soviet states, amounting to less than $10 in 1999.[8]

Political stability and support

Kyrgyzstan is a relatively heavily indebted country. Outstanding debt in the first quarter of 2000 amounted to $1409 billion.[9] Much of the Kyrgyzstan republic's debt is concessional, that is, it has been loaned by public entities as special assistance at better-than-market terms by international financial institutions such as multilateral development banks. But a considerable portion is non-concessional (i.e. it is money that was loaned by private lenders such as commercial banks). Even if Kyrgyzstan is granted special repayment terms, delays, or postponements in the repayment schedule, the burden of future debt will remain high. The Kyrgyzstan government will need to bolster its fiscal position through reducing government expenditures and increasing revenue. More competent debt management and limits on contracting of debt will help. More emphasis on government reforms may also improve the overall economic pictures by improving the investment climate and enhancing the productive and export potential of the country.

Kyrgyzstan was initially relatively unconcerned about security issues, leaving these questions to its more powerful neighbors, Kazakhstan and Uzbekistan. Security issues reemerged with the onset of the Tajikistan war, but Kyrgyzstan's commitment of peacekeeping troops in Tajikistan was merely symbolic and was soon withdrawn. Security problems reemerged in summer 1999 with a hostage crisis that focused attention on the potential for destabilization throughout the entire Central Asian region. Coordination with Uzbekistan, Russia, and other outside actors brought the hostage crisis to a conclusion, but the problems of religious extremism, terrorism, and lawlessness remained.

During the first five years immediately following independence in 1991, Kyrgyzstan cumulative output fell by about 50 percent. While the transition to a market economy opened new opportunities for private enterprise, the costs of structural adjustment were borne to a large extent by those already economically disenfranchised. By 1997 an estimated half of the population had fallen below the official poverty line, living on the equivalent of less than $0.75 per day. Although on national average only one in two persons in Kyrgyzstan is categorized as poor, 80 percent of the poor live in rural areas. The degree of poverty in rural areas has also become more severe relative to urban areas. While extreme poverty decreased from 19.1 percent of the population in 1996 to 14.8 percent in 1997, most of this resulted from a targeted poverty reduction program in urban areas only. Poverty is also distributed unevenly in the population, affecting more women than men. The Kyrgyzstan government has initiated a national poverty reduction program, the Arakat program. The government is waging major efforts to revamp its poverty-fighting strategy in coordination with major donors, including the Asian Development Bank and the World Bank.

Summary

The substantial economic challenges that Kyrgyzstan faces as a small, resource rich, but landlocked country in the heart of Asia, are in many respects overshadowed by the region's larger challenges. Lying on the fault line between West and East, Kyrgyzstan has become in past years a focus of competition of many outside powers and many competing ideologies. Insurgent and terrorist movements borne of the brutalities of the Afghanistan war (1979–89) and the Afghanistan insurrection under the Taliban (1994–96) have spilled over Central Asia. In 1999, Kyrgyzstan faced a major challenge when Islamic Rebels from the Islamic Movement of Uzbekistan shattered Kyrgyzstan's sense of neutrality by taking hostages of four Japanese mining geologists working in the southern part of the country. Later, the rebels captured several Kyrgyz villages before being repulsed by a multinational Central Asian military force (Gleason, 2001). Among the terrorists were those who sought the overthrow of the governments of Central Asia and the establishment of an Islamic Caliphate throughout the Central Asian region. Also among them were those who sought to profit from the opium trade. In the past five years, Afghanistan emerged as the world's largest producer of opium. The southern border regions of Kyrgyzstan were increasingly being used for transshipment for drugs to Russia and Western Europe.

Kyrgyzstan introduced the most determined, pro-reform policies in the Central Asian region, perhaps in the entire CIS. Largely thanks to the efforts of its pro-reform President, Askar Akaev, Kyrgyzstan's pro-reform posture quickly made the country the *Wunderkind* of the international donor community. Considerable structural reform has taken place in Kyrgyzstan, but the promised benefits of rising prosperity remain elusive for most of the population. In 2000, Kyrgyzstan ranked 98 out of 174 countries listed on the UNDP Human Development Index. Income distribution and social indicators for Kyrgyzstan fell considerably behind other countries at comparable stages of development. Nearly one-quarter of the Kyrgyzstan population was not expected to reach the age of sixty. For the first five years of independence per capita assistance dollars in Kyrgyzstan far exceeded levels in other Eurasian countries. Were it not for foreign aid, Kyrgyzstan's domestic reform efforts might not have been politically sustainable.

5 Civil war and reconstruction in Tajikistan

How have Tajikistan's economic policy choices since independence affected the country's political development? Tajikistan's economic choices have been constrained by its situation. It is probable that Tajikistan would have moved decisively in the direction of structural reform initially if the country had not fallen prey to an internal contest for power in the first year of independence. The contest plunged the country into civil war. While Tajikistan would have been classified as a lower middle-income economy in the former Soviet period, in the decade since independence it has become one of the world poorest countries.[1]

The following profile of Tajikistan surveys the distinguishing features of the country. The section on "Post-conflict reform of the state" describing the attempts at post-conflict economic reform, sets out the economic policies adopted after 1996 when the reconciliation process began. The section on "Regional pluralism and competition" analyzes the effect of these economic policy choices on government and politics in Tajikistan, emphasizing the role of regional cleavages.

Tajikistan profile

Tajikistan had an estimated population of 6.2 million people in mid-2001.[2] Tajikistan's population has been growing at 1.3 per year, a relatively modest rate. Agriculture dominates Tajikistan's economy, with cotton being the most important crop. During the first decade of independence, cotton production fell to less than half its pre-1991 level. Other agricultural output also decreased significantly in most areas except foodstuffs and cereals. Tajikistan's mineral resources include silver, gold, uranium, and tungsten, but in small amounts. Industry is limi-ted to a number of obsolete processing factories in the northern part of the country and one large aluminum plant in the southern part of the country. Coal, other minerals and aluminum production decreased significantly. Electricity production from Tajikistan's aging hydroelectric plants also decreased, although at a lower rate than other industrial output (Table 5.1(a)). Tajikistan was dependent on Russia, Uzbekistan, and on international humanitarian assistance for much of its basic subsistence needs.

Tajikistan is a landlocked country. Tajikistan's trading relationships have been constrained by politics and geography. Since 1992, Tajikistan's western access routes have been virtually blockaded by its neighbor Uzbekistan for both economic and political reasons (Table 5.1(b)). Difficult terrain and political uncertainty constrained trade with Tajikistan's eastern neighbor, China. Difficult terrain and border disputes complicated trade with Tajikistan's northern neighbor, Kyrgyzstan. Political instability and insurgency complicated trade relations with Tajikistan's southern neighbor, Afghanistan.

Tajikistan has an authoritarian government, one that has made good faith but substantially unsuccessful efforts to introduce economic and political reforms. The executive branch appears to dominate the administration, the legislature, and the judiciary. The full extent of political control by executive branch officials is thrown into question by the fact that the national government does not fully exercise control in many outlying areas of the country (Table 5.2). Some nongovernmental civic organizations are active in Tajikistan. The Tajikistan government rhetorically adheres to principles of the rule of law and the protection of civil rights. But in the charged political atmosphere of post-civil conflict and post-Afghanistan conflict, insurgency and militant regionalism are constant realities for the government. The Tajikistan government's significant counter-insurgency and counter narcotics efforts have compromised many procedural protections for civil and human rights. Tajikistan is regarded by international organizations as having a poor human rights record. The World Bank Institute governance indicators ranked Tajikistan in 2001 below the tenth percentile in all key governance measures except "voice and accountability" in which Tajikistan ranked in the twenty-seventh percentile (Table 5.3). This unusual evaluation reflects that fact that there are elements that vocally favor liberalization and reform within Tajikistan.

Post-conflict reform of the state

Tajikistan's structural reform efforts have been very much the product of the extreme circumstances the country has faced since independence.[3] Tajikistan's economy today is based primarily on subsistence agriculture, foreign assistance from donor organizations, barter relations with neighbors, and the commercial export of a few commodities. As much as 80 percent of Tajikistan's foreign exchange earnings result from sales of three commodities: aluminum, cotton, and illegal drugs. The metals and drugs sales are sources of revenue that, under Tajikistan's current conditions, have negligible or negative social welfare effects.

During the Soviet period Tajikistan's primary trading relations were structured around the import of manufactured and consumer goods from the North and the export of primary commodities, particularly aluminum and cotton, to northern markets in the former Soviet Union (Rakowska-Harmstone, 1970). Trade was channeled through a small number of corridors, all of which passed through the former Soviet Republic of Uzbekistan. Civil strife in Tajikistan interrupted shipping routes through Uzbekistan in 1992. These routes have not been reestablished for normal commercial purposes. Tajikistan's easternmost border with the People's Republic of China previously offered no commercial access to foreign markets.

Table 5.1a Tajikistan key indices: production

Item	*1991*	*1992*	*1993*	*1994*	*1995*	*1996*	*1997*	*1998*	*1999*	*2000*
Population (million; as of July 1)	5.46	5.57	5.64	5.75	5.84	5.93	6.02*	6.11*	6.20*	6.29*
Labor force (thousand; calendar year)	—	1915	1876	1886	1891	1777	1842	1855	1780*	1794*
Employed	1970	1908	1854	1854	1853	1731	1791	1796	1726*	1745*
Agriculture	881	892	949	1002	1095	1026	1145	1080	1118*	1120*
Mining										
Manufacturing	405	382	335	315	264	249	216	200	174*	170*
Others	683	634	570	538	494	456	430	516	434*	455*
Unemployed	—	7	22	32	38	46	51	59	54*	49*
Unemployment rate (%)	—	0.4	1.2	1.7	2.0	2.6	2.8	3.3	3.0*	2.7*
Production (thousand metric tons; calendar year)										
Agriculture (crop year)										
1 Seed cotton	826	515	524	531	412	210	175	183	169	180
2 Wheat	153	156	159	182	174	548	559	500	483	550
3 Potatoes	181	167	147	134	112	108	128	175	240	303
4 Cotton (lint)	247	174	180	167	130	120	104	108	103	107
5 Grapes	121	100	88	80	96	122	127	46	54	110
6 Rice	26	20	23	20	24	21	44	40	47	82
7 Barley	51	39	30	25	22	17	23	26	25	19
8 Maize	60	32	34	18	19	90	30	36	36	38
Mining										
1 Hard coal	313	214	174	106	34	14	9	8	9	9
2 Crude petroleum	100	57	49	32	24	26	26	19	19	18
3 Natural gas (Mn cu. m.)	93	72	49	33	39	47	42	32	36	40
Manufacturing										
1 Cement	1013	447	262	178	78	49	36	18	33	55
2 Wheat flour	756	628	667	360	304	271	322	417	341	307
3 Aluminum	380	345	252	237	237	198	189	196	229	269

Production indexes period averages										
Agriculture (1989–91 = 100)	—	75.8	71.5	69.3	60.4	51.8	50.2	48.4	47.4	54.3
Mining (1990 = 100)	96.0	73.0	67.0	50.0	43.0	33.0	32.0	—	—	—
Manufacturing (1990 = 100)	96.0	73.0	66.0	49.0	41.0	29.8	26.6	28.1	31.7	—
Energy (annual values)										
Crude petroleum ('000 m. t.)										
Production	99	57	39	33	26	26	26	19	19	18
Exports	—	—	—	—	—	—	—	—	—	—
Imports	—	—	—	—	—	—	—	—	—	—
Consumption	—	—	—	—	—	—	—	—	—	—
Coal ('000 m. t.)										
Production	313	214	174	106	34	20	17	19	19	22
Exports	274	186	80	42	—	14	219	—	60	—
Imports	649	422	33	14	—	—	—	—	—	—
Consumption	688	450	127	78	—	—	—	—	—	—
Natural gas (Mn cu. m.)										
Production	93	72	49	33	39	47	42	32	36	40
Exports	—	—	—	—	—	—	—	—	—	—
Imports	2	1	1	1	1	1	2	1	1	1
Consumption	—	—	—	—	—	—	—	—	—	—
Electricity (Mn kWh)										
Production	17,600	16,800	17,700	17,000	14,800	14,980	14,005	14,422	15,797	14,247
Exports	5400	5600	6400	5800	4200	4890	4247	3724	3831	3909
Imports	6900	6400	5200	4900	4900	3978	4345	3969	3641	5242
Consumption	19,100	17,600	16,500	16,100	15,500	14,068	14,103	14,667	15,607	15,580

Source: Asian Development Bank. *Key Indicators 2001: Growth and Change in Asia and the Pacific*. New York: Oxford University Press, 2001.

Note
* ADB internal estimates.

Table 5.1b Tajikistan key indices: foreign trade

Item	*1991*	*1992*	*1993*	*1994*	*1995*	*1996*	*1997*	*1998*	*1999*	*2000*
External trade (Mn US dollars; calendar year)										
Exports, fob	—	185	456	559	839	770	746	597	689	784
Imports, cif	—	240	660	707	880	668	750	711	663	675
Trade balance	—	−55	−204	−148	−41	102	−4	−114	26	109
Direction of trade (Mn US dollars; calendar year)										
Total exports	—	29.3	349.8	491.9	748.6	771.5	803.4	596.6	688.7	935.0
1 Netherlands	—	—	1.1	147.6	255.2	218.0	229.4	221.4	222.3	211.3
2 Uzbekistan	—	—	20.3	22.7	132.0	190.7	172.5	125.7	181.0	236.3
3 Russia	—	—	62.5	46.2	95.3	79.0	63.5	47.8	115.1	215.7
4 Switzerland	—	0.4	5.8	44.9	37.2	83.5	140.7	94.9	75.1	108.5
5 Kazakhstan	—	—	16.3	10.1	7.0	24.3	10.0	10.0	3.6	3.6
6 Korea, Republic of	—	—	0.9	2.9	9.3	24.9	3.2	0.2	7.4	14.5
7 Iran	—	—	—	1.4	0.7	1.7	3.5	13.6	13.5	13.5
8 Italy	—	6.8	2.5	0.4	2.4	6.6	7.8	9.8	5.1	11.6
9 Belgium	—	—	—	—	—	—	14.7	12.7	7.0	6.4
10 United Kingdom	—	—	119.9	30.3	20.7	15.2	6.5	5.1	5.5	7.1
Total imports	—	72.9	532.1	547.0	809.9	668.1	750.3	711.0	663.1	800.9
1 Uzbekistan	—	—	65.4	83.2	251.4	198.9	261.6	227.3	264.4	301.6
2 Switzerland	—	0.1	4.3	100.4	51.7	99.8	185.1	157.9	25.1	31.7
3 Russia	—	—	83.8	60.7	136.0	74.4	115.1	102.2	92.4	61.5
4 Kazakhstan	—	—	65.5	32.8	26.5	52.4	42.0	51.9	78.8	105.7
5 United Kingdom	—	—	16.4	68.0	161.2	78.3	10.1	3.8	70.5	93.2
6 Ukraine	—	—	4.4	13.6	2.2	19.2	20.7	16.6	37.7	58.7
7 Turkmenistan	—	—	26.0	39.4	57.4	26.3	29.7	31.3	15.2	15.2
8 United States	—	9.7	8.7	31.9	25.3	16.0	3.2	32.8	1.7	15.7
9 Iran	—	—	—	0.1	0.7	10.5	12.0	11.3	10.4	10.4
10 Azerbaijan	—	—	1.1	0.2	1.2	0.0	3.2	1.8	15.6	29.4

Source: Asian Development Bank. *Key Indicators 2001: Growth and Change in Asia and the Pacific*. New York: Oxford University Press, 2001.

Table 5.2 Tajikistan: political freedoms

	Nations in transit 2000 political indicators								
	1991–92	*1992–93*	*1993–94*	*1994–95*	*1995–96*	*1996–97*	*1997–98*	*1998–99*	*1999–2000*
Political rights	3	6	7	7	7	7	6	6	6
Civil liberties	3	6	7	7	7	7	6	6	6
	PF	NF	NF	NF	NF	NF	NF	NF	NF

Source: *Nations in Transit*, 2000. New York: Freedom House.

Table 5.3 World Bank Institute governance indicators for Tajikistan

Governance indicator	*Year*	*Percentile rank (0–100) in %*	*Estimate (−2.5 to +2.5)*	*Standard deviation*	*Number of surveys/ polls*
Voice and accountability	2000/01	27.6	−0.69	0.19	3
Political stability/No violence	2000/01	3.1	−1.77	0.42	2
Government effectiveness	2000/01	7.5	−1.31	0.28	3
Regulatory quality	2000/01	5.9	−1.46	0.38	3
Rule of law	2000/01	4.7	−1.25	0.22	4
Control of corruption	2000/01	9.3	−1.08	0.24	3

Source: Kaufmann, Kraay, and Zoido (KKZ), 2002. *Governance Matters II: Updated Governance Indicators for 2000–01*. World Bank Institute.

Tajikistan's southern border with Afghanistan had not been used for normal commercial purposes since the outbreak of the Afghanistan war in 1979. Only three major paved roads, each of which has high mountain passes making them unsuitable for most commercial traffic, traverse Tajikistan's northern border with Kyrgyzstan. The northern and southern sections of the country are linked by rail by only one line, which traverses Uzbekistan's territory.

Before the breakup of the USSR, Tajikistan's development prospects looked comparatively bright. Tajikistan was a relatively independent republic during the Soviet era. Centuries old traditions of mountain culture had protected the country from the loss of cultural identity (Rakowska-Harmstone, 1970; Atkin, 1989; Jawad and Tadjbakhsh, 1995; Akbarzadeh, 1996; Djalili *et al.*, 1997; Jonson, 1999). Many Tajik traditions had survived the Soviet period intact. At independence, there was an expectation that Tajikistan would simply return to its historical roots. However, by the spring of 1992 various clan-based, regional factions had become highly polarized in the competition for control over the post-communist government. The president of the country, Rakhmon Nabiev, was forced from power by an opposition government. Civil war ensued. The war was resolved in favor of the "Popular Front" coalition based in the valley region of the city of Kulob. The war resulted in a blockade of Tajikistan by its neighbors, further compressing the already collapsing Tajikistan economy. The modest level of civil normality that was maintained in Tajikistan was largely a result of the presence of foreign peacekeeping forces.

The defeated opposition, scattered in the remote mountainous regions of the country did not disarm but regrouped. Led by the Islamic Revival Party, the opposition formed into a bloc called the United Tajikistan Opposition (UTO). The Tajikistan government and the UTO entered into cease-fire negotiations in 1994. With mediation form the United Nations Mission in Tajikistan, UNMOT, a cease-fire agreement was reached in September 1994. The cease-fire was periodically violated but both sides continued to negotiate. The Russian government financed peacekeeping troops with a limited amount of assistance from other countries of the region, particularly Uzbekistan and Kazakhstan. Russian-controlled border guards were stationed along the Tajik–Afghan border. The Russian military presence was headquartered in Dushanbe, Tajikistan's capital. The peacekeeping troops claimed to remain aloof from the regional and clan-based conflicts that divided Tajikistan, although the UTO viewed the Russian presence as pro-government. A National Reconciliation Accord was signed in June 1997 bringing the war officially to an end and specifying a process of reintegration of civil-war era combatants into the Tajikistan government.

The specific shape of Tajikistan's post-conflict economic reform was very much the product of the country's civil war and post-conflict political environment. The current political leader, Emomali Rahmonov, took power as a result of the civil war. Members of parliament selected Rahmonov as chairman of the Tajikistan parliament in November 1992, in the midst of the civil conflict. Rahmonov soon thereafter acquired the title "head of state" and was popularly elected to a five-year term as president in November 1994. Tajikistan's first presidential elections were marred by numerous procedural violations and were widely considered unfair. The OSCE (then known as the CSCE, Conference on Security and Cooperation in Europe) withdrew a team of election monitors prior to the final vote count to prevent dignifying the elections with the presence of foreign monitors.[4]

Under Rahmonov's leadership, the Tajikistan government committed itself to post-conflict reconciliation and reconstruction. At the urging of the international financial institutions, the Tajikistan government agreed to undertake a comprehensive program of structural reform.[5] The government's program was established in the form of a policy matrix with timetable benchmarks. The priorities for the structural reform agenda were: fiscal reform; currency reform; improved governance; privatization; bank restructuring; land reform; and energy sector reform. Governance measures included reform of the treasury system, the establishment of a single independent auditing agency to control the efficiency of public finances and eliminate redundant inspection rights, the cessation of quasi-fiscal operations of the central bank, the prevention of unjustified intervention by public officials in the operation of private enterprises, and the completion of public procurement reform. The goal of privatization was to raise productivity and support growth targets, as well as aid in the achievement of fiscal goals by bolstering revenues and lowering direct or indirect subsidies. The goal of bank restructuring was to increase the stability of the banking system. In Tajikistan's structural reform particular emphasis was placed on measures that would lead to a greater use of monetarized commercial transactions and a reduction in inefficient and non-transparent barter relations.

Fiscal and monetary policy

The Tajikistan government committed itself to fiscal reform by adopting a new governance structure that agreed to refrain from: (1) imposing or intensifying restrictions on the making of payments and transfers for current international transactions; (2) introducing multiple currency practices; (3) concluding bilateral payments agreements that may lead to multiple currency practices; and (4) imposing or intensifying import restrictions for balance of payments reasons. To strengthen the government's control over the money supply, the National Bank of Tajikistan, the NBT, resolved to open market operations through purchases and repurchase agreements with banks. Short-term treasury bills were issued as part of the regularization of financial relations between the Ministry of Finance and the NBT.

In order to improve governance, measures were taken to prepare for the reform of the national treasury, to establish regional treasuries, to extend the treasury coverage of payments to all central and local government transactions. In order to make the treasury more effective, emphasis was placed on improving control systems on commitments and arrears, staff training, and implementation of the treasury instruction manual. The Ministry of Finance, beginning January 2001, began publishing important public budget documents, including quarterly budget execution reports, the medium-term expenditure framework, and the public investment program. In order to increase accountability and transparency, the NBT was restricted from issuing directed credits. An independent audit agency was established to inspect public financial management systems, judicial reform, and the adoption of a meritocratic civil service system.

Fiscal policy focused on improving the country's fiscal deficit, disentangling government finances from the financial activities of the NBT separating revenue and expenditure functions through the creation of a new income ministry, the Ministry of National Incomes and Duties, charged with taxation and customs, and improving revenue collection through emphasis on the value added tax (VAT) and better administration. The government established fiscal targets to reduce the deficit even as it acted to reduce subsidies. The government lowered the sales tax on cotton to 10 percent (January 2002) in order to boost agricultural incomes. The destination principle for applying the VAT was adopted in foreign trade, with the exception of gas and electricity.

The government phased out the TICEX mechanisms (The Tblisi Interbank Currency Exchange) and established competitive interbank markets. In order for an interbank foreign exchange market to develop, the role of the NBT as the sole supplier of foreign exchange was reduced. The NBT ceased all foreign exchange activities with non-banks and suspended the operations of TICEX in July 2000. Plans were made for meeting with creditors for the purpose of debt rescheduling. The government adopted the goal of avoiding external, sovereign non-concessional borrowing.

Privatization and liberalization

As early as March 1992, the Tajikistan parliament had approved land reform legislation that gave Tajikistan citizens the right to own, lease, and inherit land. Both the Tajikistan constitution and the laws on privatization guaranteed property rights, including intellectual property, real estate, and business property. Agricultural land remained under state ownership, but could be leased. Under the land code, lease rights are inheritable and can also be sold. Soviet-era privatization legislation remained on the books and formed the basis for the early years of privatization.

Price liberalization took place in Tajikistan soon after dislocation from the USSR. However, the extremely rapid fall in standards of living encouraged the government to reintroduce price controls. An anti-monopoly law was adopted in 1993 and an anti-monopoly department in the Ministry of the Economy was charged with enforcing the anti-monopoly policy. But during the period before the IMF sponsored structural reform program of 1998, little progress was made in establishing competition policy in accord with international standards. Price controls continued on farm produce, utilities, and transportation. Many prices in the formal sector were effectively set by state-owned enterprises. Financial and commodity markets were limited by size and restrictions on the banking industry.

The initial privatization process in Tajikistan moved slowly, stalled by the civil conflict, by uncertainty and by the weak banking sector. With the assistance of the World Bank and the IMF, the "Law of the Republic of Tajikistan on Privatization of State Property in the Republic of Tajikistan" was passed on May 16, 1997. The law established the framework for privatization including a legal framework, title registry, and procedural guarantees. The state property committee database listed 6974 small-scale enterprises, of which 1694 were not subject to automatic privatization. A much larger number of small-scale objects remained under the control of the consumer cooperative, Tajikpotrebsoyuz and under the farm-based enterprises.

The new privatization legislation changed the process from a bottom-up process of negotiated sale to collectives on an enterprise-by-enterprise basis, to an open and competitive top-down program with more rapid wholesale transfer of assets into the private sector. The process accelerated through 1998 and 1999. The government established as a goal the privatization of 40 percent of small and medium enterprises (SMEs), and the beginning of the implementation of a program to privatize the TADAZ aluminum smelter with the assistance of the International Finance Corporation (IFC).

By July 2000, roughly 284 of the 600 state-owned farms had been restructured into approximately 13,750 private ("dekhan") farms. These private farms were established through marketable land use certificates and land share certificates.

Local authorities managed the process with support from the State Committee for Land Resources (SCLR). In order to strengthen the land reform process, especially with regard to the independence of the newly established farms, the government created a special financing unit in the SCLR. This unit was for providing newly created farmers with agricultural extension services, including advice on their legal rights and training. The government pledged to continue the land reform process by continuous restructuring of state-owned farms at the rate of thirty farms each quarter. A system was put in place to establish a depository, title registration, and land registry system to regularize the market in land shares.

Trade and investment

Tajikistan, like all of the countries of the Central Asian region, claims to support the principle of free trade with certain reservations. However, unsatisfactory arrangements regarding government subsidies, currency controls, interbank clearing, customs and tax incompatibilities, insufficient infrastructural development, and control over access to markets continued to hamper trade in the region. At the informal level, government policy is influenced by obstacles and impediments including visas, exactions, paperwork, and red tape.

Tajikistan's trade with the outside world was heavily affected by Uzbekistan government actions. When conflict broke into the open in the northern regions of Tajikistan in spring 1992, Uzbekistan acted to establish border controls. In August 1992 the Dushanbe–Tashkent railway line was closed to passenger traffic to prevent political refugees from entering Uzbekistan. A short time afterward, Uzbek officials closed the entire border between Tajikistan and Uzbekistan. The border with the northern Tajikistan province of Leninabod remained opened for a period but then also was closed, cutting off Tajikistan almost entirely from the outside world. Customs and duty stations were hastily constructed at every border checkpoint, giving newly independent Tajikistan the character of an "embargoed society." There was no Uzbekistan Embassy in Tajikistan. The Uzbekistan–Tajikistan border has been periodically opened and closed, but has remained continuously subject to extensive regulation from the Uzbekistan side.

Banking and financial markets

In order to strengthen the legal framework and correct lax law enforcement mechanisms, the government enacted numerous laws, including the Law on Collateral, the Bankruptcy Law, and the Law on Secured Transactions. In order to reduce inter-enterprise arrears, the government established a list of high arrears enterprises and target specific measures to address the problem, including restructuring and bankruptcy. The most common forms of corruption typically involve the conditioning of a public good or public service on some form of emolument. "Baksheesh" style "speed payments" or "service payments" were the most common, widespread, and easily concealed form of corrupt practice.

In 1994 a new law "On Banks and Banking Activities" was adopted. A number of decrees were adopted that established a qualification committee of the NBT, established procedures for forming statutory capital, specified procedures for starting and terminating commercial bank activities, procedures of issuing and recalling licenses for bank audits, established procedures for bank bankruptcies, and established procedures for the operation of non-banking financial organizations that offer financial services and were licensed and regulated by the NBT.

The NBT is state-owned and carries out central bank functions. Two other state-operated banks were Khatlon Reconstruction and Development Bank and Sberbank. Sberbank had a government guarantee on its deposits from households and, with more than one million clients, led the market for individual savings. Tajikistan's largest private banks, Agroinvestbank, Tajikbankbusiness, Sberbank, Orionbank, and Vnesheconombank underwent reorganization in 1998.

A new Tajikistan tax code was adopted effective from January 1999. The elimination of several categories of exemptions in VAT took place in 1998. A reform in VAT levies, eliminating exemptions on certain items such as food, took effect in July 1999. Improvements in tax policy and tax administration contributed to an improvement in revenue in 1999. The practice of tax offsets remained a hindrance to full monetization of the economy.[6] VAT tax compliance has improved after the IMF structural reform program was introduced. But compliance rates for excise taxes, personal income taxes, and enterprise profit taxes remained low. The largest gains in revenue collection were attributable to increases in collections associated with the transition from a severance tax to an excise tax basis in aluminum and cotton. Access to consumer credit in Tajikistan remained very limited, in part as a result of low bank credit ceilings and high prudential standards.

Regional pluralism and competition

In 1999 Tajikistan celebrated the 1100 Year anniversary of the Samanid civilization in Tajikistan. Yet Tajikistan's experience as a separate, independent, and sovereign state began only with the country's declaration of national independence on September 9, 1991. Tajikistan is truly a new state in an ancient country. Tajikistan is located at the center of the Pamir Knot in the middle of Asia. The Pamirs are a unique high mountain complex located primarily in Tajikistan. The Pamir Knot is the central hub from which five great ranges of Asia radiate outward; the Himalayas extend southeast; the Karakoram range extends southeast; the Hindu Kush range extends southwest; the Tian Shan range extends northeast; and the Kunlun Shan range extends east.

Tajikistan consists of three geographically isolated regions separated by high mountain ridges. The northern region of the country is divided from the southern regions by the Hissar, Zeravshan, and Turkestan mountain ridges. There is no direct rail transportation between the north and south. Highway transportation is limited to two major roads that are closed frequently by weather conditions during winter. The eastern part of the country, Gorno-Badakhshan autonomous province, is remote and relatively underdeveloped. It is linked to the other parts of the country by road but not by rail. Weather conditions interrupt existing east–west highway transportation for long periods of time in the winter. The northern and western regions of the country have historically been more closely linked economically to other neighboring areas than to the capital and central regions of Tajikistan.

Constitutional, legal, and regulatory policy

Tajikistan's Constitution, adopted on November 6, 1994, emphasizes sovereign independence, territorial integrity, and national traditions, a strong executive branch, and the maintenance of social stability. According to Article 1 of the Constitution, Tajikistan is a sovereign, democratic, law-governed, unitary, and secular state. The Constitution affirms basic principles of limited, constitutional government, including the rule of law, the division of powers, and the protection of fundamental human rights and liberties. There are three branches of government, executive, and legislative and judicial. The president is both head of state and directs the prime minister, the head of government. The government is a presidential system. The prime minister is appointed by the president and heads a council of ministers, each of whom is appointed by the president upon approval of the parliament. The officials of the Constitutional Court, the Supreme Court, and the Arbitrage Court are elected by parliament for terms of five years on the nomination of the president.

Legislative, executive, and judicial policy

In a national referendum on September 26, 1999 Tajikistan voters approved key changes in Tajikistan's Constitution, including an extension of the presidential term of office from five to seven years and changes in the structure of the national parliament.[7] In accordance with the constitutional changes, a presidential election was held in November 1999 and parliamentary elections were held in February and March 2000. Tajikistan's president, Emomali Rahmonov was reelected in the general election of November 6, 1999 to a seven-year term.[8]

According to the Tajikistan Constitution, the president is the head of state and the commander-in-chief of the armed forces. The President has numerous executive powers including the power to sign legislation into law and to appoint, subject to the approval of parliament, the prime minister, ministerial level cabinet members, and local territorial officials. The prime minister heads the government and serves at the pleasure of the president. The prime minister is the chief implementing officer and heads the council of ministers. The bicameral parliament is made up of the lower house, or *Majlisi Namoyandagon*, consisting of sixty-three seats, and the upper house, or *Majlisi Milli*, consisting of thirty-three seats. The most recent parliamentary elections for the two houses were held on February 28, 2000 and March 23, 2000, respectively.[9]

At the national level, the judicial system includes a Supreme court, a Constitutional Court, a court of commercial appeal, and a Military Court. Regional and municipal courts exist in local jurisdictions. The judicial system is based on the Continental system. While judicial independence is a government goal, in practice constraints on government revenue limit the full implementation of the principle of judicial independence. In April 1997, the government created a Higher Economic Court. The Higher Economic Court is governed by the 1995 Legal Code and the 1994 Constitutional Law on Economic Courts. The court consists of legal, appeal, and mediation boards. Previously, one-judge arbitrage courts made decisions. Now, a verdict is delivered by a group of fifteen judges. The economic court's mandate includes any economic disputes arising from civil, administrative, business, and other economic relationships. Before a case reaches trial, plaintiffs are required to pay legal expenses of 10 percent of the suit sum, which is believed to limit the number of cases brought to the Higher Economic Court. Only legal entities, as opposed to individuals, may bring cases.

General government finance consists of the republican budget, seventy local governments, and two extra-budget funds: the Social Protection Fund and the Road Fund. The Social Fund was created in mid-1996 as a combination of the Pension, Social Insurance, and Employment Funds. One additional public finance mechanism is that the NBT has occasionally carried out quasi-fiscal operations such as directed lending to particular enterprises.

The single most important aspect of the political process in Tajikistan is the principle of coalition government that was adopted as an element in the post-conflict national reconciliation process. The principle is implemented through a process of power sharing and incremental, phased reintegration of former combatants. The program of national reconciliation prescribed a minority participation formula for the Central Electoral Commission (25 percent posts), Ministerial Cabinet posts (30 percent opposition), and the civil service.

Transparency and integrity policy

Major efforts are underway to improve the trade environment in the region. As these efforts succeed, they can be expected to exacerbate the trends in the region regarding organized crime and drug trafficking. Traffickers use legitimate transportation infrastructure and banking operations in order to move their wares and to conceal the funds derived from the trade in handguns, weapons materials, drugs, drug precursors, and production materials. In countries as poor and underdeveloped as those of Central Asia, there is little reason to expect that typical enforcement sanctions are apt to have any substantial effect on the growth of these crime syndicates unless exceptional efforts are undertaken to counter these trends.

In April 2000, the Tajikistan government's Tajik Drug Control Agency began functioning. The Tajik Drug Control Agency was principally charged with dealing with the consequences of the drug trade emanating from Afghanistan. In 1998, Afghanistan was responsible for producing 2800 tons of opium, making it the largest opium producer in the world. Afghanistan's Helmand and Nangarhar provinces, located in the south of the country, were the top producers but the largest gains in Afghanistan's opium production took place in the provinces adjacent to Tajikistan. The 1998 survey of the UN Drug Control and Crime Prevention Program noted that Central Asia, principally Tajikistan, had become a major transit zone for Afghanistan's opium and heroin trafficking. In September 2000, the UN Office for Drug Control and Prevention announced that there was no substantial change in the area under poppy cultivation in Afghanistan for the year 2000. With an overall fresh opium harvest of more than 3000 metric tons, Afghanistan remains the largest opium producer in the world.[10] The Tajik Drug Control Agency (TDCA) may play a role in improving cooperation among law enforcement bodies in Central Asia. But if the trends in collusion between drug traffickers and local government officials in other parts of the underdeveloped region are illustrative of what to expect in Tajikistan, it is clear that much more substantial efforts will be necessary to successfully confront this key challenge to government integrity in Central Asia.

Regional administrative policy

The country is administratively divided into provinces, cities, and districts. The country has three provinces, one autonomous province, one city, and seventy-four raions. The capital, Dushanbe, is under the direct control of the central government. Tajikistan is a unitary state, but within this structure the organs of local government have specific prerogatives in the areas of implementation. These formally include control over local budgets, local taxes, non-budgetary revenues, and municipal property. A republican body, the State Tax Committee, collects state taxes. Local administrations are responsible for carrying out some social service functions and many local public services.

Tajikistan's population is concentrated in the western half of the country. Population figures are approximate but a reliable index appears to be that the population is about 65 percent Tajik; 25 percent Uzbek; and 10 percent Slavic and other. Approximately 70 percent of the population live in rural areas. The official language of Tajikistan is Tajik, a dialect of Persian similar to Farsi and Dari. Many Tajikistan citizens are bilingual or trilingual, speaking Tajik, Uzbek, and Russian as well as other languages. Roughly 80 percent of the population speaks the Tajik language. Approximately 40 percent of the population in the Leninobod and Kulyob regions speaks the Uzbek language. And about 40 percent of the population and most business-persons and government officials speak or understand Russian. Tajikistan is a pluralistic country, with many different cultures and regional interests.[11] It's regional peculiarities are reflected in the capacity of government to carry out economic and political reforms. Decentralization in Tajikistan is equivalent to promoting regionalism and separatism. Centralization, on the other hand, removes formal decision-making authority from those who are most likely to make key informal decisions and to implement formal policies.

Political participation and openness

In 1990 the only legally registered political party was the Communist Party. During the period of the disintegration of the USSR new political movements appeared. Soon after Tajikistan national independence was declared, a number of political parties sought government registration. During the period of civil conflict the registration of four political parties – the Islamic Revival Party, the Rastohez National Movement, the Lali Badakhshan Movement for the Autonomy of the Pamirs, and the Democratic Party – were suspended. In 1994 the Democratic Party split into two sections and in 1995 the government registered the Democratic Party (Teheran Platform). On December 9, 1998 the Tajikistan Supreme Court banned the National Unity Party.[12]

The United Tajikistan Opposition consisted of a coalition of the Islamic Revival Party, the Democratic Party and the Lali Badakhsan Movement for the Autonomy of the Pamirs. In December 1999, in implementation of provisions of the agreements concerning post-conflict national reconciliation, the Tajikistan Ministry of Justice formally registered the Islamic Revival Party, the Rastohez National Movement, the Lali Badakhshan Movement for the Autonomy of the Pamirs, and the Democratic Party (Almaty Platform). Six Tajikistan parties were legally registered to nominate candidates to run in the 1999 presidential elections: the People's Democratic Party, the Socialist Party, the Islamic Revival Party, the Communist Party, the Democratic Party, and the Party Adolatkhoh.

Election policy

In 1999 a draft reform of the parliamentary system was developed in accordance with agreements regarding post-conflict power sharing. In December 1999 a new structure for the parliament was proposed. According to the new structure, the *Majlisi Namoyandagon*, or lower house, consists of sixty-three seats and the *Majlisi Milli*, or upper house, consists of thirty-three seats. With respect to the sixty-three seats of the *Majlisi Namoyandagon*, twenty-two seats are filled on the basis of proportional representation and forty-one seats are filled in single-seat constituencies. It was also agreed that the local elections would be conducted simultaneously with the election to the *Majlisi Namoyandagon*. With respect to the thirty-three seats of *Majlisi Milli*, twenty-five seats are filled by local Majlisi elections and eight seats are filled by appointment of the president. The term of office for both houses is five years. Tajikistan parties began the campaign process. Registration of presidential candidates required the gathering of 145,000 signatures.

On December 10, 1999 the new electoral law was adopted by parliament. On February 27, 2000 elections were held for the lower house and localities. According to the Tajikistan Central Electoral Commission, 93.23 percent of voters cast their ballot in this election. The People's Democratic Party won thirty-three seats, eighteen by direct election and fifteen through the party list. The Communist Party won seven seats, two by direct election and five through the party list. The Islamic Revival Party won two seats, both through the party list. Independent candidates won in eight constituencies, but two were declared invalid, requiring a new vote that was to be held at the end of April. In twelve constituencies, where no candidate received a majority of the vote, a run-off election was held on March 12, 2000. The People's Democratic Party won in seven constituencies.[13]

Civil and human rights

Tajikistan is a predominantly Muslim country. While Tajikistan's dominant culture is based on Islamic tradition, the Tajikistan Constitution describes a secular state. The relationship between religion and state has been the source of controversy in Tajikistan. On May 23, 1999 the *Majlis Oli* (the Tajikistan unicameral parliament until the seating of a new bicameral parliament as a result of the parliamentary elections of 2000) passed a law prohibiting the creation of political parties with a religious orientation. The opposition UTO, international organizations, and foreign governments strongly criticized the law for violating the spirit and the letter of the 1997 peace agreement. On June 2, 1999 President Rahmonov established a Special Conciliation Commission to resolve the dispute. On June 18, 1999 the Commission reported that it had devised compromise language for the law, banning political parties from receiving support from religious institutions. A new version of the law including the compromise language was passed in the November 1999 parliamentary session.

Political stability and support

The anti-government uprising in Hujand, Tajikistan, in November 1998 revealed that the conflicts of the Tajikistan war had not been completely resolved by the Tajikistan peace accord and reconciliation process. Just three months after these events, Uzbekistan was shaken by terrorist bombings in Tashkent in February 1999. The Kyrgyzstan hostage crisis in the Fergana Valley in August 1999 drew Kyrgyzstan into the situation. In August 2000, a new hostage crisis in Kyrgyzstan refocused attention on the country's vulnerability. In September 2000, an insurgent military force penetrated into Uzbekistan to within 100 kilometers of the capital.

As a result of these signs of deterioration in border security, the Uzbekistan government implemented a significant counter-insurgency program beginning in early 2000. The campaign included redoubled foreign security measures and border controls. In May 2000, the foreign ministries of Tajikistan and Uzbekistan resolved to introduce a new visa regime. The two countries introduced the mutual visa requirement in September 2000. In December 2000, the Uzbekistan Ministry of Foreign Affairs introduced a requirement that, as of January 1, 2001, citizens of Tajikistan would be required to obtain a transit visa in order to cross the territory of Uzbekistan.[14] The security measures also included the emplacement of anti-personnel landmines in the Zeravshan valley border region with Tajikistan.[15]

These and other trends in Tajikistan's national security during the period 1991–2001 illustrate that political stability remains precarious. The authoritarian nature of the Tajikistan regime calls into question the real depth of the government's apparent popular support.

Summary

While the Tajikistan government's progress at structural reform has been constrained by circumstances, key policy decisions reflect the government's abiding commitment to reform and liberalization. With the help of foreign donor assistance, Tajikistan established a three-stage economic reform process. The first stage (1995–97) focused on improvement in the legal infrastructure, reforms in the agricultural sector, privatization of small-scale enterprises, and creation of favorable conditions to attract foreign investors. The second stage (1998–2000) focused on privatizing large-scale enterprises, and establishing efficiently functioning banking, credit, and taxation systems. The third stage (2001–03) was oriented toward modernization of the economy, particularly the formation of an efficient infrastructure and the implementation of large-scale socio-economic programs.

Since the time of the disintegration of the USSR in 1991 Tajikistan has experienced the most difficult years in its modern history. Civil war, economic collapse, political divisions, social disintegration, and foreign pressures have created a range of extremely complex public policy problems. The government of Tajikistan has taken concrete steps to establish the legal and institutional framework of a democratic, market oriented society. The international community – including foreign government representation, donor organizations, and international organizations – has also sought to encourage the transition to democracy and a market-based economy. Yet these efforts too have not yet produced the desired results. The experience of Tajikistan, given the country's unique conditions, does not offer good insight into the general relationship between market change and political development.

6 Petro-dollars and "Positive Neutrality" in Turkmenistan

How have Turkmenistan's economic policy choices since independence affected the country's political development? Turkmenistan's economic system may be described as a highly administered, command-style economy, dominated by the government and the ruling political party. Structural market reforms, underway since Turkmenistan became an independent country as a result of the disintegration of the USSR in October 1991, have proceeded slowly. Economic activity in Turkmenistan is characterized above all by dominance of the agricultural sector and by a high concentration of public investment in the export-oriented natural gas sector. Turkmenistan, with an estimated 10–14 trillion cubic meters of natural gas, ranks as the world's fourth largest potential gas producer, after Russia, the United States, and Iran. Turkmenistan has substantial oil reserves. Turkmenistan also has large deposits of other natural resources, having, for instance, the world's third largest sulfur deposits. But making use of this natural wealth assumes Turkmenistan's ability to integrate into the international market, adopt modern trading practices and, above all, attract foreign investment necessary to create the physical and policy infrastructure necessary to bring these commodities to market.

The following profile of Turkmenistan surveys the distinguishing features of the country. The next section, describing the decisions of the Turkmen state to create and extend monopoly and monopsony powers in agriculture and energy, surveys the economic policies adopted during the first decade of independence. The succeeding section analyzes the effect of these economic policy choices on government and politics, emphasizing the lack of meaningful reform in Turkmenistan.

Turkmenistan profile

Turkmenistan is a landlocked country bordered by Iran and Afghanistan to the south, Kazakstan to the north, Uzbekistan to the north and east, and the Caspian Sea to the west. Sandy deserts dominate the country's physical terrain. Low lying mountain ranges in the south form the borders with Iran and Afghanistan. The northern border with Uzbekistan is in part defined by the watercourse of the Amu Darya river, one of Central Asia's most important natural resources.

Table 6.1 Turkmenistan key indices: production

Item	*1991*	*1992*	*1993*	*1994*	*1995*	*1996*	*1997*	*1998*	*1999*	*2000*
Population (million; as of July 1)	3.918	4.073	4.236	4.401	4.534	4.649	4.779	4.920	5.097	5.285
Labor force (thousand; calendar year)	1624	—	—	—	—	—	—	—	—	—
Employed	1585	1578	1628	1692	1749	1780	1816	1839	1872	—
Agriculture	675	697	713	743	789	817	850	892	—	—
Industry	168	155	169	169	177	183	203	230	—	—
Others	742	726	746	780	783	780	763	717	—	—
Unemployed	39	—	—	—	—	—	—	—	—	—
Unemployment rate (%)	2.4	—	—	—	—	—	—	—	—	—
Production (thousand metric tons; calendar year)										
Agriculture (crop year)										
1 Cotton	1433	1290	1341	1283	1293	437	635	707	1304	1300
2 Wheat	205	377	509	675	695	453	707	1245	1506	1700
3 Cotton (lint)	430	390	402	385	379	131	190	200	—	—
4 Grapes	110	125	114	147	163	165	160	177	—	—
5 Barley	128	127	198	203	207	50	100	100	—	—
6 Rice, paddy	54	64	88	92	79	60	55	55	—	—
7 Maize	124	159	214	150	121	60	50	50	—	—
8 Potatoes	30	35	32	30	21	30	28	25	—	—

Mining										
1 Natural gas (mn cu.m.)	84348	60102	65154	35722	32264	35182	—	—	—	—
2 Crude petroleum	4828	5200	4301	4083	4394	4424	—	—	—	—
3 Salt	650	483	173	—	—	—	—	—	—	—
Manufacturing										
1 Cement	904	1050	1118	690	437	438	—	—	—	—
2 Crude steel	1775	1486	—	—	—	—	—	—	—	—
3 Fuel oils	—	1942	1399	1150	1000	—	—	—	—	—
4 Wheat flour	446	453	429	429	515	374	—	—	—	—
5 Nitrogenous fertilizers, N content	—	—	79	92	90	95	110	110	—	—
Production indexes period averages										
Agriculture, 1989–91 = 100	—	88.9	99.4	105.8	103.9	68.1	78.2	85.1	99.4	94.2
Mining, 1990 = 100	96.2	—	—	—	—	—	—	—	—	—
Manufacturing, 1990 = 100	106.7	—	—	—	—	—	—	—	—	—
Energy (annual values)										
Electricity (Bn kWh)										
Production	14.90	13.18	12.64	10.50	9.80	10.10	9.50	9.42	8.86	9.85
Exports	6.30	5.45	4.44	3.69	1.50	1.50	1.50	1.20	0.40	0.90
Imports	1.13	1.15	1.25	1.04	—	—	—	—	—	—
Consumption	16.03	8.88	9.45	7.85	7.78	7.30	—	—	—	—

Source: Asian Development Bank. *Key Indicators 2001: Growth and Change in Asia and the Pacific* (New York: Oxford University Press, 2001).

The oases and river valleys of Turkmenistan have supported civilization since ancient times. But Turkmenistan's inhospitable desert climate created barriers to the development of a modern state until the past century. The contemporary national frontiers of Turkmenistan are a product of the modern period. Turkmenistan announced political independence on October 27, 1991.

Turkmenistan had an estimated population of 5.5 million people in mid-2001.[1] Turkmenistan's population is growing at a rate of 1.3 percent per year. Turkmenistan's workforce was historically predominantly agricultural and service oriented. Since independence the service workforce has diminished in size while the agricultural workforce and the industrial labor sectors have each grown by about 25 percent. Official statistical materials on economic activity in Turkmenistan supplied by the Turkmenistan government are viewed with some skepticism by outside observers. According to the statistical data provided by the Turkmenistan state, agricultural production is reported to have increased substantially in the years since independence. While cotton production is reported to have increased modestly, Turkmenistan's production of food and forage crops is reported to have increased sharply. Official Turkmenistan government data, for instance, suggest that wheat production in the country increased sevenfold between 1991 and 2001 (Table 6.1).

While agriculture is the largest employer in Turkmenistan, the country's energy sector is the largest revenue earner. Since gas and oil sectors revenues are so closely related to Turkmenistan government revenues, because of recurring allegations that gas sector revenues improperly have enriched some private individuals responsible for public decision making, and because gas sector revenues are critical to Turkmenistan's official credit rating, statistical reporting on the energy sector has come to be an item of great sensitivity for the Turkmenistan government. The Turkmenistan government began concealing production figures for natural gas in 1997. However, there are suggestions that actual output levels for gas production and other forms of industrial production in the latter 1990s were considerably below 1991 pre-independence levels. Turkmenistan foreign trade (Table 6.2) figures are similarly unreliable. Thus it is difficult to develop a clear picture of Turkmenistan's balance of payments situation. But there are suggestions that the 1998 financial crisis in Russia impacted heavily on Turkmenistan's balance of payments by leading to the cancellation of Russian gas orders and delays in outstanding payments. There are indications that after 1998 Turkmenistan ran a significant balance of payments deficit for at least three years. Thus despite Turkmenistan's great potential energy wealth, problems of administration, and governance have prevented the country from fully benefiting from its natural resource base. Turkmenistan has remained the most deprived of the Central Asian countries in terms of education, social, and economic development.

Independent Turkmenistan's first president, Saparmurad Niyazov, was the former first secretary of the Turkmenistan communist party during the Soviet period. Until the Soviet collapse, Niyazov appeared to be a staunch communist, ideologically committed to supporting communism and the Soviet Union.

Table 6.2 Turkmenistan key indices: foreign trade

	1991	*1992*	*1994*	*1995*	*1996*	*1997*	*1998*	*1999*	*2000*
External trade (mn US dollars; calendar year)									
Exports (fob)	—	2692.7	2175.8	2146.7	1681.5	751.1	593.9	1187.0	2506.0
Imports (cif)	—	1592.7	1690.1	1113.4	1011.1	1183.4	1007.5	1478.0	1785.0
Trade balance	—	1100.0	485.7	1033.3	670.4	−432.3	−413.6	−291.0	721.0
Direction of trade (million US dollars; calendar year)									
Total exports	64.3	559.4	1162.1	1880.7	1692.6	751.4	505.8	1051.4	1873.3
1 Ukraine	—	—	—	460.3	0.3	1.0	1.2	437.3	873.4
2 Russia	—	—	54.8	66.8	33.6	56.7	39.5	69.7	429.8
3 Iran	—	25.4	30.5	11.4	16.9	123.5	133.4	129.8	144.6
4 Italy	7.6	53.8	89.8	13.0	1.2	6.3	64.7	145.7	100.3
5 Turkey	—	70.9	59.7	149.6	79.3	51.0	38.2	—	—
6 Switzerland	0.2	2.3	1.7	116.8	114.8	18.2	0.1	1.1	1.2
7 Hong Kong, China	—	0.8	2.0	36.0	104.1	16.2	—	—	—
8 Kazakhstan	—	—	252.4	127.4	54.1	30.8	11.6	11.6	11.6
9 Afghanistan	—	—	—	9.1	12.9	20.9	23.8	25.2	28.3
10 Germany	2.9	33.7	36.5	32.6	17.8	2.7	27.2	42.9	14.4
Total imports	141.5	568.8	905.4	1364.0	1313.5	1227.7	965.6	922.9	1153.4
1 Uzbekistan	—	—	—	28.5	5.5	87.9	170.4	252.9	335.4
2 Ukraine	—	—	—	416.4	127.5	283.9	133.2	112.3	112.4
3 Russia	—	—	122.9	95.8	154.6	164.0	103.3	66.1	143.2
4 United States	37.8	50.1	151.1	53.5	395.2	88.0	30.8	21.8	79.5
5 Turkey	—	91.3	92.5	160.4	120.3	153.8	105.2	—	—
6 France	0.8	2.9	7.6	16.3	49.4	47.9	32.0	114.0	40.4
7 Germany	27.6	50.2	98.2	52.1	51.3	16.3	95.2	44.0	60.3
8 Iran	—	45.9	73.2	36.4	45.2	38.8	39.9	39.6	42.5
9 Kazakhstan	—	—	27.8	31.4	22.2	86.9	13.5	13.5	13.5
10 United Arab Emirates	—	—	—	13.2	10.7	25.9	26.7	26.5	28.4

Source: Asian Development Bank. *Key Indicators 2001: Growth and Change in Asia and the Pacific* (New York: Oxford University Press, 2001).

Table 6.3 World Bank Institute governance indicators for Turkmenistan

Governance indicator	*Year*	*Percentile rank (0–100) in %*	*Estimate (−2.5 to + 2.5)*	*Standard deviation*	*Number of surveys/ polls*
Voice and accountability	2000/01	6.3	−1.42	0.19	2
Political stability/no violence	2000/01	52.5	+0.11	0.49	1
Government effectiveness	2000/01	9.4	−1.23	0.32	2
Regulatory quality	2000/01	3.0	−1.73	0.38	3
Rule of law	2000/01	12.9	−1.02	0.23	3
Control of corruption	2000/01	6.2	−1.12	0.27	2

Source: Kaufmann, Kraay, and Zoido (KKZ), 2002: Governance Matters II: Updated Governance Indicators for 2000–01. World Bank Institute.

As the Soviet Union began unraveling, Niyazov changed his ideological colors, quickly assuming the position of a Turkmen nationalist. Since national independence, Turkmenistan's progress in democratization has been negligible. Most political authority is concentrated in the office of the president. There is little legislative or judicial autonomy. Non-governmental civic initiative is routinely curtailed. Political opposition figures are isolated and excluded from the political process. Human rights abuses are frequent and severe. While Turkmenistan was ranked in terms of "political stability" in the top fifty percentile in 2001 by the World Bank Institute governance indicators (Table 6.3), Turkmenistan was ranked in the bottom tenth percentile of countries in terms of the categories of "regulatory quality," "voice and accountability," and "government effectiveness."

The state as monopoly: the monopoly as state

Turkmenistan's economic activity in ancient times was restricted to oasis agriculture and animal husbandry. During the Soviet period investment was concentrated in agricultural development and the gas and oil industries. Turkmenistan agriculture heavily emphasized cotton production. Given the country's arid environment, the expansion of the Turkmenistan's cotton-based agricultural economy required the development of an extensive irrigation system. Diversion of the waters of the Amu Darya river through Turkmenistan's Garagum canal contributed to the desiccation of the Aral Sea and fueled disagreements among the Central Asian states regarding water use.

Turkmenistan's Soviet-era economy was organized in terms of the principle of cooperative production, meaning that primary commodities such as raw cotton fiber, oil, and natural gas were transported to existing manufacturing centers, located primarily in the Russian areas of the USSR, for high-value secondary processing. As a consequence, Turkmenistan served as a supplier of primary commodities while the associated processing and manufacturing took place in northern industrial centers. Turkmenistan's Soviet-era economy was based upon massive hidden subsidies. When Soviet subsidies came to an end, many industrial and agricultural enterprises immediately became insolvent. The Turkmenistan government quickly sought to liberalize prices for external trade while maintaining price supports domestically. The government adopted a development strategy that stressed increasing foreign trade earnings with assuring domestic political stability.

Turkmenistan's post-independence structural reform program has been heavily influenced by the political objectives of the current political leadership.[2] Turkmenistan's economic reform programs have been oriented around two economic sectors, agriculture, and natural gas. The key feature of Turkmenistan's economic reform is that the government has acted to maintain strict administrative and financial control over these two dominant sectors of the economy. The organizational changes in the gas sector illustrate the leading tendencies in Turkmen's development strategy, namely the reliance upon para-statal production and trading organizations in the early period of independence (1991–96) and the increasing reliance on contractual relations with international partners in the latter period (1997–2002).

Para-statal organizations are firms that appear to be private and independent but in reality are closely tied to the government either through close connections of management or financial accountability. An example is *Turkmengasprom*. This organization, an inheritance of the Soviet period, was redesigned in 1992 to attract large-scale direct foreign investment in the gas industry. At the same time, a new agricultural equipment corporation was established to compensate for the disruption in the supply of former Soviet agricultural technology. Ostensibly independent, these para-statal entities appeared to act as independent profit-maximizing firms. In reality, they functioned as disguised branches of the government.

The Turkmenistan government's dissatisfaction with the results of reliance upon para-statals in the early stages of independence due to a lack of technical capacity, led during the mid-1990s to government reappraisals of the strategy of indigenous development. In 1997, a new national law regulating on hydrocarbon resources was adopted. After 1997 a number of important major gas sector agreements for joint ventures in exploration, development, processing, and transportation were signed with major international partners and with CIS-based partners. The CIS-based partners included Russia's Gasprom and Zarubezhneft, and the active gas marketing firm Itera. International partnerships included such western firms as Bechtel, Hagler Bailly, Halliburton International, and Mobil Exploration working in cooperation with the Turkmenistan's governments' Turkmengas as well as Turkmenistan-based private sector partners such as the Turkmenbashi Oil Refinery. Foreign firms, such as England's Monument Resources Petroleum, the Middle Eastern firm Dragonoil, the Malaysian firm Petronas, and the Chinese state oil concern, the Chinese National Petroleum Company (CNPC), have been active in Turkmenistan's oil and gas exploration, development, and processing sectors. The increased activity of foreign enterprises has brought a new level of sophistication to Turkmenistan. However, despite Turkmenistan's shift to outsourcing and contracting of many of the technically most sophisticated aspects of the gas and oil industries, the Turkmenistan government has remained at the core of decision-making. The main energy policy decision-making body, referred to in Turkmenistan simply as the "Competent Body for the Use of Hydrocarbon Resources," has remained under the personal authority of President Saparmurad Niyazov.

Turkmenistan's efforts to transform into a market economy have met with little success. Russia's price liberalization in January 1992 forced Turkmenistan either to free prices or impose restrictions on exports of subsidized goods. Neither option was attractive, since exports were needed to bring rubles into the economy. Free prices, the government reasoned, would result in inflation and perhaps social dislocation. Turkmenistan's solution was to introduce rationing of basic foodstuffs, flour, rice, butter, and sugar at subsidized prices, while restricting the export of these commodities. The decision was made to undertake gradual privatization in most spheres of the economy, with the notable exceptions of energy, transportation, and public utilities such as water. Agriculture was identified as an area of gradual privatization. A State Committee on State Property and Privatization was established to oversee the process of the transition of state enterprises to private management and ownership.

While the oil and gas sectors accounted for a large proportion of foreign currency earnings, they produced incomes that were restricted to a relatively small circle and form only a small portion of overall employment. Agriculture and animal husbandry, in contrast, accounted for about 20 percent of GDP and more than 60 percent of overall employment. Turkmenistan is among the top 10 cotton producers worldwide. The production of cotton increased in 1999 to 1,200,000 tons, up from 707,000 tons in 1998 and from 630,000 tons in 1997. In an effort to establish food self-sufficiency, Turkmenistan subsidized wheat production leading to an increase to 1240 thousand tons, up from 655,000 tons in 1997.

Despite some economic gains in recent years, much of Turkmenistan's population (48 percent by World Bank estimates) is living below the poverty level.[3] The government has adopted populist policies to support the social safety net. Since 1992 the government has subsidized housing and related utilities (e.g. electricity, water, gas, sanitation, heating, and hot water) virtually free and subsidizing key consumer goods (e.g. bread, flour, and baby food). According to social indicators, however, the safety net was far from sound. Local gas and water supplies, while without cost to the consumers, are frequently interrupted. The country's infant mortality rate (39.6 per 1000 live births) is among highest in the region and life expectancy (63.9 years) is among the lowest in the former USSR.

Fiscal and monetary policy

Turkmenistan's new national currency, the *Manat*, was introduced in November 1, 1993. In December 1994, President Niyazov issued a decree requiring all companies operating in Turkmenistan to conduct transactions in the *Manat*.

In December 1995, President Niyazov announced the "President's Program for Social and Economic Development in Turkmenistan." The program focused on restructuring the economy, convertibility of the Turkment *Manat*, and foreign investment attraction measures. The proposed structural reforms including banking reform to control the expansion of credit and introduce prudential standards, expenditure management, and debt management. But the Turkmenistan government has been unwilling to enact serious post-communist structural reform by reducing the dominance of the government, liberalizing the price structure and monetarizing the economy to allow a true private sector to emerge. A weak financial and banking infrastructure continues to hobble economic growth. The government has sought to increase direct foreign investment, but has pursued this goal primarily through efforts to woo strategic investors with concessions rather than establishing a level playing field for economic activity. The government's credit policy has been expansionary, based on "directed credit programs" and sweetheart deals. This has led to lax budget constraints and resulted in a predictably high number of unperforming loans as credits are dispersed frequently not on a financial merit basis but on the basis of access to influence and power.

The Turkmenistan government continues to play a highly interventionist role in the economy. All decisions affecting business involve some political considerations. The fusion of political and economic decision making require that business people "facilitate" necessary decisions to avoid capricious and quixotic regulatory delays by offering inducements in the forms of bribes and payoffs. Rather than creating greater oversight, this form of control creates opportunities for corruption. Faced with declining tax revenues from gas exports, the Government has reduced budgetary spending by curtailing some expenditures (wages, pensions, stipends, and medicines are protected) in order to achieve fiscal balance. According to official figures, state budget deficits have not been large. The reported deficit was roughly 1.5 percent of GDP from 1994 to 1996, and a slight surplus was recorded in 1997 and 1998. But these figures are misleading. Turkmenistan's true budgetary picture is hard to assess because of a large number of extra-budgetary funds. A realistic assessment would estimate the real overall public sector deficit of 10 percent of GDP in 1999.

Privatization and liberalization

Turkmenistan was a largely underdeveloped socialist republic during the Soviet period. With the exception of the natural gas industry, the minimal economic activity that existed in Turkmenistan was maintained by Soviet central subsidies. Industry unrelated to the gas and oil complex was generally not commercially viable. The country's specialization in cotton production was based upon massive irrigation subsidies that promoted highly inefficient and environmentally damaging agriculture. As soon as Soviet-era subsidies came to an end, most of the non-subsistence agriculture and non-gas related industry immediately became insolvent. The Turkmenistan government maintained its control of the industrial service and trading industries related to the gas, oil, and the chemical industries. Together these made up about 80 percent of Turkmenistan's industrial economy. The architect of the para-statal strategy in the gas industry, Valerii Otchertsov, argued that Turkmenistan's privatization program would stress small businesses in trade, the service sector, and the petroleum and gas refining and processing industries. Otchertsov explained to his fellow citizens that these industries were "within the government sector" in most market economy nations.[4]

The Turkmenistan government adopted the Law on Foreign Concessions in 1993. According to this law, foreign concessions can be granted for onshore and offshore areas containing natural resources, and for investment in industrial enterprises that explore, develop, extract, and use natural resources. The law provides for competitive tendering of concession rights for periods from five to forty years. A new Law on Hydrocarbon Resources adopted in March 1997 granted concessions to multinational energy companies to participate in the development of Turkmenistan's large oil and gas reserves through production sharing agreements and joint venture agreements. There is a substantial presence of foreign multinational energy and energy supply companies in Turkmenistan.

The Turkmenistan government announced major privatization initiatives in 1996. Government ministries were required to bring forth lists of subordinate state-owned entities for privatization. A mass privatization program was announced and a voucher style privatization was planned for entities with more than 330 employees. Auctions for privatization of many of the most attractive assets, however, were delayed and then apparently cancelled. The energy sector was excluded from the initial stage of privatization.

Under Turkmen law, individuals have the right to own land, including agricultural land. However, Turkmenistan has only a small number of private farmers as most agricultural land continues to be leased by the government on long-term use agreements. Large state-owed farming associations still dominate the agricultural landscape. The Turkmenistan government maintains a state order system of agricultural procurement that provides for monopsony control over prices.

In sum, the transfer of the state's most valuable assets to the private sector – privatization – has been slow and unsuccessful. While small-scale trading and service operations have largely been privatized, the Turkmenistan government has delayed transfer to the private sector of medium- and large-scale enterprises, preferring to hold these as state managed trusts or para-statals enterprises.

Trade and investment

The cornerstone of Turkmenistan's future economy is its energy wealth. With an estimated 2.7 trillion cubic meters in natural gas reserves and additional potential reserves estimated at 14 trillion cubic meters, Turkmenistan is the second largest natural gas producer in the former Soviet Union and the fourth largest producer in the world. Turkmenistan also has an estimated 1.1 billion tons of oil reserves and is the fourth largest oil producer in the region. In 1998,

Turkmenistan produced 13,284 million cubic meters of gas, down from against 17,322 million cm in 1997. Turkmenistan produced 6280 thousand tons of oil in 1998, down from 4481 thousand tons in 1997.

Turkmenistan's gas industry is not limited by capacity. Turkmenistan can expand the output of natural gas with the turn of a valve. The constraints on production arise from the physical transport capacity. In late 1997, Turkmenistan began exporting gas to Iran through a newly completed pipeline. The Turkmenistan government has also sought to develop new pipelines for access to external gas markets. The Turkmenistan government has lobbied hard for international cooperation in the construction of a gas pipeline across the Caspian, through Azerbaijan, Georgia, and through the Turkish port of Ceyhan to Western consumers.

Turkmenistan's hydrocarbon resources offer great long-term potential for economic development. But, if past management practice is any indicator of future practices, it also implies certain developmental vulnerabilities. Turkmenistan was an early beneficiary of price liberalization after the disintegration of the USSR. This enabled Turkmenistan to charge world market prices for the gas it supplied to its former Soviet era customers in Ukraine, Georgia, Russia, and other countries. On the other hand, the existing transportation infrastructure made Turkmenistan dependent upon customers in countries that were not in a position to pay. Accordingly, gas was supplied sporadically on credits that exceeded the consumers' ability to pay. A large proportion of Turkmenistan's gas sales were conducted on an inefficient barter basis. This led to serious problems of external arrears and led to a declining gas output. The total of arrears – mainly to Armenia, Azerbaijan, Georgia, and Ukraine – rose to $1.2 billion and the Turkmenistan government interrupted some gas exports in 1997, greatly exacerbating political tensions in the region. Following complex negotiations involving trading partners, governments, commercial banks, and international organizations, many of the debts were rescheduled and the Turkmenistan government resumed gas exports.

For several years in the late 1990s, Turkmenistan was a major player in the effort headed by the US government to promote a pipeline under the Caspian Sea for the purpose of exporting Turkmen gas to the Turkish domestic market. The partners in the initiative included Turkmenistan, Georgia, Azerbaijan, and Turkey. By the summer of 2000 the Turkmen political leadership essentially abandoned the idea in favor of separate arrangements with Russian gas transporters and new arrangements with Iran.

Banking and financial markets

The Turkmenistan banking sector is small and access to finance for commercial purposes on the basis of commercial criteria is highly limited. The Central Bank of Turkmenistan (CBT) carries out central bank functions. Several other large state-owned banks carry out commercial bank functions, including two large banks, Turkmen-Vnesh-Econom-Bank and Sberbank. Some sixty smaller banks carry out consumer banking functions. The Turkmenistan government holds majority shares in most of the commercial banks and directly or indirectly controls almost all of the financial system's assets.

Mirage of reform

Turkmenistan is a highly authoritarian state with a highly authoritarian political culture. Turkmenistan's President, Sapamurad Niyazov, popularly known simply as Turkmenbashy, or "Head of the Turkmen," leads Turkmenistan's single functioning political party, the Turkmenistan National Democratic Party. An engineer by training, Niyazov climbed the administrative latter in the old Soviet system. Niyazov became the republic's Prime Minister in 1985 and served during the final days of Soviet power as the first secretary of the Communist Party of Turkmenistan, the highest political official in the country. The parliamentary delegates elected Niyazov chairman of the Turkmenistan Supreme Soviet in January 1990. Niyazov was elected president of the Soviet Socialist Republic of Turkmenistan in October 1990.

At the time of Turkmenistan's national independence on October 27, 1991, Niyazov sought to bolster his political image at home and abroad by holding popular elections. Niyazov was elected president of Turkmenistan for a five-year term in elections held on June 21, 1992, running without opposition. Niyazov's term was extended for an additional five years by a national referendum held on January 15, 1994. On December 28, 1999, Turkmenistan's parliament approved an amendment to the Turkmenistan Constitution allowing the President to remain president for an unlimited period, effectively making Niyazov "president for life." Turkmenistan has recognized its president by naming numerous institutions, including cities, irrigation canals, numerous schools, streets and buildings, in his honor. Even the famed "Lenin Karakum Canal" of Turkmenistan was renamed the "Niyazov Garagum Canal." A new medal of Turkmenistan National Distinction was introduced to honor extraordinary service to the Turkmenistan state. President Niyazov was honored as the first bearer of this new distinction.

Constitutional, legal, and regulatory policy

Turkmenistan moved more swiftly than the other Central Asian countries to accommodate the circumstances of independence, adopting a new post-Soviet Constitution that went into effect in May 1992. The new constitution described a "presidential democracy." The constitution paid lip service to a tripartite distinction of executive, legislative, and judicial powers. In reality, however, there was no separation of power. The legislature and the judiciary possessed only advisory powers. Virtually all authority was concentrated in the executive branch.

Niyazov is a populist political figure, claiming to rule in the interests of the people. During his 1992 presidential campaign, Niyazov offered Turkmenistan citizens a number of inducements for their support, including a promise that after October 27, 1992 – the first anniversary of Turkmenistan's independence – electricity, gas, and water would be provided to all Turkmenistan citizens free of charge. In return for public support, President Niyazov announced a "10 Years to Prosperity Program," claiming that the standard of living in Turkmenistan would soon approach that of Kuwait and that Turkmenistan would pursue a policy of "Positive Neutrality" in foreign affairs, establishing good relations with all countries.

The Chairmen of the Supreme Court, the members of the Supreme Economic Court, and the Prosecutor General serve at the President's pleasure. The President appoints judges at all levels. The President has the power to disband the local governing bodies and the *Mejlis* (the national parliament) in the event that there is a no-confidence vote twice in eighteen months. The concentration of power in the president's hands was initially defended as a temporary expedient, necessary in the circumstances of post-communist transition.

Turkmenbashy has repeatedly pointed out that the Turkmenistan constitution was the first legal document in any of the Central Asian states to explicitly endorse private property. The constitution guaranteed citizens the right to capital, land, and other material or intellectual property.[5] However, there were no provisions in the constitution regarding the source from which this private land is to come, nor was the creation of a land fund announced. Niyazov stated that "until the people have learned to be property owners, the government will hold all resources in its hands and use them in the interests of the entire society."[6] The new constitutional provisions did little to establish a land market. Furthermore, in order to dissuade non-Turkmen citizens from selling their assets and migrating to Russia, *Turkmenbashy* issued a series of decrees that effectively made the sale of apartments illegal. Subsequent legal provisions made it possible for Turkmenistan citizens to "own" land, but placed restrictions on alienation and other forms of transfer that are typically thought to be inherent in the right of ownership.

Legislative, executive, and judicial policy

The government is managed on a top-down principle, contending that accountability and responsiveness in Turkmenistan should be maintained not through the electoral process but through the paternalism of the head of state. The Cabinet is composed of Deputy Chairman of the Cabinet of Ministers, usually eight in number, each with responsibilities in a broadly defined functional area. Beneath the level of the Cabinet are the Ministers leading Ministries defined by functional areas. While number of ministries varies from time to time, the list includes functional areas familiar from Soviet-era government administration such as Foreign Affairs, Defense, Internal Affairs, Justice, Finance, Education, Energy and Industry, Oil and Gas.

Other high officers of government include the chairmen of the national parliament, the *Mejlis*, the members of the Supreme Court, the members of the Supreme Economic Court, and the Prosecutor General. The Cabinet members and the other officers of government serve at the President's pleasure. The President appoints judges at all levels.

The legislative branch consists of the *Halk Maslhaty*, the Peoples Council. The *Halk Maslhaty* is intended to be a public information institution rather than a true deliberative assembly. The *Halk Maslhaty* includes the President, the high officers of government including high court justices, fifty elected members of the *Mejlis*, fifty elected members to the *Halk Maslhaty* from territorially defined single voter districts, and certain other appointed local officials. In the *Mejlis* elections held in December 1994, the Central Electoral Commission reported a 99 percent voter turnout. In this election, fifty new *Mejlis* deputies were elected in uncompetitive, single-candidate districts. All the candidates were registered members of the Turkmenistan National Democratic Party, the party headed by *Turkmenbashy*. In the most recent parliamentary elections, held on December 12, 1999, the parliamentarians were elected in the same way and all seats went to candidates of the Turkmenistan National Democratic Party.

The Turkmenistan president is head of state and the chief executive officer of the government. There is no Vice-President or Prime Minister. While the Turkmenistan Constitution pays lip service to the principle of separation of powers, in fact no system of checks and balances functions in the country. Since declaring national independence, Turkmenistan has made minimal progress in the movement towards establishing an independent judiciary, promoting a truly deliberative legislature, conducting competitive elections, promoting institutions of democratic accountability, defending civil rights, or allowing the free operation of the freedom of association. The public and private sector remain as closely interdependent today as during the period of state communism. This fusion of political and economic decision-making in Turkmenistan creates constraints on the normal operation of business and provides a fertile ground for petty economic corruption.

Transparency and integrity policy

Transparency refers to freedom from deceit and misrepresentation. Transparent government refers to public decision-making in a context in which information is available to the public in such a way as to reduce the likelihood of concealed transactions. Traditionally, openness and honesty in government have been supported by a free and open media, by a legal and regulatory order that separates the public from the private sectors, and by clear and uniformly enforced regulations regarding nepotism, cronyism, favoritism, and the influence of special interests. No single set of policies and no single legal framework can ensure that the objectives of transparency and honest government can be assured because societies differ greatly in their expectations about what is appropriate interaction between the public and private sectors. But governments that are interested in reducing misunderstanding, suspicion and compromise regarding the use of public resources undertake activities to promote transparency and openness. In this light, the Turkmenistan government's efforts ranks poorly in terms of measures of transparency and integrity.

Historically in Turkmenistan authority has been highly personalistic. The concentration of substantial political authority in the hands of the executive branch in modern Turkmenistan reinforces the use of public resources for political purposes. Consequently, Turkmenistan's post-independence government has evolved in the direction of a patronage system. In Turkmenistan, as in some other areas of Central Asia, position of authority and influence were historically bought and sold. This practice continues today. Many government services that are nominally free of cost are in fact paid for by under-the-table transactions.

Accountable modern government rests upon the transparency of executive branch implementation, particularly in such areas as government procurement, distributive policy, and intergovernmental relations.

Turkmenistan has strict anti-corruption laws that specify criminal sanctions for violations of the public trust such as embezzlement, bribe-taking, kickbacks, and illegal forms of favoritism. However, these laws are applied sporadically and non-uniformly in ways that suggest that political considerations outweigh objectivity and neutrality.

Turkmenistan was not ranked in the most recent corruption indices published by Transparency International.

Regional administrative policy

The former territorial divisions of Soviet days into oblasts and raions have been replaced by the more traditional organizations, the *velayet* and *etrap*, respectively, although no territorial borders were actually changed. The territorial units are ruled by the local *hakim* and *archin*. The local bodies of government were renamed the *gengesh*. Only ethnic Turkmen could head the *gengesh*.

Political participation and openness

Turkmenistan has not succeeded in recognizing the importance of institutional pluralism in the modern period. Formal opposition political parties are outlawed. Small, unofficial parties and opposition movements are dealt with harshly by government security services. Fundamental freedoms of speech, press, assembly, movement, and confession (Table 6.4) are routinely subordinated by the state to the prevailing definition of the national interests as determined by the leader of the government. Only Islam and Russia Orthodoxy are registered religions. Authorities have intimidated, arrested, and otherwise persecuted individuals and groups outside of these government-supervised structures.

The Turkmenistan government maintains that the country is "not ready" for openly functioning political parties working in a context of open contestation of values, ideals and policies as in most developed democratic countries. The government prefers to avoid social tensions, conflicts, and bloodshed by outlawing democratic institutions. While elections have been held in Turkmenistan, these have been instruments designed to legitimize the existing power structures rather than to express popular will.

Table 6.4 Turkmenistan: political freedoms

	Nations in transit 2000 political indicators								
	1991–92	*1992–93*	*1993–94*	*1994–95*	*1995–96*	*1996–97*	*1997–98*	*1998–99*	*1999–2000*
Political rights	6	7	7	7	7	7	7	7	7
Civil liberties	5	6	7	7	7	7	7	7	7
	PF	NF	NF	NF	NF	NF	NF	NF	NF

Source: *Nations in Transit*, 2000 (New York: Freedom House).

Election policy

Turkmenistan does not pass the "election test," that is, it does not reflect a situation in which "the government can be changed by elections as opposed to one where elections are changed by the government." (Lewis)

Civil and human rights

Turkmenistan is not tolerant toward opposition perspectives. The Turkmen communist party had it last meeting in the morning of December 16, 1991. At that meeting the party faithful agreed to disband the communist party. The assembled ex-Party members then went to lunch together and reconvened afterwards in a session that established the "Peoples Democratic Party of Turkmenistan." Within months the new Turkmenistan Democratic Party had a membership of nearly 52,000 members, 48,000 of whom were former communist party members. *Turkmenbashy* became the president of the democratic party.

Small and fragmented opposition parties have emerged from time to time. For instance a group called *Agzybirlik* (Solidarity) nominated it head, Nurberdy Nurmamedov, as republican presidential candidate in 1992, but Nurmamedov was not allowed to register in the presidential election. An alternative Democratic Party, headed by Durdy Murad Khadzhi-Mukhamed, was tolerated by the government, but not allowed to organize as an official opposition party. Clandestine political opposition exists within the existing political structures, however. It can be assumed to play a more important role than the visible opposition.

International Human rights organizations have been highly critical of the Turkmenistan political system as failing to meet minimal standards of progress toward international standards of policy and practice. There has also been criticism of the influence of the foreign community.

The international development community has not been satisfied with Turkmenistan's progress toward the adoption of democratic norms of policy and practice. In April 2000, the EBRD took the unprecedented step of suspending its public sector lending programs to Turkmenistan on the basis of the government's unwillingness to take to implement agreed upon structural reforms.[7] Turkmenistan's economic development in the years ahead rests upon the country's ability to break out of the cycle of excessive government controls and crony capitalism toward a modern economy based upon international standards. The US government and other major world powers have been criticized for turning a blind eye to Turkmenistan's record by virtue of the goal of promoting the development of Turkmenistan's fabulous gas potential.[8]

Political stability and support

The Turkmenistan government is the most precariously poised of the governments of Central Asia. Few opportunities for legitimate political change, monopoly political power of the existing leadership, the dissatisfaction of previous high-level politicians including Ministers of Foreign Affairs, and the extremely high financial stakes involved in a government overthrow, would suggest the Turkmenistan government remains in power not as a result of public support and inherent sources of political stability such as legitimacy, but merely by virtue of coercion and control.

Summary

The general principle of *Turkmenbashi*'s foreign posture was called "Positive Neutrality." According to the policy of Positive Neutrality, Turkmenistan sought to remain aloof and "Neutral" with respect to all relationships that might be risky or costly and to remain engaged and "Positive" with respect to all relationships that might be beneficial and reliable. While such a formula might be ideal, the real world choices of foreign economic and security relations in a context as highly nuanced as that of the Caspian basin make avoiding all risk impossible without forbearing all possibility of benefit.

In practice, Turkmenistan's Positive Neutrality was initially designed to provide that, first, Turkmenistan could maintain as much distance as possible from Russia without giving up access to northern and European gas markets that, for the first few years of independence at least, would continue to be under Russian control by virtue of geography. Second, the policy of Positive Neutrality was designed to promote the expansion of trade with Turkmenistan's southern and western neighbors on the basis of Turkmenistan's self-interest. Third, the policy was designed to make it possible for Turkmenistan to attract foreign direct investment to the extent possible to revitalize the gas-related industry and build a Kuwait-style emirate in the country while not relinquishing Soviet-style controls over the political system.

None of these goals of Positive Neutrality were achieved by the end of the first decade of independence. In 2000, the Russian natural gas monopoly, Gazprom, resumed purchasing Turkmen gas. This resulted in increased export revenue and contributed to improved political relations with Russia but it also resulted in Turkmenistan's losing a substantial degree of control over the export route of

Turkmenistan's most important commodity. A decade of debate over equitable trade arrangements in the Caspian Basin did not result in substantial improvements of trade relations with Turkmenistan's western and southern neighbors. With the elimination of the Taliban regime in Afghanistan, the Turkmenistan government could seek to rekindle interest in a trans-Afghanistan gas pipeline that would offer Turkmenistan gas an inexpensive egress route to the Indian Ocean. But the political and financial complexity of shipping gas across war-torn and unstable Afghanistan offered no early prospects of success. Meanwhile, with the lack of success in solving domestic governance problems and with Turkmenistan's failure to establish collaborative and cooperative relations with its immediate neighbors, the goal of establishing a Kuwait-style emirate with economic growth sustained by gas export revenues has proved elusive. High inflation, large government deficit, and a persistent lack of capacity continue to make Turkmenistan's dreams of economic transformation seem like a mirage.

The Turkmenistan government rhetorically encouraged foreign direct investment and joint ventures with foreign firms. However, actual government policies did not adequately support this rhetorical commitment. A large portion of formal economic activity, some analysts say as much as 90 percent, continued to be under the direct or indirect control of the government. A highly restrictive currency exchange system acted as a major inhibitor to participation of foreign firms. Excessive and quixotic government regulation, local unfamiliarity with international business practices, and most of all, the absence of a stable, established rule of law, with procedures for equitable dispute resolution undercut the capacity of the state to carry out its rhetorical commitment to international standards.

7 Economic self-reliance and the "Uzbek Path"

How have Uzbekistan's economic policy choices since independence affected the country's political development? At the time of independence, the Uzbek economy was more diversified than the economies of the other four Central Asian states. It included agriculture, light industry, heavy industry, and important branches in primary commodities. In the first decade of national independence, the Uzbek government articulated its principal goals as promoting social justice, achieving political stability, and establishing secular rule in accordance with international standards. The Uzbek government committed itself to promoting the growth of a market economy. The Uzbek government also made rhetorical commitments to principles of democracy and public sector accountability. These commitments notwithstanding, the early years of independence witnessed the emergence of a distinctive Uzbek style of rule, drawing partially on Soviet-era practices, partially on development models borrowed from the successful Asian "Tigers," and partially on the personalistic politics of Uzbekistan's political leader, Islam Karimov. Uzbekistan's economic strategy championed stability over market forces, placing state institutions at the hub of financial, commercial, and industrial management. Uzbekistan's political strategy championed public order over popular participation, leading to the elaboration of a highly authoritarian political order (Karimov, 1998).

The following profile of Uzbekistan surveys the distinguishing features of the country. The section "Uzbek Path," describes the unique set of policy choices adopted by the state in Uzbekistan during the first decade of independence. The section "The politics of economic self-reliance" analyzes the effect of these economic policy choices on government and politics, emphasizing the political consequences of Uzbekistan's policy of national economic self-reliance.

Uzbekistan profile

Uzbekistan occupies the dominant geographical, political, and cultural position in Central Asia. Bordered by rugged mountains to the east and inhospitable deserts along its western, northern, and southern borders, Uzbekistan is home to Central Asia's most productive agricultural oases, river valleys, and irrigated lowlands. Uzbekistan is a double landlocked country. There are many landlocked countries in the world, but Uzbekistan is one of the very few countries distinguished by the feature that every one of its neighboring countries is itself a landlocked state. Uzbekistan's southern border with Turkmenistan is, in part, defined by the watercourse of the Amu Darya river, one of Central Asia's most important natural resources. To the north, Uzbekistan's country's border with Kazakhstan is defined by the watercourse of the Syr Darya river. In the northwest, the Aral Sea, languishing form overuse of the region's water resources, defines the country's border. Uzbekistan's Fergana Valley, lying in the mountainous, protected eastern part of the country between Kyrgyzstan and Tajikistan, is one of the most productive agricultural regions in the world. The celebrated Uzbek cities of Bukhara, Khiva, Kokand, and Samarkand have supported civilization and agriculture since ancient times.

Uzbekistan had an estimated population of 25.1 million people in mid-2001.[1] Uzbekistan's population has the highest rate of natural increase among the Central Asian countries. Uzbekistan's workforce has traditionally been oriented toward the largest sector, agriculture. Over the past decade, however, while the agricultural workforce has grown somewhat, the largest employment growth has occurred in light industry, processing, and service sectors. Cotton remains the mainstay of Uzbekistan's agriculture, but some crop diversification has occurred, as Uzbekistan agricultural officials have placed greater emphasis on the production of cereals and grains in response for the demand for foodstuffs. Industrial diversification reflecting market forces has also occurred. Coal production has fallen substantially while oil, natural gas, and electricity production has increased (Table 7.1(a)). Uzbekistan has sought to diversify its trade patterns, trading with numerous and shifting trade partners. Uzbekistan foreign trade began to develop in the early 1990s, but the import of manufactured goods and luxury items led to trade deficit in 1996. To restrain the deficit, promote domestic production, and curb capital fight, the Uzbekistan government introduced import substitution measures in 1996. Between 1996 and 2001, Uzbekistan's self-reliance measures had profound impact on both Uzbekistan's domestic and foreign markets (Table 7.1(b)) .

Uzbekistan is widely regarded as an authoritarian country. The executive branch dominates the administration, the legislature, and the judiciary. The activities of non-governmental civic organizations are tightly monitored and controlled by the government. The media are tightly monitored and controlled. Fundamental freedoms of speech, association, and political expression are highly limited by the government (Table 7.2). Strident political opposition, fueled by insurgency movements originating in the events of the Afghanistan war and the Tajikistan civil conflict, grew increasingly active over the first decade of Uzbekistan's independence, breaking into violent opposition to the regime in the late 1990s. In response to the growth of political opposition, the Uzbekistan government mounted significant counter-insurgency efforts. These efforts have had the effect of chilling even modestly enforced protections of civil and human rights. The World Bank Institute governance indicators ranked Uzbekistan in 2001 in the bottom third percentile in all six key governance measures (Table 7.3).

The "Uzbek Path"

Uzbekistan's economic reform program has been distinguished by the effort to retain the state as the key actor and manager in the Uzbekistan economy.[2] At the time of independence, the Uzbek economy was more diversified than the economies of the other four Central Asian states. Uzbekistan had a well-educated and technically trained population (Lubin, 1984, 1995). It included agriculture, light industry, heavy industry, and important branches in primary commodities. It was a country rich in variety of natural resources including coal, copper, gold, natural gas, oil, silver, and uranium. Primary commodities, together with cotton fiber, accounted for about 75 percent of merchandise exports, with cotton alone accounting for about 40 percent.

Following the disintegration of the Soviet Union, Uzbekistan sought to insulate itself from the economic contraction that afflicted other former Soviet states. Uzbekistan President, Islam Karimov championed the view that economic development, not European style civil rights, was the true benefit of national independence. Karimov announced that Uzbekistan was "pro-business." The Soviet communist system was immediately rejected. But it was replaced by an indigenous, state-controlled economy. In the years to follow, the Uzbekistan government stressed a graduate, step-by-step approach to macroeconomic reform and market-oriented structural transformation with one primary goal – national economic self-reliance (Gleason, 1993). The Uzbek self-reliance strategy emphasized establishing self-sufficiency in energy and food grains, developing manufacturing for domestic consumption, creating an internally oriented services market, and exporting primary commodities, particularly cotton and gold. Uzbekistan shifted some of its crop acreage from cotton to grains to boost food self-sufficiency. The Uzbekistan government established targeted subsidies for industries and clamped rigid price controls on key consumer goods and services. While these steps produced positive outcomes in terms of limiting the immediate effects of the economic contraction, they had the long-term result of delaying the structural reforms that Uzbekistan's neighbors, particularly Kazakhstan and Kyrgyzstan, implemented (Akiner, 1992; Pomfret, 1995; Kaser, 1997; Degtiar, 2000).

At the close of the Soviet era, economic linkages were primarily within the larger post-Soviet geographic space. The Commonwealth of Independent States sought to maintain a single "economic field" on the territory of the former USSR. But market relationships shifted rapidly in the wake of the Soviet collapse. Russia made the decision to free retail prices on many goods and services in January 1992. Kazakhstan, moving more slowly toward the market, was also determined to introduce price liberalization and trade reform. Small, neighboring Kyrgyzstan, whose territory physically surrounded about 65 percent of Uzbekistan's Fergana Valley, moved forward with liberalization even more swiftly than Kazakhstan.

The actions of Uzbekistan's neighbors imposed upon Uzbekistan the necessity to do one of two things: either free prices and liberalize or impose restrictions to

Table 7.1a Uzbekistan key indices: production

Item	*1991*	*1992*	*1993*	*1994*	*1995*	*1996*	*1997*	*1998*	*1999*	*2000*
Population (million; as of July 1)	20.96	21.46	21.95	22.38	22.79	23.22	23.66	24.05	24.41	24.75
Labor force (thousand; calendar year)	—	—	10,739	10,975	11,222	11,376	11,665	11,999	12,297	12,469
Employed	8111	8271	8259	8150	8449	8561	8680	8800	8885	8903
Agriculture	3291	3612	3667	3603	3485	3505	3533	3467	3220	3090
Mining					65	68	68	69	—	—
Manufacturing	1867	1147	1166	1067	727	653	591	650	530	—
Others	2953	3512	3426	3480	4172	4335	4488	4614	5135	5813
Unemployed	—	—	—	—	—	28	29	33	39	35
Unemployment rate (in %)	—	—	—	—	—	0.3	0.3	0.4	0.4	0.4
Production (thousand metric tons; calendar year)										
Agriculture (crop year)										
1 Seed cotton	4646	4128	4235	3938	3934	3350	3646	3206	3639	3002
2 Wheat	610	964	876	1362	2347	2742	3073	3556	3602	3532
3 Rice	515	539	545	498	328	450	386	346	421	160
4 Barley	324	361	292	300	321	203	144	83	111	86
5 Corn	431	367	404	276	186	137	137	124	168	131
6 Potatoes	351	365	472	567	440	514	692	691	658	731
7 Vegetables	—	3494	3039	2975	2725	2497	2384	2403	2680	2645
Mining										
1 Coal	5948	4680	3807	3732	3054	2837	2946	2952	2955	2500
2 Crude petroleum	1384	1748	2406	3500	7586	7622	7891	8104	8116	7500
3 Natural gas (Bn cu. m.)	41.881	42.805	45.036	47.283	49	49	51	55	56	56

Manufacturing										
1 Cement	6191	5934	5177	4780	3419	3277	3286	3358	3331	3284
2 Steel	—	—	611	364	367	466	379	357	355	416
3 Rolled steel	—	—	572	337	322	423	350	322	325	372
Production indexes period averages										
Agriculture, 1989–91 = 100	—	97.9	100.2	100.2	101.2	91.7	95.2	98.6	97.8	96.3*
Mining, 1990 = 100	96.1	—	—	—	95.1	98.9	102.6	107.3	105.6	107.7
Manufacturing, 1990 = 100	102.2	—	—	102.0	94.2	96.5	101.0	104.4	111.8	117.7
Energy (annual values)										
Natural gas (Mn cu. m.)										
Production	—	—	45,035	47,181	48,626	48,987	51,245	54,790	55,581	56,400
Exports	—	—	5753	2111	5624	9076	9897	5228	5700	6857
Imports	—	—	7378	4912	1416	4200	2760	1062	2126	1621
Consumption	—	—	42,093	40,862	42,001	43,594	44,266	47,348	49,364	51,288
Electricity (Mn kWh)										
Production	54,160	50,910	49,148	47,755	47,454	45,421	46,056	45,935	45,372	46,864
Exports	18,080	16,400	15,214	14,815	14,199	12,826	11,488	10,642	11,114	—
Imports	17,700	15,910	15,621	16,175	12,908	13,918	12,417	10,818	12,305	—
Consumption	71,870	50,420	48,741	46,395	46,163	46,513	46,985	46,111	46,563	—
Retail prices (Sums/litre)										
Gasoline, premium	—	—	0.35	7.96	12.39	19.80	28.21	44.00	72.00	104.36
Diesel	—	—	—	—	—	—	—	—	—	—

Source: Asian Development Bank. *Key Indicators 2001: Growth and Change in Asia and the Pacific*. New York: Oxford University Press, 2001.

Note
* ADB internal estimate.

Table 7.1b Uzbekistan key indices: foreign trade

Item	*1992*	*1993*	*1994*	*1995*	*1996*	*1997*	*1998*	*1999*	*2000*
External trade (Mn US dollars; calendar year)									
Exports, fob	—	—	2689.9	3719.9	4590.2	4387.5	3528.2	3235.8	3264.7
Imports, cif	—	—	2609.5	2892.7	4721.1	4523.0	3288.7	3110.7	2947.4
Trade balance	—	—	80.4	827.2	−130.9	−135.5	239.5	125.1	317.3
Direction of Trade (Mn US dollars; calendar year)									
Total exports	161.6	688.6	1990.8	2717.9	2618.1	2889.8	2440.6	2184.2	2709.3
1 Russia	—	—	773.9	807.9	592.7	923.3	473.7	423.2	602.0
2 Tajikistan	—	—	75.7	228.5	180.8	237.8	206.6	240.4	274.2
3 Italy	35.9	82.5	113.7	196.7	231.3	197.2	147.8	136.9	172.8
4 Turkmenistan	—	—	—	25.9	5.0	79.9	154.9	229.9	304.9
5 Korea, Republic of	—	—	—	—	—	—	129.8	189.8	249.8
6 Germany	25.3	272.0	282.0	167.2	125.0	121.1	117.4	72.7	65.4
7 Kazakhstan	—	—	—	245.0	81.2	59.6	87.6	115.9	144.3
8 Kyrgyz Republic	—	52.9	57.9	63.6	119.5	116.9	111.1	46.0	43.0
9 Ukraine	—	—	44.7	89.5	55.3	114.9	27.0	79.4	131.7
10 France	16.4	49.1	97.1	118.8	103.9	92.2	87.7	52.2	48.1
Total imports	300.1	915.7	2522.0	3030.3	4869.8	4538.4	3054.5	2681.7	2579.0
1 Russia	—	—	917.4	906.5	1191.3	962.2	533.2	264.1	301.9
2 Korea, Republic of	—	76.6	153.1	269.7	559.6	742.9	442.2	376.2	376.2
3 Germany	74.2	149.4	354.1	389.4	522.3	483.2	303.6	291.7	230.9
4 United States	57.0	80.6	98.5	69.5	387.0	257.6	162.3	386.7	182.7
5 Tajikistan	—	—	24.9	145.2	209.8	189.7	138.2	199.1	259.9
6 Turkey	—	238.7	70.9	74.3	251.7	231.6	171.7	109.1	111.1
7 Kazakhstan	—	—	304.3	168.4	222.0	163.2	131.1	132.4	133.7
8 Ukraine	—	—	75.8	151.6	196.6	259.5	153.5	85.4	85.4
9 Iran	—	—	29.5	76.9	137.1	114.6	114.6	114.6	114.6
10 France	35.3	33.9	28.7	55.8	147.1	70.1	151.6	67.8	73.5

Source: Asian Development Bank. *Key Indicators 2001: Growth and Change in Asia and the Pacific*. New York: Oxford University Press, 2001.

Table 7.2 Uzbekistan: political freedoms

	Nations in transit 2000 political indicators								
	1991–92	*1992–93*	*1993–94*	*1994–95*	*1995–96*	*1996–97*	*1997–98*	*1998–99*	*1999–2000*
Political rights	6	6	7	7	7	7	7	7	7
Civil liberties	5	6	7	7	7	6	6	6	6
	PF	NF	NF	NF	NF	NF	NF	NF	NF

Source: *Nations in Transit*, 2000. New York: Freedom House.

Table 7.3 World Bank Institute governance indicators for Uzbekistan

Governance indicator	*Year*	*Percentile rank (0–100) in %*	*Estimate (−2.5 to +2.5)*	*Standard deviation*	*Number of surveys/polls*
Voice and accountability	2000/01	13.2	−1.18	0.18	5
Political stability/No violence	2000/01	13.0	−1.17	0.29	4
Government effectiveness	2000/01	21.3	−0.86	0.22	5
Regulatory quality	2000/01	11.2	−1.17	0.37	4
Rule of law	2000/01	27.6	−0.71	0.20	6
Control of corruption	2000/01	29.2	−0.66	0.20	5

Source: Kaufmann, Kraay, and Zoido (KKZ), 2002. *Governance Matters II: Updated Governance Indicators for 2000–01*. World Bank Institute.

prevent the effects of liberalization to be felt in Uzbekistan. Uzbekistan opted in favor of the latter. Restrictions were immediately placed upon exports and prices for many goods and services. At the same time, the government resolved to create quasi-private manufacturing and trading organizations in the form of parastatals. These typically were an institutional hybrid linking the government with the private sector. The parastatals had special access to credit and government protection, but were supposed to run on a commercial basis. The Uzbek Ministry of Trade was transformed into a Uzbek State Stock Association called *Savdo*. The presidential gave the local executive officials, known as *Hakims*, the right to run the regional branches of *Savdo* on a regional basis. At the same time, a State Committee on State Property and Privatization was established to oversee the process of the transition of state enterprises to private management and ownership.

Fiscal and monetary policy

In the early years of independence, the government approached questions of structural reform cautiously and relied upon administrative measures and government controls to soften the shock of the interruption of Soviet-era commerce. On the plus side, rapid growth in 1992–95 in oil and gas production allowed Uzbekistan to eliminate oil imports and increase gas exports. But on the minus side, rapid growth in unregulated trade during this same period raised concerns over loss of market shares in manufacturing and industry, concerns over low quality products that appeared on the market, avoidance of tax and customs duties, and capital flight.

In September 1996, in connection with a shortfall in foreign reserves, the Uzbekistan Ministry of Finance imposed a system of import contract registration. The goal of the system was to ensure that scarce foreign currency was used primarily to import capital rather than buy consumer goods, particularly luxury goods and items. However, in practice the system severely limited the availability of foreign exchange for all sectors of the economy and retarded economic activity. In subsequent years the Ministry of Finance periodically acted to make the system yet more rigorous as foreign currency reserves continued to dwindle. Foreign companies in Uzbekistan reported that the currency restrictions constituted the most serious obstacle to doing business in the country.

An overvalued currency tends to channel trade into narrow and more easily managed sectors. It thus may appear to offer a solution to capital flight. However, there are great efficiency losses associated with currency overvaluation. It requires strict regulation of financial transactions, imposing a heavy burden of monitor and sanctions. Well-connected parties with access to cheap, government-financed foreign exchange and import licenses benefit greatly from this situation. These parties can be expected to lobby to maintain the situation despite great efficiency losses and the corresponding damage to the public interest.

The bureaucratic burden of maintaining strict currency controls can be expensive and it unavoidably creates an unfavorable climate for trade. A policy of overvaluation creates a rationale for extending police sanctions even to the extent of replacing the goal of public safety with that of regulating private behavior. It can give rise to an incentive structure in which private parties have an interest in avoiding or evading the legal framework through various forms of side-payments and inducements. An overvalued currency also can be expected to lead to the depletion of foreign reserves, which, in turn, can bring about pressures for severe import restrictions and, eventually, the collapse of the free trade policy.

International donor organizations urged Uzbekistan to rethink its currency policies. The International Monetary Fund (IMF), which Uzbekistan joined in 1992, suspended credits to Uzbekistan in November 1996 as a result of the country's adoption of the overvalued, artificial currency exchange rate. Since that time, the IMF has continued to work with the country, but has restricted its assistance to technical counsel. The IMF urged the Uzbekistan government on repeated occasions to abandon the multiple exchange rate regime.[3] President Karimov announced in 1999 that the country's currency would be fully convertible as of January 1 2000.[4] Some improvements were introduced. In May 2000 the Uzbek government took a major step by devaluing the official exchange rate for government transactions by about 50 percent, setting the Uzbek *Som* at 231 to the US dollar and establishing a system for regular weekly modifications of the official and commercial exchange rates based on market factors. On November 1, 2001, the Uzbek government devalued the official exchange rate for all fiscal transactions in an effort to fully free the *Som*. The official rate was set at 680 *Som* to 1 US dollar. International financial institutions immediately praised the Uzbek government for this step to ease the country's monetary policy. Finally, in January 2002 the Uzbekistan government announced its intention to abolish the multiple exchange rate regime by mid-year.

Privatization and liberalization

Privatization legislation was passed during the Soviet period although it was not widely implemented in Uzbekistan. After independence, the Uzbekistan government established the basic framework for private property rights and private commercial activity. The State Property Committee (SPC) was created by a presidential decree of February 1994 on the basis of the Committee for State Property Management and the State Property Fund subordinated to the Ministry of Finance. The SPC was given responsibility for use and maintenance of state property, development of the privatization legal framework, maintaining the state's packet of shares in joint equity stock companies, determining forms of denationalization and privatization, selling property. The regulations of the SPC defined a property as privatized if it has been reconfigured as a joint stock company regardless of the ownership of the shares. Consequently, a joint stock company, 100 percent of the shares of which were owned by the government, would be considered to be a privatized company. Using this definition, privatization reassigned ownership but did not in many cases exert a substantial effect upon actual management, financial practice, or incentives. Also, given this definition of privatization, estimates of the proportion of property in private as opposed to public hands may be somewhat misleading.

Trade and investment

Under the leadership of President Islam Karimov, many elements of the Soviet system were quickly rejected (Karimov, 1998). But at the same time many elements of the Soviet-era administrative system merely were replaced by an indigenous, state-controlled administrative system that was itself top-heavy and stultifying. In the years to follow, the Uzbekistan government pursued foreign economic policies that stressed a gradual, step-by-step approach to the adoption of macroeconomic reform and market-oriented structural reforms. This conservative transition strategy emphasized establishing self-sufficiency in energy and food grains, exporting primary commodities, particularly cotton and gold, and creating an internally oriented services market.

Given Uzbekistan's rhetorical pro-business posture, the government moved to boost foreign trade through a number of mechanisms. A presidential decree in May 1992 provided that agricultural enterprises would be relieved of the Value

Added Tax (VAT). A decree designed to attract direct foreign investment came into effect on a few months later. According to the decree, enterprises that included a specified amount of foreign investment were exempt from income tax during their first five years of operation. A major law on foreign investment was signed into effect in May, 1994. The law was designed to create confidence among foreign investors that profits could be withdrawn from the country.

Foreign trade, however, was stymied by the lack of access to foreign markets. Uzbekistan had no natural ports, no developed foreign trade infrastructure, and little foreign trade expertise. Moreover, political relations with bordering countries forced Uzbekistan into a reflexive withdrawn posture. For instance, as conflict broke into the open in the northern regions of Tajikistan in spring 1992, Uzbekistan acted to establish border controls. In August 1992 the Dushanbe–Tashkent railway line was closed to prevent political refugees from entering Uzbekistan. A short time afterward, Uzbek officials closed the entire border between Tajikistan and Uzbekistan. The border with the northern Tajikistan province of Leninabad remained open for a period but then it was also closed, cutting off Tajikistan almost entirely from the outside world. Customs and duty stations sprouted at every border checkpoint, giving newly independent Uzbekistan the character of a "closed society."

Banking and financial markets

The National Bank of Uzbekistan (NBU), is government owned. The NBU works in association with the Ministry of Finance to carry out central bank functions. The NBU also carries out commercial bank activity. At the end of 1997, the NBU was responsible for about 70 percent of all commercial and foreign bank transactions.[5] Banking reform was originated in Uzbekistan with the creation of self-regulating organization for the banking sector, the Banking Association of Uzbekistan (BAU) in July 1995. In November 1995, the Cabinet of Ministers delegated to the BAU responsibility for conducting the National Banking Sector Development Program. Enterprises, organizations and the government dominate deposits in Uzbekistan's banks. Private citizens hold fewer than percent of bank deposits. This reflects the low citizen confidence in the banking system and the suspicion that bank deposits may be subject to review by government officials. To increase the savings rate, the government adopted an initiative in September 2000 to guarantee secrecy of deposits and protect savings. The measures require that banks process transactions in both cash and non-cash and give cash to depositors on demand.[6]

The Uzbekistan republican stock exchange was established in March 1994 by a presidential degree. Other stock markets include the Tashkent, Bukhara, Namangan, Samarkand, and Ferghana exchanges. The markets provide a platform for trade in commodities and financial instruments. Public trading is regulated by the Uzbekistan Center for Regulation of the Securities Market (CRSM). Public offerings require that the firm first submit the prospectus for review by the CRSM. The legal framework provides for trade in joint-stock company securities, government bonds (i.e. treasury notes, both national and local), corporate bonds, and promissory notes (state, commercial, common, and transferable). The volume of trading on the Uzbek Republican Stock Exchange and regional exchanges totaled 26.4 billion Uzbek *Som* ($114.2 million at the May 2000 official exchange rate after devaluation) in comparison with 8.1 billion Uzbek *Som* ($35 million) during the first six months of 1999.[7] However, the volume of trade figures are misleading because most of these contracts are prearranged by government transactions and do not represent free market forces. As a consequence, the volume of trade is low and most securities are illiquid. The Uzbekistan government announced plans to boost trade volumes and liquidity through measures to enhance transparency in secondary market operations and by establishing transparent and efficient settlement, clearing, and registration.

In August 2000 a Presidential decree established the Uzbekistan State Committee of Demonopolization and Competition Development. The purpose of the Committee was to carry out the provisions of the previously law "On Competition and Restriction of Monopoly Activity in Commodity Markets." The legislation was designed to establish a healthy competitive environment, create favorable legal and economic conditions for competition development, prevent attempts to monopolize the domestic market, improve the anti-monopoly legislation, and protect consumers' rights. The Committee was charged with monitoring consumer goods prices and cooperating with consumer protection organizations in taking measures to prevent artificial price growth and sale of low-quality goods and services. The Committee had the right to impose fines on companies and their executives, as well as on government officials.[8]

The politics of economic self-reliance

Uzbekistan, stressing economic self-sufficiency and state-sponsored welfare programs, has resisted counsel from international organizations and economic specialists to liberalize prices, abandon government subsidies, adopt a tradable currency, and open its borders to trade. Instead, Uzbekistan has maintained restrictions on trade and currency movement, closed its borders with war-torn Tajikistan, established government-controlled trading companies, and developed an elaborate system of subsidies and price supports for industry and agriculture. The Uzbek government also made rhetorical commitments to principles of democracy and public sector accountability. These instrumental pronouncements notwithstanding, the early years of independence witnessed the emergence of a distinctive Uzbek style of rule, drawing partially on Soviet-era practices, partially on development models borrowed from the successful Asian "Tigers," and partially on the personalistic politics of Uzbekistan's political leader, Islam Karimov (Critchlow, 1991; Gleason, 1991, 1993; C [pseudonym], 1993; Starr, 1996; CSCE, 2000).

Soon after national independence the Uzbekistan government took on a personalistic tone, with the president, former first secretary Islam Karimov, at the center. Born in 1938, Karimov was a communist party official who rose through the financial bureaucracies of the Uzbek republic. He had worked in the party, served as party first secretary of the Kashkadaria oblast committee, and then rose in the republican party bureaucracy. Karimov was not an Uzbek nationalist, but neither was he a socialist cosmopolitan in the mold of Nazarbaev or Akaev.

Although Karimov was known as a staunch supporter of Moscow authority, he quickly changed his coloration after independence, arguing in favor of a nationalist policy agenda. As Karimov amassed power, the legislature continued to function, but a July 1992 decree authorized the president to withdraw the immunity of a parliamentarian who was charged with "anti-constitutional actions aimed at undermining the state structure" (Interfax, 30 July 1992). The president presided over a presidential council, the economic ministries, a new system of regional administration, and the legislature. In the summer of 1992, a Consultative Council was established. The Council included the ministry officials and the new presidentially appointed regional bosses, the *hakims*.

Constitutional, legal, and regulatory policy

Uzbekistan's Constitution was adopted by the parliament in December 1992. The Constitution consists of a preamble and six main divisions, including 26 chapters and a total of 128 articles. The divisions concerned the sovereignty of the republic, civil rights, the social contract, and the state legislative, administrative and judicial systems. According to the constitution, the existing supreme soviet (parliament) was replaced by the *Oliy Majlis* (Supreme Council). The judiciary adopted a three-tiered system consisting of Constitutional Court, Supreme Court, and Arbitrazh Court. In theory, the judiciary is independent; in practice, however, the capacity of the judiciary to function as an independent branch of government was limited. The branches were not coequal or balanced; the executive branch is dominant in virtually all matters.

The Constitution describes a secular, democratic state in which "the people are the sole source of state power." According to the rhetoric of the Constitution, the highest organ of power is the legislature. But according to the blueprint of government, the Constitution describes a unitary, "presidential form of government." The president is identified as the "head of state and executive authority" in the republic and there are no meaningful lower tiers of independent authority (i.e. no federal divisions). The preamble to the Constitution notes that one of the principal goals of the people of Uzbekistan is to "create a humane and democratic rule of law." The Constitution is written in Uzbek with parallel text published in Russian and other languages. The Constitution guarantees rights of freedom of speech, free assembly, religion, as well as the rights to express one's national heritage. What the Constitution does not say is also important; The vice president is not mentioned in the Constitution and no relationship is specified in the Constitution between the president and a political party.

Included among the president's powers is the right to form a government and head it and appoint and dismiss the prime minister and cabinet ministers, to appoint and recall diplomats, to establish and dissolve ministries, to appoint and dismiss the Procurator-General and his deputies; to nominate appointees to the Constitutional Court, Supreme Court, and Board of the Central Bank, to appoint and dismiss judges of regional, district, city, and arbitration courts, to appoint and dismiss *Hakims* for violations of the law, to suspend or repeal acts of *Hakims*, to sign all laws of the *Oliy Majlis* or return them for reconsideration, to declare a state of emergency, to serve as Commander-in-Chief of the armed forces, to declare war, award orders and medals, to rule on matters of citizenship, to issue amnesty and pardons, and form and dismiss heads of the national security service. The president enjoys "personal immunity" (Article 91). Parliamentary deputies also enjoy immunity from prosecution, but are subject to the sanction of the parliament. No such restriction is placed on the immunity of the president.

The three-tiered judicial system is subordinated to the Ministry of Justice. The court system is funded from the state budget. In order to avoid partisanship, no judge may be a member of any political party. The Procurator's office represents the prosecutorial arm of the justice system. It is responsible for public observance of the laws. Procurators are appointed by the president and are restricted from any political or party activity during period of service. There are local and neighborhood conflict resolution committees – the Mahalla – which are reported to function effectively on a local level in many areas, particularly rural areas.

The president is elected by direct, secret, but not necessarily competitive, election for a term of five years. According to the Constitution, a president can hold the office no more than two terms. After state service, the President becomes a lifetime member of the Constitutional Court. Islam Karimov was elected president in March 1990 by Uzbekistan's Soviet-era parliament. He was re-elected in December 1991 in a popular election, running opposed and winning 86 percent of the votes. A March 1995 referendum extended the president's term of office to January 2000, matching the Parliament's and allowing him to stand again for election.

The Uzbek constitution outlines the powers of the *Oliy Majlis*, calling it the political authority of the country (Chapter 17). It is charged with initiating and passing legislation, as well as executing policies through committee work. It meets on a regular basis – two times a year plus any special sessions – and has both public and closed sessions. At the same time, similar authority is given to the president, putting into question the actual powers of the legislature. In addition, the legislature spends most of its two sessions per year discussing and passing presidential proposals and decrees, suggesting that it is not the *de facto* rule-making body of Uzbekistan.

Legislative, executive, and judicial policy

The fundamental regulatory instruments establishing the ground rules of political competition include the law on the Elections for the *Oliy Majlis*, the law on the Central Election Commission, the law on political parties, and the laws regulating the functioning of the mass media. The key is the nomination process, which is carefully monitored and controlled by the government through the activity of the electoral commissions. The Central Electoral Commission (CEC) is a fourteen-member board established by the parliament on the advice of the president. The CEC is responsible for oversight of the nomination process, the campaigning, and the organization of the election. Campaign financing and campaign publicity is managed by the CEC.

On May 25, 2000 Islam Karimov proposed in a speech to the *Oliy Majlis* deputies that the unicameral legislature be reformed to create a second, higher chamber (Oliy Kengash or Supreme Council) and transform the *Oliy Majlis* to a "professional" legislature that would meet more frequently than the present legislature. This "upper house" would represent the interests of the country's various regions.

The judiciary system in the Republic of Uzbekistan consists of the Constitutional Court, the Supreme Court, the Supreme Economic Court of the Republic of Uzbekistan, along with the Supreme Court, and the Arbitration Court of the Republic of Karakalpakstan. Judges of these courts are elected for a term of five years. The judicial branch also includes regional, district, town, city, Tashkent city courts, and arbitration courts appointed for a term of five years.

In theory, the judiciary is independent; in practice, however, the capacity of the judiciary to function as an independent branch of government is limited. While the Constitution describes the legislature as the highest organ of power, in fact the country has a unitary, "presidential form of government." In reality, the branches are not coequal or balanced; the executive branch is dominant in virtually all matters. The president acts as the "head of state and executive authority" in the republic and there are no meaningful lower tiers of independent authority (i.e. no federal divisions). According to Article 117 of the Constitution, all defendants are entitled to legal assistance. A number of opposition figures, including Shukhrullo Mirsaidov, the former vice-president of Uzbekistan, have been convicted of crimes. Although many of Karimov's opponents were amnestied, their criminal records remain, technically disallowing their possible candidacies for high public office. A new law regulating the courts was passed in 2000.

Transparency and integrity policy

There is separation of public and private roles, but the lines tend to be drawn on an *ad hoc* basis. The president withdrew from party participation, citing the need to maintain a separation of powers and noting that it would be inappropriate for a sitting president to also influence party competition. Major officials may not play a role in politics. Lobbying is considered illegal. However, these superficial rules do not relate well to a political culture that rests above all on personal interactions. Since medieval times in certain oasis cities of Central Asia government positions were sold, rather than earned. While it may seem backwards that a person has to pay in order to receive a job, in fact this could be economically rational in many cases because government positions carry high prestige and an official can earn an income to pay his superiors by levying "extra" taxes, fines, and service fees. In Central Asian cities this was considered a standard practice. Such practices are alive today. They continue and constitute a drain upon the efficiency and equity of government. As one observer noted "At almost every level of government, 'extra' rates and tariffs are set for otherwise free services, and no query can be resolved without under-the-table cash. The mechanisms that were created to cope with corruption do not punish the wrongdoers but only serve to eliminate the undesirables."

The Uzbekistan government has undertaken a number of initiatives to respond to the negative reporting regarding the prevalence of official corruption. The government announced in September 2000, an analysis of investigations concerning 11,430 cases of customs violations by business people. This number included 9300 cases by organizations and 176 cases of officials who committed violations. Of these cases 1319 involved smuggling or drug trafficking. A customs whistleblower hotline was established to identify violations (*Russia Today*, September 28, 2000).

The bureaucratic burden of maintaining strict currency controls can be expensive and it unavoidably creates an unfavorable climate for trade. A policy of overvaluation creates a rationale for extending police sanctions even to the extent of replacing the goal of public safety with that of regulating private behavior. It can give rise to an incentive structure in which private parties have an interest in avoiding or evading the legal framework through various forms of side-payments and inducements. An overvalued currency also can be expected to lead to the depletion of foreign reserves, which, in turn, can bring about pressures for severe import restrictions and, eventually, the collapse of the free trade policy. The Transparency International 2001 Corruption Perceptions Index measures perceptions of the degree of corruption as seen by business people, risk analysts, and the general public. The values on the index range between ten (highly clean) and none (highly corrupt). Uzbekistan, with a score of 2.7, ranked 74 out of 91 ranked countries.

Regional administrative policy

In terms of territorial organizations, Uzbekistan has a centralized political system of government with ultimate authority resting at the national level. Within this system, there are twelve *veliyats* (provinces), one autonomous region, and one city government (Tashkent). The president has the power to appoint and dismiss the highest executive officers in the veliyats, the *Hakims*. All policies made and enforced at the *veliyat* level must comply with national laws. This also holds true for policies made and enforced at the level of the Autonomous Republic of Karakalpakstan. *Hakims* serve at the pleasure of the president. In turn, local officials serve at the pleasure of the *Hakims*. In 1997 alone, over half of the regional *Hakims* were dismissed for a variety of reasons, usually due to poor harvests figures from their respective *veliyats*.

The system of government recognizes a national (countrywide) level, the level of autonomous republic (Karakalpakstan); and wiloyat (province) level. Subnational political institutions below the *veliyat* level are not considered to be part of the government as such but to be a sphere of "local control." The most important administrative change in the recent period was the revitalization of an ancient institution, the Mahalla Committees, following an April 1999 decree by President Islam Karimov. According to Uzbekistan legislation and tradition, the Mahalla level is local self-rule and is not considered part of the government. In 1999, the Uzbekistan government shifted greater emphasis to local public order activities by adopting a community-based approach to public law and order. Its novelty lies in the intensification of preventive measures in local communities and residential areas. This work is carried out by "prevention inspectors;" local officials who combine the duties of a neighborhood police officer, public health inspector, and a Good Samaritan. In a short period of time these organizations have obtained a level of autonomy that has not been known for many years.

The financial system is unitary. *Veliyat* and municipalities are responsible for collection of government revenue (taxes and other mandatory payments) but expenditure decisions are made at the national level. Very few categories of legitimate own-source revenue are available to local officials for purposes of local policy programming. On the other hand, local officials wield exceptional interference powers. Lower level bureaucrats, firms, and private parties that do not see eye-to-eye with local political officials find great difficulty in acquiring the necessary government approvals, licenses, or permits to carry out their activities. Official government positions are highly sought after. Professional training institutions such as the Academy of Public Administration provide training in the theory and practice of government. However, the selection of government officials has not yet been shifted to a meritocratic basis. The Uzbekistan national tax system is centrally administered and implemented at the local (*veliyat*) level. The Uzbekistan Tax Code was adopted by the *Oliy Majlis* in April 1997 and came into effect on January 1, 1998.

Political participation and openness

The most visible opposition movements in early post-independent Uzbekistan were *Birlik* (Unity) and *Erk* (Will). *Birlik* gained its support through spearheading protest efforts, drawing attention to pressing problems, and generally awakening Central Asian citizens from a state of political passivity. *Birlik*'s leaders defined the organization's main goals as achieving economic and political sovereignty while restoring the cultural values of the people of Uzbekistan. *Birlik* started as only a small group of intellectuals, but quickly discovered broad popular support. Timur Valiev, a member of the presidium of *Birlik*'s Central Council and one of the founders of the group, observed that members were surprised by the number of people from all over the republic who approached them asking what *Birlik* intended to do to help the rural workers.

Religious political opposition groups also existed in Uzbekistan. The goal of the Islamic Renaissance Party (IRP), for instance, was to establish an Islamic state in Uzbekistan. But the form of the state that this movement envisaged, according its chairman, Abdullakh Utaev, more closely resembled the modern state of Pakistan than that of Iran or Saudi Arabia. According to the Pakistan model, the Muslim style of life would be preserved by law. Such practices as drinking, drug use, and prostitution would be illegal, and the official Islamic clergy that was allowed to operate under the Soviet regime – and was thus considered by the IRP to have compromised itself – would be replaced. But, within the broad outlines of an Islamic state, the government would observe international standards of human rights, including the right to freedom of speech and religion as a matter of individual choice.

In addition to the nationalist and religious opposition, there was some opposition based on policy differences. For instance, Faisulla Ishakov, Chairman of the Organizing Committee of the Uzbek Social Progress Party, opposed the Uzbekistan government on the grounds that it essentially continued to pursue the policies of the Soviet government. Ishakov favored a new agricultural policy that included handing over land to peasants. But even Ishakov, reflecting widespread fears that land privatization would result in racial stratification, claimed that there should be no right to resell the land for twenty years. In the *Otechstvo Party* was established in Uzbekistan. It was a party which claimed to be modeled upon Western liberal-democratic parties. The goal of the party, according to its general secretary, Uzman Azim, was to achieve the economic and spiritual independence of Uzbekistan.

Official an unofficial harassment of the opposition parties took a variety of forms during 1992. The newspapers *Halk Suzi* and *Narodnoe Slovo* were closed down in early 1992. President Karimov was harshly criticized by Russian and other foreign observers for attempting to silence political opposition and allowing opposition leaders to be isolated and even physically beaten. Karimov defended his policy as the only means to avoid what he termed the "Tajik variant." He stated publicly that his model of leadership would be that as Indonesia's Suharto. Suharto, Karimov claimed, may have brooked little political opposition but he would be revered in history for setting his country on the road to economic modernization.

Election policy

Uzbekistan's first post-independence presidential elections took place on December 29, 1991, when Islam Karimov defeated Muhammed Salih of the opposition party *Erk* (Will) by a margin of 86 to 14 percent.[9] Limitations on Salih's election campaign raised questions of the fairness of the election regarding restriction on pre-election rallies, dissemination of information, and media attention. The post-independence Uzbekistan constitution was ratified in December 1992. It includes term limit of two consecutive terms for the president. On March 26, 1996, a referendum was held to extend President Karimov's term in office until the year 2000. It passed with over 99 percent voter turnout and over a 99 percent vote in favor of the extension. The *Oliy Majlis* rejected Karimov's suggestion that this extension be considered his "second term." As a consequence, Karimov was eligible to run for reelection in 2000. There is speculation that the 2000 presidential election may be technically considered to be Karimov's first term, given that the 1991 election was prior to the adoption of the current constitution. This interpretation would allow Karimov to stand for reelection in a second term in 2005. The extension of Karimov's term by the 2002 referendum would further extend this second election date to 2007. Karimov was born in 1938 in Samarkand. He remains in good health.

Uzbekistan's presidential elections were held on January 9, 2000. Najmiddin Komilov, Chairperson of the Uzbekistan Central Election Committee later announced the results of the presidential election. The total number of registered voters was 12,746,903. The total number voting was 12,123,199 or 95.10 percent of votes. There were 11,147,621 votes for Karimov, or 91.90 percent of the total number of votes. Abdulhafiz Dzhalalov, won 4.17 percent of the vote or 505,161 votes. Leading international organizations did not send observers to avoid dignifying the voting process. The elections were widely regarded as neither free nor fair and a travesty of the democratic process.

As the numbers suggest, voter turnout in Uzbekistan elections is exceptionally high. This high turnout, however, reflects not political participation but rather the ceremonial and representational qualities of Uzbekistan's elections. Elections are seen not as a plebiscite on public policy choice but as an opportunity to demonstrate patriotism. Manipulation, coercion, falsification, and the "family" voter phenomenon suggest that figures are inflated.

The political process is carefully monitored and controlled. The Central Electoral Commission (CEC), a fourteen-member board established by the parliament on the advice of the president, is responsible for oversight of the nomination process, the campaigning, and the organization of the election. Campaign financing and campaign publicity is managed by the CEC. According to the election law passed in December 1993, the right to nominate candidates was reserved to registered political parties, the *veliyat* legislative councils, and the Karakalpakistan parliament. Moreover, political parties must satisfy the additional condition that they must have been registered with the Ministry of Justice no less than six months prior to the election and have collected 50,000 voters' signatures supporting the party's participation in the election. These and other restrictions on the nomination process make it possible for the government to exercise a determinative influence on the pre-selection of candidates.

The People's Democratic Party (PDP), the successor to the Communist Party, is the dominant party and explicitly supports the president and the government. Other political parties include the Fatherland Progress Party, the Adolat Social Democratic Party, the Democratic National Rebirth Party, and the Self-Sacrificers Party (Fidokorlar). In 1996, Karimov withdrew from the National Democratic Party of Uzbekistan, claiming that the president should be above partisan politics.

The Islamic Renaissance Party and Adolat (not to be confused with the Adolat Social Democratic Party) have not been allowed to register by the Ministry of Justice on the grounds that they do not comply with the constitutional mandate of separation of Church and State and the September 16, 1996 law on political parties. The Islamic Renaissance Party was headed by Abdulla Utaev until his disappearance December 1992. Since that time, the party's leadership has remained in exile or in hiding. *Birlik* and *Erk* have active informational programs in exile.

Provisions regulating the registration of political parties severely limit possibilities for the development of new parties. Provisions regarding the registration of candidates favor self-recruitment and government manipulation. Key provisions on election administration fail to guarantee true independence and impartiality. The law on Election for the *Oliy Majlis* establishes unequal conditions for the nomination of candidates, in effect creating three classes of candidates with different requirements. The candidates who were not nominated by legislative bodies faced difficulties in collecting the required number of signatures unless they have the support of local authorities. They also encounter significant difficulties during the signature verification phase.

Executive power, in particular through its local branches, unduly interfered with the election process. The *Hakims* (governors and mayors), having both legislative and executive powers, and *Hakimiats* (executive apparatus) at regional, district, and city levels exercised determinative influence on the electoral process, including playing a key role in the nomination of candidates and the conduct of the elections. After registration, candidates faced further impediments from the *Hakimiats* and election commissions during the campaign period. Some candidates are subjected to pressure by *Hakimiats* to withdraw from the election in favor of other candidates.

Party membership in Uzbekistan is difficult to gauge, especially if one is trying to include membership in unregistered parties. The HDP claims membership between 300,000 and 400,000, and the WTP declares that it has at least 35,000 members. These numbers are quite possibly inflated, with most political organizations membership numbers in the low thousands. The existence of multiple parties in Uzbekistan has not led to political competition.

Civil society in Uzbekistan lags far behind the standards for countries in similar stages of economic development. A "citizen–subject" orientation rather than a "citizen–participant" orientation combines with Soviet-era traditions of a single hierarchical social structure to make independent citizen initiative psychologically difficult. In Uzbekistan government approved NGOs are often indistinguishable from government organized NGOs. The Uzbekistan government, in particular the Ministry of Justice, has failed to appreciate the role that civic organizations can play a critical role in establishing democratic, market-based economies by encouraging grass roots, constituency-based citizen involvement.

In the early stages of national independence in Uzbekistan a number of NGOs formed around social and political issues. But the social movement "Birlik," the Committee to Save the Aral Sea, and Samarkand (an organization to assist ethnic Tajiks) were seen by the government as possessing political rather than social goals and were denied registration. The Human Rights Society of Uzbekistan (HRSU) and the Independent Human Rights Organization of Uzbekistan (IHROU) have unsuccessfully attempted to register. According to the Uzbekistan Ministry of Justice, in 2000 there were 2300 registered NGOs in Uzbekistan. This number includes 287 international and republican public organizations, of which sixty-two are international and 225 are republican. The total number also includes 2023 local public organizations that have been registered by the Ministry of Justice of the Republic of Karakapakstan, Boards of Justice of regions, and the city of Tashkent.

There are three main types of civic organizations in Uzbekistan. The first category includes indigenous civic organizations that play a public service role endorsed by the Uzbekistan government. These NGOs include nation-wide organizations such as the Mahalla Foundation, the Association of the Disabled, and the Veteran's Fund "Nuroniy." There are also specialized organizations that focus on key environmental or social issues. These organizations often are organized at government initiative and receive special privileges from the government.

Political stability and support

Toward the mid-1990s a significant political opposition emerged, fueled by popular dissatisfaction with stagnating incomes, excessive government intervention in the economy, and a dearth of opportunities for meaningful participation in public affairs. As the Uzbek government consolidated political control during the mid-1990s with heavy-handed methods, political opponents either left the country or went underground. Many of the government's underground opponents were drawn to Islam as a natural counterforce to the secularism of the Uzbek government. The government's opponents viewed President Karimov, a former communist party first secretary, as a holdover from what was widely regarded as a period of foreign occupation by Russia. The Uzbek government began to fear that its opponents were attempting to shield themselves by cloaking their opposition in the garb of Islam. The Uzbek government began a series of campaigns to isolate and neutralize opponents of the regime, branding them as criminals and "Wahhabists," that is, Islamic political fanatics (Filipov, 2000). The government's counter-insurgency campaign cast a wide net, ensnaring the regime's legitimate and illegitimate opponents alike. Numerous cases of violations of human rights and Uzbekistan civil law at the hands of Uzbekistan law enforcement authorities were reported by international human rights organizations. The Uzbekistan government did not offer authoritative figures as to the numbers of those caught up in the anti-terrorist dragnet, but third parties have given an indication of the scale of the counterinsurgency detentions. Uzbekistan human rights activists estimated the number to be as high as 7600.[10] Journalists estimated the number to be as high as 6000.[11] The US State Department estimated that by the end of 2000 well over 5000 persons were in prison as a result of the crackdown.[12]

Civil and human rights

The preamble of Uzbekistan's Constitution (adopted December 8, 1992) notes that one of the principal goals of the people of Uzbekistan is to "create a humane and democratic rule of law." The Constitution guarantees rights of freedom of speech, free assembly, religion, as well as the rights to express one's national heritage. According to a poll conducted by an Uzbekistan government-sponsored public opinion center (*Izhtimoiy Fikr*) on the topic "Uzbekistan – Our Common Home," 87 percent of the population believes that the rights and freedoms of Uzbek citizens are protected regardless of their nationality or religion. Every second respondent thought that the individual's rights were fully observed. Fewer than 5 percent of the respondents reported that their constitutional rights and freedoms were not observed (Izhtimoiy Fikr, 2000).

The constitution lists a wide range of rights (Chapters 7–10), which include the rights to assembly, free speech, freedom of religion, due process, ownership of property, and gender and ethnic equality. However, Chapter 11 provides that individual rights shall be interpreted in terms of the greater interests of the state. The constitution (Chapter 12) also guarantees the right to engage in business and commercial activity and protects private property rights. The right to own property is listed in Chapter 9 of the constitution and Chapter 12 provides for freedom to engage in business. Legislation has progressed on these fronts, especially since 1996. In that year, new laws of private property ownership, setting up businesses, and taxation of business were introduced. Economic rights, as outlined in the constitution, have been of particular importance as the government continues to entice foreign investment in Uzbekistan.

The government severely restricts freedom of speech and the press, and an atmosphere of repression stifles public criticism of the government. Although the Constitution expressly prohibits it, press censorship continues, and the government sharply restricts citizens' access to foreign media. A 1999 decree requires all Internet service providers to route their connections through a government server. The primary purpose of this measure, according to the government, is to prevent access to information that the government considers harmful. Despite the law, private Internet providers have proliferated during the year.

The government limits freedom of assembly and association. The government continues to ban unauthorized public meetings and demonstrations. The government has not yet implemented a 1999 law that improves the formal legal framework for the formation, registration, and operation of NGOs.

The US government has repeatedly expressed concern over human rights in Uzbekistan. In November 2000, the US House of Representatives expressed concern over human rights violations and the use of terrorism as a pretext for political repression in urging the urging the Uzbekistan government, which "engaged in military campaigns against violent insurgents, to observe international law regulating such actions, to keep civilians and other noncombatants from harm, and not to use such campaigns to justify further crackdowns on political opposition or violations of human rights commitments under Organization for Security and Cooperation in Europe (OSCE)".[13] Throughout 2001 and early 2002 the Uzbekistan government the Uzbekistan government committed serious civil rights abuses. Testimony indicates that Uzbekistan policy and security forces tortured, beat, and harassed suspects. The security forces arbitrarily arrested or detained pious Muslims and other citizens on false charges, frequently planting narcotics, weapons, or forbidden literature on them.

The NGO registration process is complicated and threatening. There is a widespread assumption within the Ministry of Justice and the Tax Service that not-for-profit enterprises are merely fronts for tax evasion. There is an assumption within the public order ministries that the NGOs are fronts for political organizations. The distribution of income in contemporary Uzbekistan precludes many citizens from engaging in direct public interest activities. As a result of this, local NGOs have a keen appreciation for the significance of the approaching horizon of the decline of foreign donor assistance. However, there are few creative attempts to realistically confront this eventuality. Proposals for the establishment of externally funded, local NGO support centers have met with caution due to concerns about the interference of the government (or other actors) after the withdraw from a management role of the foreigners.

Trade unions exist in Uzbekistan as an instrument of management rather than as a means of interest-group based collective bargaining. About 25 percent of Uzbekistan's labor force is in the main Trade Union that is under the aegis of the Ministry of Labor. Farmers groups and small business associations also exist, but are primarily mechanisms for the dissemination of information rather than interest promotion.

The NGOs represent a spectrum of activities ranging from the governance oriented (such as election monitoring) to the civic-initiative and advocacy oriented (such as women's self-help associations) to the broadly social (such as child health collectives). Social needs in the region are exceptional and urgent. Structural change in government processes has been top-down in origin and orientation.

The Uzbek government exerts direct control over Uzbekistan's print and electronic media. The Uzbek government restricts citizens' access to foreign media. The scope of government control leads to an atmosphere of self-censorship and repression, stifling public criticism of the government. A 1999 decree requires all Internet service providers to route connections through a government server. The government maintains that the primary purpose of this measure is to prevent access to information that the government considers harmful. However, private Internet providers have increased in number, taking advantage of the technological ease of circumventing the law. A new media law, adopted by the Uzbek parliament in late 2000, established new definitions for terrorist activity as well as a streamlined bureaucratic and legislative system to be enforced in the event of a national emergency. The law restricts and sanctions media coverage of anti-terrorist and counterinsurgent activities by the police (IWPR No. 36, January 16, 2001). Uzbekistan is a challenging political environment for press and media. Government sponsored-media dominate the information areas. Government censorship, both active and passive, confronts independent journalists and media managers on a daily basis. This creates an atmosphere that chills free expression of views and opinions and limits access to facts and information.

Uzbekistan has an equally challenging economic environment for private commercial media organizations. Low advertising income results in unfair competition as the private organizations struggle to maintain the technical standards of the government organizations. The newspaper distribution system remains under government control. Libel, public defamation of the president, and irresponsible journalism, that is, spreading falsehoods, are all subject to financial penalty and possible imprisonment. This was underscored in the December 1997 *Law on Media*. The law specified responsibilities and obligations of journalists. The Uzbek government has criticized foreign journalists, principally Russia-based journalists, for reporting libelous stories and have either pressured them to leave the country or prohibited the distribution of their papers. This has been the case for journalists working for *Nezavisimaya gazeta, Izvestiia,* and Interfax.

Freedom House's *2001 Survey on Press Freedom* ranks Uzbekistan's treatment of the media in its most repressive category (Freedom House, 2001). Laws and guarantees do not have the effect of protecting the independence of the media but have the effect of using media as an instrument of state policy. Political pressures and controls over the media are ranked as pervasive. Economic conditions reinforce media's dependence upon the state. Repressive state actions, including failure to protect, discriminate use of legal protections, censorship, chilling mechanisms reinforcing self-censorship, and physical violence are reported.

The Uzbekistan criminal code of Uzbekistan was revised in 1994. The law initially included thirteen articles envisaging capital punishment. In 1998, five of these articles were removed. In October 2001, the government announced that Uzbekistan had amended the Criminal Code to narrow the range of crimes punishable by the death penalty from eight to four. Death penalty now may apply only to crimes of first-degree murder and terrorism. The government also announced a reduction in prison terms and an increase in the number of offenses punishable by fines rather than prison sentences. The government enforces criminal law energetically.

Summary

Uzbekistan's approach to foreign economic policies created conditions that constrained the country's ability to democratize internally. Although the Uzbekistan government, pursued policies designed to promote economic self-reliance, in practice these policies have isolated Uzbekistan from its neighbors and trading partners, have inclined Uzbekistan toward conflictual responses to its neighbors' liberalization initiatives, and have retarded well-balanced economic development within Uzbekistan. The unpopularity of the consequences of the Uzbekistan government's policies has not called forth moderation on the part of the government but, in contrast, has brought forth repressive and coercive state responses to what is broadly perceived as challenge to the basic principles of Uzbek rule.

A decade after independence, Uzbekistan's politics is far from pluralistic, competitive, or dynamic. The political process is carefully monitored and controlled. Restrictions on the electoral registration process make it possible for the government to exercise a determining influence on the pre-selection of candidates and the outcome of the elections. While Uzbekistan's Constitution describes the legislature as the highest organ of power, in fact the country has a unitary, "presidential form of government." In reality, the branches are not coequal or balanced; the executive branch is dominant in virtually all matters. The judiciary, independent in theory, is subordinate and defensive in practice. Uzbekistan's record on human rights over the first decade of independence suggests that the government has virtually abandoned a true commitment to basic civil and human rights when these are regarded as inconvenient. The Uzbekistan government routinely circumscribes rights to speech, association, assembly, and religion without due process. There are documented cases in which the security forces have arbitrarily arrested or detained human rights activists, religious activists, and ethnic group activists on false charges in the interests of state security.

8 Political reform and structural stability

The principal development challenge in the Central Asian countries that emerged from communism is one of transforming previously authoritarian, centrally planned societies into open democratic polities and market-led economies with the institutions and processes of a civil society. This is what the political leaders of the former communist countries have themselves announced as the goal of their strategies. It is not simply a discretionary policy choice. It is a requirement of today's continuously expanding network of global interactions in law, commerce, communication, and culture. It is a requirement imposed by the nature of the international community at the beginning of the twenty-first century. Only by making this transition can the former communist countries of Central Asia escape the negative legacies of communism, avoid a descent into syndromes of bad government and autarkic, exploitative economics, and participate in the international community as full partners.

Recognizing the principal development challenge of the era, the political leaders of the Central Asian states embarked upon economic reform and invited national and international assistance organizations to help them in this undertaking. As a condition of this economic assistance, the countries pledged to also undertake political reforms. More than ten years have passed since serious reform was commenced. What lessons can be drawn regarding the impact of market reforms on political change? What lessons can be drawn from the Central Asian experience with respect to the theoretical relationships between markets and politics? What lessons can be drawn with respect to the most auspicious policies for sustaining and deepening programs of reform?

The influence of markets on politics

When the international donor community moved into the former Soviet arena following the collapse of the USSR, it was still very much in the sway of the "small is better" minimalist approach to structural reform. The consensus among policy specialists was that "top-heavy" Soviet state apparatuses created conditions that could only be overcome through downsizing and right-sizing to unload excessive public sector burdens, eliminate state subsidies, and improve the efficiency of government. The rapid reduction in the size and scope of the state was required, leading program designers argued, in order to achieve a better balance between the public and private sectors. Donor organization planners also believed that this would facilitate a sorting out of the distribution of tasks among public and private entities. The post-communist states with the greatest reductions in size and the greatest focus on core functions, this line of reasoning maintained, would become the most efficient and would be expected to reap the greatest gains in the transition process. Policy advisors maintained that success in terms of economic output could be expected to be roughly proportional to success in implementing reform measures.

Kazakhstan undertook fundamental macroeconomic reforms and was rewarded by increases in economic output. Kazakhstan benefited considerably from the adoption of international standards. Kazakhstan drew praise from the international community for its success in economic reform. Improvements in tax administration and public expenditure management greatly strengthened the country's fiscal position. In 2000, Kazakhstan achieved a budget surplus and even took the unusual step of repaying IMF loans ahead of schedule. In 2001 Kazakhstan's economic growth reached 13 percent, the highest growth rate in the CIS. Along with accolades, however, the Kazakhstan government also began receiving messages of caution that too swift a course toward an oil-based economy may carry economic and political risks. Too heavy a reliance on primary commodity exports could lead to the so-called "Dutch disease" – a situation in which oil-rich countries draw in large amounts of foreign capital for needed oil industry development but find that the resulting strong exchange rates hinder the country's ability to competitively price its other goods and services.

These warnings were particularly germane as Kazakhstan's oil industry began gearing up for a decade of steep growth. Kazakhstan oil production rose to over 800,000 barrels per day in 2001, with nearly 70 percent of production bound for export. Major new oil fields were scheduled to come on line in the years ahead, including the giant Kashagan oil field that represents the world's largest new find in the past forty years. An overdeveloped energy sector, critics observed, could end up dominating other branches of the economy, both economically and politically. As powerful constituencies became ensconced in key decision-making positions, Big Oil's influence over economics and politics threatened to become self-perpetuating.

Kyrgyzstan, which at least initially introduced the most determined, proreform policies in the Central Asian region, was not rewarded by the expected gains in economic activity. Kyrgyzstan, as the first to introduce a national currency, the first to privatize, and the first country of the CIS to join the World Trade Organization, distinguished itself as a leader in reform. But Kyrgyzstan's narrow resource base and *cul de sac* location limited its ability to actively integrate into the international community. The promised benefits of rising prosperity remained elusive for the majority of the country's citizens. Competition over scarce resources gradually drew into question the political stability of the Kyrgyzstan government and the country's commitment to the reform path.

Uzbekistan, stressing economic self-sufficiency and state-sponsored welfare programs, resisted counsel from international organizations and economic specialists to liberalize prices, abandon government subsidies, adopt a tradable currency, and open its borders to trade. Instead, Uzbekistan maintained restrictions on trade and currency movement, closed its borders with war-torn Tajikistan, established government-controlled trading companies, and developed an elaborate system of subsidies and price supports for industry and agriculture. The contraction of Uzbekistan's foreign trade in the 1997–2002 period reflected the consequences of the country's illiberal trading policies. Initially, Uzbekistan's commitment to social welfare programs did have a beneficial impact on political stability. Gradually, however, the slowdown in economic development was reflected in increasing levels of social desperation and anti-state political activism. The Uzbekistan government's tendency to counter confrontation with coercion may have played a role in further polarizing society. The government's reevaluation of the development strategy in late 2001 suggested the beginnings of a markedly different economic and political evolution.

Turkmenistan, like Uzbekistan, resisted counsel from international donors to open its economy, relying on its expected gas revenues as a panacea for development. In so doing, the country postponed much needed governance reforms. Turkmenistan's efforts to transform into a market economy met with little success and produced negligible liberalizing effects on the political sphere. Turkmenistan's insistent efforts to intimidate and isolate all forms of political opposition neutralized any benign effects of economic reform.

The smallest and most constrained of the countries of the Eurasian region was Tajikistan. While it would have been classified as a lower middle-income economy in the former Soviet period, by the end of the first decade of independence Tajikistan had become one of the world's poorest countries. Tajikistan's economic and political situation was complex. The dominant features in Tajikistan's economic and political evolution were the consequences of the Afghanistan conflict (1979–89), the Tajik civil war (1992–94), the post-conflict power-sharing arrangement imposed upon the Tajikistan government, the Taliban-era trade in narcotics and weapons (1994–2001), and the nature of Tajikistan's geographically divided and regionally split government. The Tajikistan government undertook economic reforms in good faith, but was only marginally successful in translating these reforms into action. It should be observed that the Tajikistan case is unique. It serves poorly as a basis for general conclusions about the relationship between economic reform strategies and political development.

The influence of markets on politics is most evident in terms of the impact of standards of living on politics. No significant progress toward a free society can be achieved in countries marred by severe poverty, financial instability, social disparity, and manifest economic injustice. Political debating societies are of little intrinsic interest among peoples suffering from malnutrition, disease, and abject poverty. As standards of income, health care, and education have deteriorated among some populations in Central Asia over the past decade, these changes have exerted a direct influence on politics. Many analysts argue that the resulting social desperation has fueled the rise of insurgency and extremist political doctrines. Subsequent economic reform programs will need to more directly address the mounting problems associated with the growth of poverty and increasing disparities in income.

Market reform programs in some cases in Central Asia took place without much direct economic, let alone political impact. For instance, Kazakhstan reformed its banking system. Kyrgyzstan privatized its manufacturing and processing industries. Uzbekistan adopted legislation establishing a stock market. Kazakhstan citizens found that new banking services were available, but few of these services affected the day-to-day economic of most citizens and there was no appreciable affect on political conditions. Kyrgyzstan citizens found that the newly privatized industries remained under the control of small numbers of people closely associated with the government and witnessed no appreciable affect on the country's political conditions. The Uzbekistan government physically created a stock exchange but was unsuccessful in breathing financial vitality into it. During the first decade of independence, the Uzbekistan stock exchange served only as a convenience for the government and did not engage the hurly burly trading activity of a true stock market. Uzbekistan citizens drew few benefits from the government's efforts to create an Uzbekistan stock exchange beyond the ability to admire the architecture of what is one of the world's most artfully designed stock exchange buildings.

The influence of politics on markets

History provides examples both of revolutions and reforms. These two modes of social change are different, each having its own mechanisms, consequences, advantages, and disadvantages. The bitter irony of the Soviet collapse is that the countries of Central Asia endured many of the disadvantages of revolution without managing to benefit from the advantages of reform. A revolution is a sudden and sweeping change of the principles of a society. A revolution substitutes a new set of principles as the basis for governance. Reform, by way of contrast, implies incremental change. It affirms the basic soundness of the principles of governance but seeks adjustments or compensations to improve equity, efficiency, or some other values. Conducting a revolution implies replacing a government. Reforming a government implies conducting a step-by-step, incremental transition from one way of getting to the agreed upon goals to another way of getting there. It means changing the "rules of the game," but not necessarily eliminating the opposition or purging "incorrect" ways of thinking.

Many politicians lament that reform is more difficult than revolution. "The worst way to cross a chasm," unsuccessful reformers point out, "is in small steps." Because political reform goes forward in piecemeal steps, at each juncture in the reform process groups have an opportunity to reorganize to protect their interests. In so doing, they change the *terra politica* in ways unexpected by the reform agenda. Groups and individuals seeking to protect their own interests begin to anticipate the reformers' next steps in order to position themselves for the next round of change. Responding to this anticipation, leaders dedicated to democratic reform may begin to resort to the tactic of surprise or subterfuge to achieve their goals. As reformists grow more desperate in their efforts to out maneuver their opposition, they act in ways that limit participation, transparency, and even the consent of the governed. In this way, political leaders seeking to attain the ends of reform often abandon democratic means. This explains what may otherwise seem paradoxical: why Central Asian leaders who publicly championed democratic ideals and the transition to market economic relations so frequently fell back on authoritarian methods and statist economic policies for bringing about their vision of change. The social shock of the post-communist revolution took place while the politics of reform reassigned power and privilege to a well-ensconced few.

Politics continued to be dominated by personalities in Central Asia. The Soviet-era leaders almost effortlessly assumed power after the collapse of the USSR in the new states of Central Asia except Tajikistan. In all cases the political systems of the Central Asian states have remain dominated by the countries' presidents. This may have been partially a carryover from the communist period, in which, despite all the rhetoric of scientific communism and the primacy of ideology, politics was always in the shadow of heroic political figures, whether a Marx, Lenin, Mao, or Fidel. But the prominence of particular politicians may also be attributed to some extent to the strength of nationalist and ethnic inclusiveness and the extraordinarily strong sense of family obligation in indigenous Central Asian society. The post-communist transition has taken place without a resolution to that most important problem of politics, the succession problem.

From the very beginning of the transformation, the governments of Central Asia were less enthusiastic about implementing political reforms than they were about economic reforms. The governments had negligible success in carrying out political reforms. Elections in Central Asia have been less than free and fair, government has not grown more accountable, and human and civil rights have not satisfied international standards. Even in the instances in which the governments have moved to adopt formal political institutions based on foreign models, the institutions have often been artificial. To merely adopt Potemkin style democratic institutions and expect that democratic process will follow is to engage in a self-deceptive practice in which the imperfect structures of democracy themselves become the basis for bias, exclusion, and dominance.

Central Asian policy makers were heavily invested in their particular practices, heavily dependent on the paths they were following. Path dependence, that is, the idea that inefficient practices can be preferable to efficient ones if the cost of shifting from one to the other is high, would suggest why Central Asian officials were so reluctant to support external reform programs. Reforms are risky, indifference is less so, and non-action is the least conspicuous course of all. Central Asian officialdom was threatened by the prospect of political reform as government officials who saw their own Soviet-era sinecures evaporating. Central Asia's structural reform programs, whatever their goals, whatever the intentions of the international financial institutions that sponsored them, whatever the intentions of the country leaders who agreed to them, were implemented by the government officials whose livelihoods were most immediately affected by them, usually to their detriment.

Another key domestic political question during the past decade in the Central Asian countries, as in the other Soviet countries, was the competition for control over Soviet-era assets. Privatization of assets in many cases simply meant reassignment of assets. In many cases privatization simply put in place mechanisms for collective economic rents and for distributing these rents to their clients. The public interest is by no means easily defined and pursued even in the best of circumstances. Moreover, benign oligarchies exist and function in some circumstances in ways that promote a nation's economic development and even social justice. But the likelihood of oligarchy and hierarchy in the end defeating the public interest in favor of sectarian and private interests is overwhelming.

Reform is not costless. Comparative studies have drawn attention to the crucial question of how reform is financed (Levi, 1988; Burnell and Ware, 1998; Burnell, 2000). Yet we still have far too little understanding of the relationship between markets and the process of financing political reform in Central Asia. Only one succinct scholarly work, Cummings' study of Kazakhstan's regional decision-making, offers any systematic insight into how Central Asian sources of revenue are related to reform (Cummings, 2000).

While the Central Asian states became politically independent entities after the collapse of the USSR in 1991, in fact they continued to be heavily dependent upon one another in terms of history, culture, infrastructure, and trade ties. The relations among Central Asian states, in particular the relations among the heads of state and the high level officialdom, played an important role. But the states were not successful in turning their close connections to their common benefit. Over the first decade of independence, interregional Central Asian trade actually declined as the states found it easier to conduct trade with countries outside the region. Throughout the first decade of independence the Central Asian states pursued policies that were uncoordinated and frequently conflicting (Kubichek, 1997; Gleason, 2001). As Richard Sakwa and Mark Webber have noted, the countries of Central Asia were parties to many of the CIS regional cooperation agreements that were designed to lead to forms of "equitable and mutually beneficial cooperation" (Sakwa and Webber, 1999: 379). But the fact that the countries moved forward toward a market economy at different rates and relied upon different measures, created market competition, and political animosity among the countries (Gürgen *et al.*, 1999). The lack of cooperation was reflected in other areas, such as transboundary resources (Kobori and Glantz, 1998; Micklin, 2000).

Lessons of reform

In Chapter 1 of this book we surveyed the theoretical propositions of classical liberal economic and political theory. We noted the close association between economic and political liberalism. We noted that it is tempting to suppose that economic change and political change are two sides of the same coin. Liberal theory describes a situation in which the constitutional order undergirds a legal and regulatory structure that protects a private sphere of activity in which individuals and groups of individuals act to pursue their interests as they define them in terms of their preferences. The sphere of private activity is separated from the public sphere. In the realm of economic activity, the legal and regulatory structure protects the private sphere in which individuals, households, partnerships, enterprises, and corporations pursue their interests through voluntary transactions. In the realm of political activity, this private sphere is where individuals, groups, parties, and nongovernmental organizations pursue their interests through open expression, voluntary association, and collective action. Civil and commercial codes, business law, and government regulatory law prescribes the rights and obligations of parties in the economic sphere. Civil law, human rights legislation, and administrative law prescribe the limits of the state and the rights and obligations of individuals and groups in the political sphere. To the extent that these theoretical conditions are fulfilled in practice, it would be natural to assume that economic reform and political reform are conceptually linked and would reinforce one another in practice. Improvements in the economic sphere could be expected to have a spill over effect that would improve the policy environment of the political sphere. Likewise, improvements in the political sphere could be expected to have a spill over effect that would improve the policy environment of the economic sphere. Enduring reform, one would be led to suppose, could be equally well promoted by political or by economic progress.

To what extent does the experience of the Central Asian countries bear out these theoretical expectations? The analysis of the first decade of post-communist development in the Central Asian states provided in the preceding chapters leads to three primary insights regarding the link between economic and political processes.

First, the analysis of the preceding chapters provides support for the general conclusion that political reform programs in the absence of structural reform and economic change do not appear to have been productive in the context of Central Asia. Political liberalization in the Central Asian countries has been thwarted and derailed in numerous cases by constituencies who themselves have been the principal beneficiaries of the economic changes introduced by structural reform efforts. Indigenous Central Asian political values, lingering Soviet-era political assumptions and practices, and the influence of domestic political constituencies have had the effect of undermining or neutralizing political reform activities of foreign donor organizations and even political reform initiated by Central Asian government leaders. These kinds of political reform activities have been viewed by Central Asians in the best of cases as unwanted intervention and in the worst of cases as unacceptable interference in domestic political affairs. Political reform efforts, one may conclude, in the absence of parallel economic liberalization, are not apt to be very productive.

Second, the analysis provides some evidence to support the conclusion that the adoption of liberal economic policies as features of structural reform is apt to lead to conditions that promote liberal political domestic conditions, but do not guarantee political liberalization. The international financial institutions are charged in part with providing technical assistance to aid their member countries in development efforts. The charters of the international financial institutions preclude them from interference in domestic political affairs. The donor institutions provide non-political technical assistance in structural reform programs that is designed to increase capacity and bring countries into closer conformance with the demands of the international community. In so doing, the international financial institutions operate under restrictions that are designed to strengthen state sovereignty. The structural reform programs of the international financial institutions, therefore, are designed to be as non-political as possible. They seek to improve governance, assuming that improvements in governance will make improvement in government more likely. But in the background there is the assumption that, given economic liberalization, sooner or later, political liberalization will take place.

Economic reform programs improve the policy environment for individual actors, for entrepreneurship, for commerce and industry. They introduce "best practices" in the economic sphere that then can be replicated in other spheres of life. They improve the policy environment for political change by introducing habits of cooperation and participation, as well as standards of transparency, accountability, probity, and responsiveness. It is true that market practices may put people in the mood to be more democratic. And it is true that free people tend to thrive in circumstances of open markets. But this does not necessarily imply that, for societies struggling to break free of despotism, the surest path to political freedom is through creating markets. Reformers cannot assume that economic reform by itself will lead to desired political changes. Not all best practices are always the most suitable or effective. As a recent World Bank report argues, the idea of "best practices" may be a flawed concept for many developing countries (World Development Report, 2002: 4–5). Many institutions and policy reforms that led to desired outcomes in developed, industrial countries cannot be assumed to produce analogous results in countries undergoing transformation from within. The evidence is clear that markets do not breed democracy by magic. Promoting the conditions of economic change is not the same as promoting political change itself. While improvement in the conditions for political change may be a necessary requirement of political change, it is not a sufficient condition.

Third, the analysis of the experience of the Central Asian states leads to the conclusion that, while political reform alone has not been productive and that, while economic reform can create the conditions for political liberalization it does not necessarily do so in all cases, there are nevertheless grounds for concluding that some forms of economic reform can produce desired political change. The key to the impact of market reforms on political reforms is that market reform programs change the circulation of financial flows within the society, generating winners and losers. Structural reforms introduce changes that benefit some sectors and disadvantage others. Market reforms that underwrite monopolies, cloistered and controlled sectors of the economy, sympathetic and special relationships between government officials, and narrow business sectors, are sure to defeat the purposes of broad public inclusion in the political process. The reciprocal linkages between markets and politics are such that the more efficient and "flat" the markets, the more inclusive the economic playing field, the more invested the numbers of people, and the more likely that people will petition, lobby, vote, and insist upon democratic rights and freedoms. Economic reform is most durable when it leads to changes in the size and influence of political constituencies that capture the benefits of reform. This explains why some economic reform has further empowered the powerful, bypassed the disenfranchised, and had even negative effects on fundamental freedoms (Luong and Weinthal, 2002).

The critical issue is how economic and political reforms are linked in terms of policy cycles. Development strategies emphasizing a dominant economic sector under close government control run the risk of the political analog to what economists refer to as the "Dutch disease." Even if highly promising future oil, gas, mineral, cotton, or hydroelectric, revenues can be expected to financially support the government in the absence of broadly based and relatively unpopular forms of taxation, the political consequences of government control of the easily monopolized dominant sector are likely to defeat political liberalization. Government control of these dominant sectors can be expected to lead to policies that conceal incomes, compromise fiscal transparency, and benefit insiders rather than the public interest.

The future may be different than the past. But to the extent that the record of the first decade of post-communist transition offers lessons for future practice, a few general conclusions may be drawn. The experience of the Central Asian countries during the first decade of independence illustrates that neither economic reforms nor political reforms are apt to produce enduring change in the absence of the other. The benefits of economic reform in the absence of political reform are likely to be captured by groups who have no interest in furthering political liberalization. Attempts at political reform in the absence of economic reform offer little prospect of sustaining true liberalization. Reforms that reinforce open competition, diminish the influence of the state in natural monopolies of all kinds, promote transparent transactions between actors and the state and among non-state actors, and generally broaden political constituencies for reform are most likely to lead to virtuous cycles of policy reform. Central Asian governments that are serious in their efforts to spur mutually reinforcing and enduring economic and political liberalization would be wise to adopt reform policies that emphasize service, trade, small enterprises, and public benefits. Governments adopting these priorities will find the wait for democracy in Central Asia much shorter and far more tolerable.

Notes

1 Economic and political reform

1 The rationale for a detailed case study approach to the analysis of the relationship between markets and politics is that the margins of error associated with cross-national composite estimates of such difficult to measure phenomena as political inclusion, participation, transparency and so on, are typically so large as to induce caution with respect to the conclusions that can be drawn. At least until our ability to measure these phenomena has substantially improved, systematic investigation of case studies will continue to be necessary.

2 Nursultan Nazarbaev, President of Kazakhstan, is the former first secretary of the Kazakhstan republic communist party organization. Islam Karimov, president of Uzbekistan, is the former first secretary of the Uzbekistan republic communist party organization. Saparmurad Niyazov, President of Turkmenistan, is the former first secretary of the Turkmenistan republic communist party organization. Emomali Rahmonov, President of Tajikistan, is a former Kuliab region communist party official. His predecessor as president, Rakhmon Nabiev who died under mysterious circumstances in May 1993, was the former first secretary of the Tajikistan republic communist party organization. Among the Central Asian presidents, only the president of Kyrgyzstan, Askar Akaev, does not belong to the former party *nomenklatura* although in some respects even Akaev, a physicist who was trained in Leningrad and who worked as the head of the communist party organizational department in Kyrgyzstan, can also be considered to be a member of the former party elite.

3 Lindblom specifies the core rules as guaranteeing: freedom to form and join organizations; freedom of expression; right to vote; eligibility for public office; right of political leaders to compete for support; right of political leaders to compete for votes; alternative sources of information; free and fair elections (open, honestly conducted, one man-one vote), which decide who is to hold top authority; and institutions for making government policies depend on votes and other expressions of preference. Charles E. Lindblom, *Politics and Markets: The World's Political-Economic Systems*. New York: Basic Books, 1977, p. 133.

4 Political theory refers to various kinds of social compacts. Sometimes these compacts are explicit, as in the case of constitutions and other forms of written agreements. Sometimes they are simply understood. What I have called "Lindblom compact" is a barter arrangement between business interests and government, exchanging support for support. Neither party precisely knows the exact terms of the bargain. It is a risk venture. Business interests have no explicit guarantee that if they continue to favor free elections, the electorate will return to power political leaders sympathetic to their interests. Political leaders have no guarantee that inclusive political policies, civil and human rights, and other democratic processes will continue to advantage business interests. Both sides are taking a gamble and are engaged in an open-ended bargain.

5 Civil society is rooted in reliance upon individual initiative and assumes a limited role of the state in the private affairs of its citizens. The key institutional or "structural"

elements of the civil society include: (1) the rule of law supported by an independent judiciary; (2) a respect for democratic proceduralism as reflected in competitive elections with secret ballots; (3) recognition of the inviolable rights of individuals and groups, in addition to rights of collectivities; (4) representative government with public accountability provided for by an independent press and media; (5) a market-based economy with limits on the scope and powers of government intervention; (6) and a separation of Church and State (secular and theocratic values). Civil development refers to the development of civil society based on limited government, the rule of law, and the protection of the civil rights of private parties. Civil development requires a government that is committed to protecting the civil rights of its citizens and protecting private property as an institution.

6 Daniel Kaufman, Aart Kraay, and Pablo Zoido-Lobaton, "Governance Matters II: Updated Indicators for 2000/01." Policy Research Working Paper No. 2772. The World Bank, Development Research Group and World Bank Institute, Governance, Regulation, and Finance Division (February 2002).

2 Post-communist structural reform

1 All of the Soviet republics except the large Russian republic had separate party organizations.

2 Tajikistan initially was constrained by civil insurrection and by the country's unique geography. In 1990, Tajikistan was an underdeveloped Soviet republic, but would have been classified as a lower middle-income country. By 1994, the Tajikistan government was heavily dependent upon international donor organizations and the Russian Federation. By 1998, Tajikistan had become one of the world's poorest countries. Its foreign policy choices were constrained accordingly.

3 The prevailing trend in studies of structural reform is to assess the top-down impact of reform packages imposed from outside. While this indeed may be the salient aspect of reform, the focus of this book is on the impact of the reform provisions that the state itself adopts; that is, the local effects of the reform provisions.

4 Collectively the international financial institutions constitute the most important pillars of the international donor community. The international financial institutions have differing mandates and strategic approaches. For instance, the International Monetary Fund's (IMF) mandate is to coordinate monetary policy among states. The IMF achieves this goal through conducting monitoring (or what it calls "surveillance") of monetary affairs in its member countries, providing technical assistance, and offering loans to redress short-term disequilibria in its member countries' balance of payments. The member countries own the IMF. A board composed of twenty-four representatives from the member nations manages the IMF. In contrast, the World Bank's mandate is to promote development through poverty reduction. The World Bank achieves this through grants, loans, and technical assistance. The member countries own the World Bank.

In both these cases and in the cases of the other major donor organizations, the political legitimacy of the organization derives from the legitimacy of the member states. Therefore, when viewed in terms of principal–agent relationships of contract law, the member states are the principal and the international financial institution is the agent charged with carrying out tasks. Accordingly, the IFIs are not charged with giving instructions, but with carrying them out. The host state is the client. Host country client states are quite sensitive to issues of subordination and political authority involved in the lending and technical assistance activities that IFIs carry out on their territory.

5 There is no single template for reform activities. The international donor community is large and varied in its values, approaches, methods, and constituencies. Accordingly, the international donors often speak with many voices. But there are

some common elements. In much of their recent analysis, World Bank researchers have emphasized five key strategic objectives that are critical to reform. These are:

- Establishing a foundation of law
- Maintaining a non-distortionary policy environment
- Investing in basic social services and infrastructure
- Protecting the vulnerable
- Protecting the environment.

While not all countries put equal weight on all of these elements of a reform program, all countries pursue strategic objectives that can be viewed in terms of this framework (*World Development Report 1997*, hereinafter *WDR*, 1997: 4).

6 A newly emerging country does not necessarily need to adopt its own new currency; a country may do very well by simply relying on a foreign currency that is stable. The key is not a national currency as such, but stability in currency transactions.

7 In societies where states are highly competent but corruption, bribery, or abuse of public office are commonplace, the reduction in the arena of control of the state may be justified. In many emerging societies, however, disestablishing the state may lead directly to detrimental effects on the least powerful and advantaged sectors of the society. Those closest to the state are apt to be able to circumvent the effects of reduced size and influence, transferring the costs of downsizing or functional redesign to those less politically influential. In many cases, reducing the capacity of the state may only result in the incapacity of the state to carry out core functions. Thus, in many cases, reduction in the size of the public sector cannot by itself be considered an appropriate formula for establishing a more efficient, more equitable state.

8 Freedom House is an international philanthropic research organization established in 1937. The Freedom House Annual Surveys measure progress toward democratic ideals on a seven-point scale for political rights and for civil liberties (with one representing the most free and seven the least free). Changes in countries' scores from year to year are monitored via annual surveys. The political rights measurement addresses the degree of free and fair elections, competitive political parties, opposition with an important role and power, freedom from domination by a powerful group (e.g. military, foreign power, totalitarian parties), and participation by minority groups. The civil liberties measurement addresses the degree to which there is a free and independent media; freedom of discussion, assembly and demonstration; freedom of political organization; equality under the law; protection from political terror, unjustified imprisonment and torture; free trade unions, professional and private organizations; freedom of religion; personal social freedoms; equality of opportunity; and freedom from extreme government corruption.

9 The US Department of State is instructed by Congress annually to prepare a report on the observance of international standards of Human Rights in all the major countries of the world. See the US Department of State's *Report on Human Rights Practices for 2000* (released by the Bureau of Democracy, Human Rights, and Labor, February 2001).

3 Kazakhstan and globalization

1 Population Reference Bureau 2001 World Population Data Sheet. Available on-line at <http://www.prb.org>.

2 The Kazakhstan government's structural reform program consists of internal initiatives and external program support. The two largest donors are the IMF and the World Bank. The scope and scale of their program support provides insight into the government's program. The Kazakhstan's IMF sponsored program began in July 1996 with a three-year $446 million credit under the IMF Extended Fund Facility (EFF) to

support the Government's medium-term economic reform program for 1996–98. The IMF support followed the acceptance by the Kazakhstan government of the IMF Article VIII conditions that provide for responsible currency transactions. In December 1999 the IMF extended a second three-year $453 million credit for Kazakhstan to support the government's economic program for 2000–02. This EFF was suspended in early 2002 when a scheduled review of program indicators was not completed. Analysts seeking a comprehensive statement of the Kazakhstan structural reform program should consult the November 22, 1999 "Memorandum on Economic Policies of the Government of Kazakhstan and The National Bank of Kazakhstan Through December 31, 2002" submitted to the IMF.

Kazakhstan became a member of the World Bank in July 1992. A country assistance plan was approved in 1993 and operations started in 1994. The Bank's lending program was designed to support the government's efforts to build a market economy through balance of payments support for macroeconomic stabilization; structural reforms through enterprise restructuring, financial sector reforms, and privatization; protection of vulnerable groups through an effective social safety net; and sectoral reforms through operations in energy, agriculture, infrastructure, environment, institution building, and reinforcement of the government's implementation capacity. In the first decade of operations, the World Bank approved $1.8 billion covering twenty-two projects in Kazakhstan, including five adjustment operations, two technical assistance loans, and fifteen investment loans.

3 The names of many cities in Kazakhstan were changed after the country became independent in December 1991. Almaty was known as Alma-Ata until 1992 when the city changed its name to reflect the native Kazak language spelling. Almaty had been the capital of Kazakhstan since the Soviet Republic's formal establishment in 1936. A Presidential decree of September 15, 1995 announced that the capital would be moved from Almaty to the city of Akmola. Akmola, known as Tselinograd until 1992, officially became the capital of Kazakhstan on December 10, 1997. Akmola was renamed Astana in May 1998. Astana is located 1300 km north of Almaty, approximately in the center of the country.

4 Kazakhstan's 6800-kilometer border with Russia is the longest continuous bi-national border in the world (excluding the US–Canadian border which is discontinuous). Kazakhstan's 5000 kilometers of borders with China, Kyrgyzstan, Turkmenistan, and Uzbekistan span desolate and hard to reach regions. The customs and border control issues facing Kazakhstan are unparalleled by those of any other country.

5 See Nazarbaev's speech to the Kazakh SSR Supreme Soviet, December 10, 1997, "Nash Vybor – Tsivilizovannoe Demokraticheskoe Obshchestvo." [Our Choice – A Civilized Democratic Society] *Pyat' let Nezavisimosti* [Five Years of Independence] (Almaty: Kazakhstan, 1996), pp. 19–24.

6 The Kazakhstan parliament voted on October 7, 1998 in favor of legislation changing the terms of deputies in the Majlis from four to five years and in the Senate from five to six years. The parliament also voted to increase the president's term in office from five to seven years and set presidential elections for January 1999, a year ahead of schedule. The parliament voted to lift the restriction that held that the president may not be over sixty-five and may not serve more than two terms in office.

7 In 1997 an American businessman with close ties to the Kazakhstan government was implicated in facilitating questionable trade practices in the oil sector. The questionable practices involved oil swaps between Kazakhstan producers and refineries in Iran. By late 2001 the political scandal over the oil swaps reached the highest levels of Kazakhstan government.

The oil industry frequently uses oil swaps as a way to reduce the cost of transporting crude oil to refineries. A swap usually involves the exchange of title to oil in one location in favor of an equivalent value of oil in another location. The arrangement also provides a way to get oil from remote oil fields and isolated nations, such as

Kazakhstan, to market. International oil companies used swaps frequently in the Middle East and in the Caspian oil region. However, the US, Iran–Libya Sanctions Act of 1996 imposed sanctions on companies that engage in specified economic transactions with Iran or Libya. The law was intended to deny Iran and Libya revenues that could be used to finance international terrorism; to limit the flow of resources necessary to obtain weapons of mass destruction; and, to put pressure on Libya to comply with the UN resolutions that, among other things, call for Libya to extradite for trial the accused perpetrators of the Pan Am 103 bombing. The law sanctions foreign companies that provide new investments over $40 million for the development of petroleum resources in Iran or Libya. The law sanctions foreign companies that violate existing UN prohibitions against trade with Libya in certain goods and services such as arms, certain oil equipment, and civil aviation services. If a violation occurs, the US President may impose two out of seven possible sanctions against the violating company. These sanctions include: denial of Export–Import Bank assistance; denial of export licenses for exports to the violating company; prohibition on loans or credits from US financial institutions of over $10 million in any twelve-month period; prohibition on designation as a primary dealer for US government debt instruments; prohibition on serving as an agent of the United States or as a repository for US government funds; denial of US government procurement opportunities (consistent with WTO obligations); and a ban on all or some imports of the violating company. The Iran–Libya Sanctions Act was renewed in 2001. In 1999 Swiss banking officials discovered that some $85 million destined for a Kazakhstan government account had been linked to the American businessman implicated in the questionable oil swaps. Swiss authorities passed the evidence to the US Department of Justice. A US investigation was begun.

In 2000 the Kazakh parliament passed a law granting Kazakhstan president Nursultan Nazarbaev lifetime immunity from prosecution stemming from all his actions in office, with the exception of high treason. Later the Kazakhstan parliament, with Nazarbaev encouragement, adopted amnesty legislation giving Kazakhstan citizens the right to bring money into the country for a specified period of time with no questions asked – and no tax assessed. Leaders of Kazakhstan's political opposition claimed that the legislation amounted to little more than legalized money laundering.

8 In the territorial consolidation, part of the Torgai Region was transferred to the Akmola Region and part was transferred to the Kostanai Region. The Taldykorgan Region was consolidated into the Almaty region, the Semipalatinsk Region was consolidated into the East-Kazakhstan Region, the Zhezkazgan region was consolidated into the Karaganda Region, and the Kokchetau Region was consolidated into the North-Kazakhstan Region.

9 Kazakhstan's two standard statistical reference handbooks discontinued reporting ethnicity figures. See RSEK, *Regional'nyi Statisticheskii Ezhegonik Kazakhstana* (Almaty: Committee on Statistics and Analysis, Agency for Strategic Reform, 1997) and SEK, *Statistickheskii Ezhegodnik Kazakhstana* (Almaty: National Statistical Agency of the Ministry of Economics and Trade, 1997).

4 Kyrgyzstan and the reform path

1 Population Reference Bureau 2001 World Population Data Sheet. Available on-line at <http://www.prb.org>.

2 In July 1994 the IMF sponsored a $105 million enhanced structural adjustment facility (ESAF) for Kyrgyzstan for the period 1994–96. This was later increased to $131 million and later the term was extended until 1998. A new three-year ESAF for $86 million was issued to support the government's economic program for 1998–2000.

In March 1999 Kyrgyzstan received a $12 million supplement to this ESAF. In February 2000, a Poverty Reduction and Growth Facility (PRGF) of $29 million was issued for 2000. In November 2001 a new three-year PRGF of $93 million was approved to support the government's 2001–04 economic program. The Kyrgyz government accepted IMF Article VIII obligations in March 1995. Analysts seeking a comprehensive statement of the Kyrgyzstan structural reform program should consult the January 22, 2000 "Memorandum of Economic and Financial Policies of the Government and the National Bank of the Kyrgyz Republic for 2000" submitted to the IMF.

Kyrgyzstan became a member of the World Bank in September 1992. Following the approval of a country assistance plan in 1993, the World Bank undertook projects to facilitate restoration of economic growth, particularly in rural areas; foster an appropriate legal and regulatory environment to support the private sector; assist the government in reducing poverty and protecting vulnerable segments of society during the transition; and promote good governance and strengthen institutional capacity. The World Bank also supported regional environmental initiatives such as the Central Asia Transboundary Biodiversity Project. A Governance Structural Adjustment Credit and a Governance Technical Assistance Credit focus on improving efficiency and transparency in government by implementing civil service and administrative reform, and improved public expenditure management. In the first decade of operations, the World Bank has approved commitments of about $607 million for 27 projects.

3 "Kyrgyz Republic – Recent Economic Developments," International Monetary Fund (IMF) Staff Country Report No. 99/31 (May 5, 1999).

4 See "Kyrgyz Republic: Report on the Observance of Standards and Codes. Fiscal Transparency Module." International Monetary Fund Report No. 02/54 (March 2001).

5 See "Kyrgyz Republic: Selected Issues and Statistical Appendix." International Monetary Fund Staff Country Report No. 00/131 (October 2000), p. 74.

6 "Final Report: Kyrgyz Republic Parliamentary Elections, 20 February and 12 March 2000." Organization for Security and Cooperation in Europe, Office for Democratic Institutions and Human Rights, Warsaw, Poland (April 10, 2000).

7 "Final Report: The Kyrgyz Republic Presidential Elections, 29 October 2000." Organization for Security and Cooperation in Europe, Office for Democratic Institutions and Human Rights, Warsaw, Poland (January 16, 2001).

8 "Kyrgyz Republic: Selected Issues and Statistical Appendix." International Monetary Fund. IMF Staff Country Report 00/131 (October 2000), p. 57.

9 *Op. cit.*, p. 113.

5 Civil war and reconstruction in Tajikistan

1 International Monetary Fund. "Republic of Tajikistan: Recent Economic Developments," International Monetary Fund Staff Country Report No. 00/27 (March 2000).

2 Population Reference Bureau 2001 World Population Data Sheet. Available on-line at <http://www.prb.org>.

3 In May 1996 the IMF sponsored a $22 million stand-by credit for Tajikistan for 1996. A $10 million emergency post conflict assistance credit was sponsored in December 1997 followed by a second $10 million credit in April 1998. In June 1998 a $128 million Enhanced Structural Adjustment Facility (ESAF) was sponsored for the period 1998–2001. In February 2002 the IMF assessed that it had been provided with inaccurate information regarding Tajikistan government debts and concluded, as a result, that two previous IMF disbursements were not in compliance. Tajikistan was called upon to repay two disbursement totaling $31 million before March 2003. Analysts seeking a comprehensive statement of the Tajikistan structural reform

program should consult the June 17, 1999 "Memorandum of Economic Policies for 1999–2000" and the "Memorandum of Economic and Financial Policies for the Period January 1 to June 30, 2002" submitted to the IMF.

Tajikistan joined the World Bank in June 1993. World Bank programs have supported economic transformation efforts, poverty reduction, and post-conflict assistance. This has been achieved through a combination of policy advice, increased field presence, institutional capacity building, and supporting post-conflict activities through rehabilitation and reconstruction operations. During the first decade of Tajikistan independence, the World Bank has approved assistance totaling $261 million for fourteen operations.

4 The fact that OSCE abjured from monitoring the 1994 presidential elections in noted in "Final Report: The Republic of Tajikistan Elections to the Parliament, 27 February 2000." Organization for Security and Cooperation in Europe, Office for Democratic Institutions and Human Rights, Warsaw, Poland (May 17, 2000), p. 3.

5 This description of the government's structural reform agenda is based upon the government's agreements with the international financial community regarding structural change. These agreements are described in memoranda and government policy planning papers. See particularly: Supplementary Memorandum of Economic Policies, Supplement to the Letter of Intent of the government of Tajikistan to the IMF, June 17, 1999; Enhanced Structural Adjustment Facility Policy Framework Paper (1999–2002) prepared by the Tajikistan Authorities in Collaboration with the Staffs of the International Monetary Fund and the World Bank (June 18, 1999); Supplementary Memorandum of Economic Policies, Supplement to the Letter of Intent of the government of Tajikistan to the IMF, December 30, 1999; and Supplementary Memorandum of Economic Policies, Supplement to the Letter of Intent of the government of Tajikistan to the IMF, October 11, 2000; and Memorandum of Economic and Financial Policies for the Period January 1 to June 30, 2002 under the Staff Monitored Program, Supplement to the Letter of Intent of the government of Tajikistan to the IMF, March 28, 2002.

6 Tax offsets occur when enterprises that supply the government with goods and services are not paid in cash but in compensating reductions of tax payments. Non-monetized transactions are more likely to lack transparency that cash transactions.

7 The Head of the Tajikistan Central Electoral Commission, Mirzoali Boltuyev, announced on September 27, 1999 that 68 percent of voters favored the constitutional amendments and that over 90 percent of the eligible electorate of 2.9 million took part in the referendum. Voters were called upon to approve or reject a package of three constitutional amendments. The first amendment established a bicameral legislature. The second amendment extended the presidential term from five to seven years. The third amendment legalized political parties having a religious orientation.

8 Emomali Sharipovich Rahmonov was born in the city of Dangara, Tajikistan on October 5, 1952. Rahmonov served in the Soviet navy during the period 1971–74. In Tajikistan Rahmonov worked as electrician, commercial representative, and administrator of trade union and communist party committees. During the period 1988–92 he was Director of a Sovkhoz in Dangar region. In 1992, he became Chairman of the Kulyob Regional Executive Committee. Emomali Rahmonov's service as a national political leader began when he was elected chairman of the parliament on November 16, 1992 at an election held in the northern Tajikistan city of Hujand.

9 The previous parliament, the *Majlisi Oli*, consisted of 181 parliamentarians elected by popular vote to serve five-year terms. Parliamentary elections were last held on February 26, 1995 and March 12, 1995. See "Final Report: The Republic of Tajikistan Elections to the Parliament, 27 February 2000." Organization for Security and Cooperation in Europe, Office for Democratic Institutions and Human Rights, Warsaw, Poland (May 17, 2000).

10 UNODCCP, "Afghanistan Opium Cultivation in 2000 Substantially Unchanged: Country Still the Largest Opium Producer in the World." UNIS/NAR/696 (September 15, 2000). United Nations Office of Drug Control and Crime Prevention.
11 Languages spoken in Tajikistan (1995 estimates) include Armenian 6000; Balochi 4842; Bashkir 5412; Kazakh 9606; Kirghiz 64,000; Korean 13,000; Osetin 8000; Russian 237,000; Shughni 35,000; Tajiki 3,344,720; Tatar 80,000; Turkmen 13,991; Ukrainian 41,000; Uyghur 3581; Uzbek 873,000; Wakhi, 7000; and Yazgulyam, 4000. Barbara F. Grimes (ed.), *Ethnologue: Languages of the World*. 13th edn. (Dallas, TX: Summer Institute of Languages, 1999) <http://www.sil.org/ethnologue/>.
12 The National Unity Party had previously been headed by former Tajik Prime Minister Abdumalik Abdullojonov. At the time Abdullojonov was wanted by Tajik law enforcement agencies for his contribution to the November 1998 coup attempt in northern Tajikistan.
13 UN Secretary General, Interim Report of the Secretary-General on the situation in Tajikistan (S/2000/214).
14 *Asia Plus-Blitz*, December 14, 2000.
15 Bruce Pannier, "Central Asia: Kyrgyz, Tajiks Complain About Uzbek Landmines," *RFE/RL Weekday Magazine* (November 29, 2000).

6 Petro-dollars and "Positive Neutrality" in Turkmenistan

1 Population Reference Bureau 2001 World Population Data Sheet. Available online at <http://www.prb.org>.
2 Turkmenistan's cooperation with the International Monetary Fund has been minimal. By the end of the first decade of independence, the IMF had extended no credits to Turkmenistan. Turkmenistan joined the World Bank in 1992. The World Bank program sought to implement structural reform through technical assistance and institution building, particularly in debt management, energy exports, public expenditures, health and agriculture sectors, international accounting standards implementation, taxation, and the preparation of an environmental action program. World Bank sponsored programs in Turkmenistan in the first decade of independence total less than $100 million.
3 "Turkmenistan: Recent Economic Developments," International Monetary Fund Staff Country Report No. 99/140 (December 10, 1999).
4 V. Kuleshov, "Turkmenistan gotov prodat' svoi gaz Ukraine po tsenam, priblizhennym k mirovym," *Izvestiia* (March 6, 1992): 1.
5 *Turkmenskaia Iskra* (May 19, 1992): 2.
6 Portnikov, *op. cit.*
7 "EBRD Cuts Turkmen Loans, Slams Political System," Reuters, April 18, 2000.
8 Statement of Christopher H. Smith, Chairman, Commission on Security and Cooperation in Europe, Hearing on Democratization and Human Rights in Turkmenistan, March 21, 2000, Washington, DC.

7 Economic self-reliance and the "Uzbek Path"

1 Population Reference Bureau 2001 World Population Data Sheet. Available on-line at <http://www.prb.org>.
2 The IMF sponsored a $74 million systemic transformation facility (STF) to support the macroeconomic stabilization and systemic reform in Uzbekistan for 1995 and 1996. In December 1995 the IMF extended this to a $259 million package of programs to support economic reform. In late 1996, as a result of a dispute over compliance with Article VIII of the IMF Articles of Agreement, the IMF's direct financial support for

economic reform programs in Uzbekistan came to a standstill. When the IMF field representative in Uzbekistan was due to return to headquarters after completing the standard field assignment, the IMF announced that it would not replace him. Negotiations regarding renewed IMF activity continued throughout 2001 until the terrorist attack on September 11 stimulated a much higher level of participation by Uzbekistan in the international community. On January 31, 2002, the Uzbekistan government submitted a letter of intent to the IMF announcing that Uzbekistan intended to comply as of July 2002 with Article VIII of the IMF Articles of Agreement by discontinuing policies that allowed for multiple exchange rates. See the Uzbekistan government's "Memorandum of Economic and Financial Policies for the period January 1–June 30, 2002" submitted to the IMF.

Uzbekistan joined the World Bank in September 1992. The World Bank's program in Uzbekistan have focused on: improving the policy framework for foreign exchange and trade liberalization; strengthening the environment for private sector development; increasing the efficiency of resource allocation and use especially in social infrastructure; and reinforcing the effectiveness of the country's irrigation and drainage infrastructure. Between the start of World Bank programs in 1994 and mid-2002, bank support amounted to $534 million.

3 "IMF Pressures Uzbekistan To Make Currency Convertible." REF/RL Newsline June 29, 2000.
4 "Uzbekistan Promises Currency Will Become Fully Convertible." RFE/RL Newsline December 2, 2000.
5 "Republic of Uzbekistan: Recent Economic Developments." IMF Staff Country Report No. 98/116 (October 1998), 104.
6 *Pravda Vostoka* (October 3, 2000), 1.
7 "Stock Exchanges in Uzbekistan are Thriving." *The Times of Central Asia*, Vol. 2, No. 31 (August 3, 2000), 3.
8 *The Times of Central Asia*, Vol. 2, No. 32 (August 10, 2000), 1.
9 Muhammad Salih is the pen-name of Salai Madaminov.
10 Saidjahon Zainabutdinov, "Uzbek Women Plead for Religious Prisoners." Institute of War and Peace Reporting (RCA No. 64, August 10, 2001).
11 Galima Bukharbaeva, "Uzbek President Frees Jailed Activist." Institute for War and Peace Reporting (RCA No. 35, January 9, 2001).
12 Uzbekistan: Country Reports on Human Rights Practices – 2000 Bureau of Democracy, Human Rights, and Labor (February 2001) <http://www.state.gov/g/drl/rls/hrrpt/2000/eur/index.cfm?docid=858>.
13 Congressional Resolution 397, US House of Representatives, 106 Congress, November 1, 2000. Also see "Uzbekistan: US Expresses Deep Concern On Death of Human Rights Activist." Statement by Richard Boucher, July 12, 2001. US Department of State, 2001.

Bibliography

Akbarzadeh, Shahram. 1996. "Why Did Nationalism Fail in Tajikistan?" *Europe-Asia Studies* 48, 7: 1105–29.

Akchurin, Marat. 1992. *Red Odyssey: A Journey Through the Soviet Republics*. New York: Harper Collins.

Akiner, Shirin. 1986. *Islamic Peoples of the Soviet Union: An Historical and Statistical Handbook*. New York: Kegan Paul International.

Akiner, Shirin, ed. 1992. *Economic and Political Trends in Central Asia*. New York: Routledge & Kegan Paul.

Alchian, A. and H. Demsetz. 1973. "The Property Right Paradigm." *Journal of Economic History* 33, 1: 16–27.

Alesina, Alberto. 1997. *Political Cycles and the Macroeconomy*. Cambridge: MIT Press.

Allworth, Edward. 1967. *Central Asia: A Century of Russian Rule*. New York: Columbia University Press.

Allworth, Edward, ed. 1973. *The Nationality Question in Soviet Central Asia*. New York: Praeger.

Almond, Gabriel A., and G. Bingham Powell. 1966. *Comparative Politics: A Developmental Approach*. Boston: Little Brown.

Anderson, John. 1999. *Kyrgyzstan: Central Asia's Island of Democracy?* London: Harwood Academic Publishers.

Anderson, Lisa. 1999. *Transitions to Democracy*. New York: Columbia University Press.

Anderson, Richard D., M. Steven Fish, Stephen E. Hanson, and George W. Breslauer. 2001. *Postcommunism and the Theory of Democracy*. Princeton: Princeton University Press.

Anspanger, Franz. 1989. *The Dissolution of the Colonial Empires*. London: Routledge.

Åslund, Anders. 1995. *How Russia Became a Market Economy*. Washington: Brookings Institution.

Åslund, Anders. 2001. *Building Capitalism: The Transformation of the Former Soviet Bloc*. Cambridge: Cambridge University Press.

Atkin, Muriel. 1989. *The Subtlest Battle: Islam in Soviet Tajikistan*. Philadelphia: Foreign Policy Research Institute.

Bacon, Elizabeth. 1980. *Central Asians under Russian Rule: A Study in Culture Change*. Ithaca: Cornell University Press.

Bahry, Donna. 1987. *Outside Moscow: Power, Politics, and Budgetary Policy in the Soviet Republics*. New York: Columbia University Press.

Balcerowicz, Leszek. 1995. *Socialism, Capitalism, Transformation*. Budapest: Central European University.

Banuazizi, Ali and Myron Weiner, eds. 1994. *The New Geopolitics of Central Asia and Its Borderlands*. Bloomington: Indiana University Press.

Bates, Robert H. 1981. *Markets and States in Tropical Africa: The Political Basis of Agricultural Policies*. Berkeley: University of California Press.

Becker, Seymour. 1968. *Russia's Protectorates in Central Asia: Bukhara and Khiva, 1865–1924*. Cambridge: Harvard University Press.

Beissinger, Marc. 2002. *Nationalist Mobilization and the Collapse of the Soviet State: A Tidal Approach to the Study of Nationalism*. Cambridge: Cambridge University Press.

Bennigsen, Alexandre and S. Enders Wimbush. 1986. *Muslims of the Soviet Empire*. Bloomington: Indiana University Press.

Bhagwati, Jagdish. 2002. *Free Trade Today*. Princeton: Princeton University Press.

Blanchard, Olivier. 1997. *The Economics of Post-Communist Transition*. Oxford: Clarendon Press.

Bova, Russel. 1991. "The Political Dynamics of the Post-Communist Transition: A Comparative Perspective." *World Politics* 44, 1: 114–21.

Boycko, Maxim, Andrei Shleifer, and Robert W. Vishny. 1995. *Privatizing Russia*. Cambridge: MIT Press.

Brada, Josef C., Michael P. and Claudon, eds. 1991. *The Emerging Russian Bear: Integrating the Soviet Union into the World Economy*. New York: New York University Press.

Brada, Josef. 1996. "Privatization is Transition. Or is It?" *Journal of Economic Perspectives* 10, 2: 67–88.

Brada, Josef C., Ed. A. Hewett, and Thomas A. Wolf, eds. 1989. *Economic Adjustment and Reform in Eastern Europe and the Soviet Union*. Durham: Duke Press University Press.

Brady, Rose. 1999. *Kapitalizm: Russia's Struggle to Free Its Economy*. New Haven: Yale University Press.

Braguinsky, Serguey and Grigory Yavlinsky. 2000. *Incentives and Institutions*. Princeton: Princeton University Press.

Bransten, Jeremy. 1997. "Kyrgyzstan: A Democracy Only For The Rich," RFE/RL Newsday (14 October).

Breslauer, George, Josef Brada, Clifford Gaddy, Richard Ericson, and Carol Saivetz. 2001. "Russia at the End of Yel'tsin's Presidency." *Post-Soviet Affairs* 16, 1: 1–33.

Bromley, Daniel W. 1992. *Making the Commons Work: Theory, Practice, and Policy*. San Francisco: Institute for Contemporary Studies.

Bunce, Valerie. 1995. "Should Transitologists be Grounded?" *Slavic Review* 54, 1: 111–27.

Bunce, Valerie. 1999a. "The Political Economy of Postsocialism," *Slavic Review* 58, 4: 756–93.

Bunce, Valerie. 1999b. *Subversive Institutions: The Design and Destruction of Socialism and the State*. Cambridge: Cambridge University Press.

Burnell, Peter, ed. 2000. *Democracy Assistance: International Co-Operation for Democratization*. London: Frank Cass & Co.

Burnell, Peter and Alan Ware, eds. 1998. *Funding Democratization*. Manchester: Manchester University Press.

Butler, William Elliott. 1999. *Tadzhikistan Legal Texts: The Foundations of Civic Accord and a Market Economy*. London: Simmonds & Hill.

C (pseudonym). 1993. "One Man Rule in Uzbekistan: A Perspective from Within the Regime." *Demokratizatsiya* 1, 4: 44–55.

Carothers, Thomas. 1999. *Aiding Democracy Abroad: The Learning Curve*. Washington: Carnegie Endowment for International Peace.

Carrère D'Encausse, Hélène. 1989. *Islam and the Russian Empire: Reform and Revolution in Central Asia*. Berkeley: University of California Press.

Chao, Sui-Sheng, ed. 2000. *China and Democracy: The Prospects for a Democratic China*. London: Routledge.

Coase, R.H. 1937. "The Nature of the Firm." *Economica* 4: 386–405.

Coase, R.H. 1960. "The Problem of Social Cost." *Journal of Law and Economics* 3, 1: 1–44.

Colomer, Josep Maria. 2000. *Strategic Transitions: Game Theory and Democratization*. Baltimore: Johns Hopkins University Press.

Colton, Timothy J. 2000. *Transitional Citizens: Voters and What Influences Them in the New Russia*. Cambridge: Harvard University Press.

Commission on Security and Cooperation in Europe (CSCE). 2000. Human Rights and Democratization in Uzbekistan and Turkmenistan. Washington: US Government Printing Office.

Compton, Robert W. Jr. 2000. *East Asian Democratization: Impact of Globalization, Culture, and Economy*. New York: Praeger Publishers.

Craumer, Peter R. 1994. "Agricultural Change, Labor Supply, and Rural Out-Migration in Soviet Central Asia." pp. 132–80 in Robert A. Lewis, ed., *Geographic Perspectives on Soviet Central Asia*. London: Routledge.

Crawford, Beverly, ed. 1995. *Markets, States, and Democracy: The Political Economy of Post-Communist Transformation*. Boulder: Westview Press.

Critchlow, James. 1991. *Nationalism in Uzbekistan: A Soviet Republic's Road to Sovereignty*. Boulder: Westview.

Culpeper, Roy. 1997. *The Multilateral Development Banks: Titans or Behemoths?* Boulder: Lynne Rienner.

Cummings, Sally N. 2000. *Kazakhstan: Centre-Periphery Relations*. London: The Royal Institute of International Affairs.

Dahl, Robert. 1989. *Democracy and Its Critics*. New Haven: Yale University Press.

Dawisha, Karen and Bruce Parrott, eds. 1997a. *Conflict, Cleavage, and Change in Central Asia and the Caucasus*. Cambridge: Cambridge University Press.

Dawisha, Karen and Bruce Parrott. 1997b. *Democratic Changes and Authoritarian Reactions in Russia, Ukraine, Belarus and Moldova*. Cambridge: Cambridge University Press.

Degtiar, Mikhail. 2000. "Clans, Cotton and Currency." *The Central Asian Times*, 2: 41: 2.

Demsetz, Harold. 1967. "Toward a Theory of Property Rights." *American Economic Review* 57, 2: 347–59.

Diamond, Larry and Marc F. Plattner, eds. 1995. *Economic Reform and Democracy*. Baltimore: Johns Hopkins University Press.

Dispatch. 1992. Public Information Service, US Department of State. 3, 4: 57–60, p. 57.

Djalili, Mohammed-Reza, Frederic Grare, and Shirin Atkiner, eds. 1997. *Tajikistan: The Trials of Independence*. New York: St. Martin's Press.

Dorian, James P. 1994. "The Kazakh Oil Industry: A Potential Critical Role in Central Asia." *Energy Policy* 22: 685–98.

Dornbush, Rudiger and Sebastian Edwards, eds. 1991. *The Macroeconomics of Populism in Latin America*. Chicago: University of Chicago Press.

Dryzek, John S. 1996. "Political Inclusion and the Dynamics of Democratization." *American Political Science Review* 90, 1: 475–96.

Duquette, Micchel. 1999. *Building New Democracies: Economic & Social Reform in Brazil, Chile, & Mexico*. Toronto: University of Toronto Press.

Easter, Gerald. 2000. *Reconstructing the State: Personal Networks and Elite Identity in Soviet Russia*. Cambridge: Cambridge University Press.

Easterly, William. 2001. *The Elusive Quest for Growth*. Cambridge: MIT Press.

Eckstein, Harry, Frederic J. Fleron Jr., Erik P. Hoffmann, and William M. Reisinger. 1998. *Can Democracy Take Root in Post-Soviet Russia: Explorations in State–Society Relations*. Lanham, MD: Rowman & Littlefield.

Eggertsson, Thrainn. 1990. *Economic Behavior and Institutions*. New York: Cambridge University Press.

Elster, Jon, Claus Offe, and Ulrich K. Preuss. 1998. *Institutional Design in Post-Communist Societies: Rebuilding the Ship at Sea*. New York: Cambridge University Press.

Ely, Jr, James W. 1992. *The Guardian of Every Other Right*. New York: Oxford University Press.

Esposito, John L. 1992. *The Islamic Threat: Myth or Reality?* New York: Oxford University Press.

Fainsod, Merle. 1958. *Smolensk under Soviet Rule*. Cambridge: Harvard University Press.

Fierman, William, ed. 1991. *Soviet Central Asia: The Failed Transformation*. Boulder: Westview Press.

Filipov, David. 2000. "Uzbek Government Cracks Down on Islamic Rebel Groups: Officials Fear Muslim Uprising." *The Boston Globe* (31 December): 1.

Fish, M. Steven. 1996. *Democracy from Scratch*. Princeton: Princeton University Press.

Fish, M. Steven. 1998. "The Determinants of Economic Reform in the Postcommunist World." *East European Politics and Societies* 12, 2: 31–78.

Fox, Jonathan. 1993. *The Politics of Food in Mexico: State Power and Social Mobilization*. Ithaca: Cornell University Press.

Freeland, Chrystia. 2000. *Sale of the Century: Russia's Wild Ride from Communism to Capitalism*. New York: Crown Business.

Freedom House. 2001. *Press Freedom Survey 2001*. New York: Freedom House.

Friedman, Milton. 1963. *Capitalism and Freedom*. Chicago: University of Chicago Press.

Gaddy, Clifford and Barry W. Ickes. 1998. "Russia's Virtual Economy." *Foreign Affairs* 70, 5: 53–67.

Geddes, Barbara. 1994. *Politician's Dilemma: Building State Capacity in Latin America* Berkeley: University of California Press.

Ghadbian, Najib, Michael W. Suleiman, and John P. Entelis, eds. 1997. *Democratization and the Islamist Challenge in the Arab World*. Boulder: Westview Press.

Gill, Graeme. 2000. *The Dynamics of Democratization: Elites, Civil Society, and the Transition Process*. London: Palgrave.

Glasser, Bradley Louis. 2001. *Economic Development and Political Reform: The Impact of External Capital on the Middle East*. Cheltenham: Edward Elgar.

Gleason, Gregory. 1991. "Fealty and Loyalty: Informal Authority Structures in Soviet Asia." *Soviet Studies* 43, 4: 613–28.

Gleason, Gregory. 1992. "The Federal Formula and the Collapse of the USSR." *Publius* 22, 3: 141–63.

Gleason, Gregory. 1993. "Uzbekistan: from Statehood to Nationhood?" pp. 331–60 in Ian Bremmer and Ray Taras, eds. *Nations And Politics in the Soviet Successor States*. New York: Cambridge University Press.

Gleason, Gregory. 1997a. "Uzbekistan: The Politics of National Independence." pp. 572–96 in Ian Bremmer and Raymond Taras, eds. *New States, New Politics*. Cambridge: Cambridge University Press.

Gleason, Gregory. 1997b. *The Central Asian States: Discovering Independence*. Boulder: Westview.

Gleason, Gregory. 2001. "Inter-state Cooperation in Central Asia from the CIS to the Shanghai Forum." *Europe-Asia Studies* 53, 7: 1077–95.

Gleason, Gregory. 2001. "Why Russia is in Tajikistan." *Comparative Strategy* 20, 1: 77–89.

Gleason, Gregory and Susan J. Buck. 1993. "Decolonization in Former Soviet Borderlands: Politics in Search of Principles." *PS: Political Science and Politics* 26, 4: 522–5.

Glenn, John K. 2001. *Framing Democracy: Civil Society and Civic Movements in Eastern Europe*. Stanford: Stanford University Press.

Gorbachev, M.S. 1988. *Pravda*, January 13, 1988: 1.

Grimes, Barbara F., ed. 1999. *Ethnologue: Languages of the World*. Thirteenth Edition. Dallas, TX: Summer Institute of Languages.

Guerrieri, Paolo. 1995. "Trade Integration of Eastern Europe and the Former Soviet Union into the World Economy: A Structuralist Approach." pp. 103–29 in Beverly Crawford, ed., *Markets, States, and Democracy: The Political Economy of Post-Communist Transformation*. Boulder: Westview Press.

Gürgen, Emine, Harry Snoek, Jon Craig, Jimmy McHugh, Ivailo Izvorski, and Ron van Rooden. 1999. "Economic Reforms in Kazakhstan, Kyrgyz Republic, Tajikistan, Turkmenistan, and Uzbekistan." Washington: International Monetary Fund Occasional Paper No. 183.

Haggard, Stephan. 1990. *Pathways from the Periphery: The Politics of Growth in the Newly Industrializing Countries*. Cornell: Cornell University Press.

Haggard, Stephan and Robert R. Kaufman. 1995. *The Political Economy of Democratic Transitions*. Princeton: Princeton University Press.

Haghayeghi, Mehrdad. 1995. *Islam & Politics in Central Asia*. New York: St Martin's Press.

Hardin, Garrett. 1968. "The Tragedy of the Commons." *Science* 162: 1243–8.

Hayek, Freidrich A. 1944. *The Road to Serfdom*. Chicago: Chicago University Press.

Hayek, Freidrich A. 1948. *Individualism and Economic Order*. Chicago: University of Chicago Press.

Hayek, Freidrich A. 1960. *The Constitution of Liberty*. Chicago: University of Chicago Press.

Hayek, Freidrich A. 1972. *The Road to Serfdom*. Chicago: Chicago University Press.

Haynes, Michael and Rumy Husan. 1998. "The State and Market in the Transition Economies: Critical Remarks in the Light of Past History and the Current Experience." *The Journal of Economic History* 27, 3: 609–44.

Helliwell, James. 1994. "Empirical Links between Democracy and Economic Growth." *British Journal of Political Science* 24: 225–48.

Hellman, Joel. 1998. "Winner Takes All: The Politics of Partial Reform in Postcommunist Transition." *World Politics* 50, 2: 203–34.

Hiro, Dilip. 1994. *Between Marx and Muhammad: The Changing Face of Central Asia*. London: HarperCollins Publishers.

Hirschman, Albert O. 1972. *Exit, Voice, Loyalty*. Cambridge: Harvard University Press.

Hollifield, James F. and Calvin Jillson, eds. 1999. *Pathways to Democracy: The Political Economy of Democratic Transitions*. London: Routledge.

Hopkirk, Peter. 1994. *The Great Game: The Struggle for Empire in Central Asia*. London: Kodansha International.

Hough, Jerry F. 1969. *The Soviet Prefects*. Cambridge: Harvard University Press.

Hough, Jerry F. and Michael H. Armacost. 2001. *The Logic of Economic Reform in Russia*. Washington DC: Brookings Institution.

Hunter, Shireen T. and Marie Bennigsen Broxup. 1996. *Central Asia Since Independence*. Westport: Praeger Publishers.

Huntington, Samuel P. 1993. *The Third Wave: Democratization in the Late Twentieth Century*. University of Oklahoma Press.

Huntington, Samuel P. 1997. *The Clash of Civilizations and the Remaking of World Order*. New York: Penguin.

Huntington, Samuel P. 1969. *Political Order in Changing Societies*. New Haven: Yale University Press.

International Helsinki Federation (IHF). 2001. " Mission to Central Asia (Kazakhstan, Kyrgyzstan and Uzbekistan), 7–16 June 2001." Vienna: International Helsinki Federation.

Izhtimoiy Fikr. 2000. "Uzbekistan – Our Common Home." *Narodnoe Slovo* (3 October): 1.

Jawad, Nassim and Shahrbanou Tadjbakhsh. 1995 *Tajikistan: A Forgotten Civil War*. Minority Rights Group.

Jonson, Lena. 1998. *Russia and Central Asia: A New Web of Relations*. London: The Royal Institute of International Affairs.

Jonson, Lena. 1999. *The Tajik War: A Challenge to Russian Policy*. London: The Royal Institute of International Affairs.

Karimov, Islam. 1998. *Uzbekistan on the Threshold of the Twenty-first Century*. London: St Martin's Press.

Kasenov, U.T. 1998. *Bezopasnost Tsentralnoi Azii: natsionalnye, regionalnye, i globalnye problemy*. Almaty: Kainar.

Kaser, Michael. 1997. *The Economies of Kazakhstan and Uzbekistan*. London: Royal Institute of International Affairs.

Kazhegeldin, Akezhan. 2000. "Shattered Image: Misconceptions of Democracy and Capitalism in Kazakhstan." *Harvard International Review*, 22, 1.

Kienle, Eberhard. 2001. *A Grand Delusion: Democracy and Economic Reform in Egypt*. London: IB Tauris and Company.

Kim, Samuel S. 1999. "East Asia and Globalization: Challenges and Responses." *Asian Perspective* 23, 4: 5–44.

Kobori, Iwao and Michael H. Glantz, eds. 1998. *Central Eurasian Water Crisis: Caspian, Aral, and Dead Seas*. New York: United Nations Publications.

Kohli, Atul. 1990. *Democracy and Discontent: India's Growing Crisis of Governability*. Cambridge: Cambridge University Press.

Kornai, Janos. 1992. *The Socialist System: The Political Economy of Communism*. Princeton: Princeton University Press.

Krasner, Stephen D. 1985. *Structural Conflict: The Third World against Global Liberalism*. Berkeley: University of California Press.

Krueger, Anne O. 1974. "The Political Economy of the Rent-Seeking Society." *American Economic Review* 64, 3: 291–303.

Krueger, Anne O. 1993. *Political Economy of Policy Reform in Developing Countries*. Cambridge: MIT Press.

Krueger, Anne O. 2000. *Economic Policy Reform: The Second Stage*. University of Chicago Press.

Kubicek, Paul. 1997. "Regionalism, Nationalism, and Realpolitik in Central Asia." *Europe–Asia Studies* 49, 4: 637–65.

Kuleshov, V. 1992. "Turkmenistan gotov prodat' svoi gaz Ukraine po tsenam, priblizhennym k mirovym." *Izvestiia* (6 March 1992): 1.

LaPalombara, Joseph. 1974. Politics Within Nations. Englewood Cliffs, NY: Prentice Hall.

Lavigne, Marie. 1995. *The Economics of Transition: From Socialist Economy to Market Economy*. London: Macmillan.

Leitzel, Jim. 1995. *Russian Economic Reform*. London: Routledge.

Levi, Margaret. 1988. *Of Rule and Revenue*. Berkeley: University of California Press.

Lewis, Bernard. 2001. *What Went Wrong: Western Impact and the Middle East Response*. Oxford: Oxford University Press.

Lewis, Bernard. 1996. "A Historical Overview." *Journal of Democracy* 7, 2: 52–63.

Lijphart, Arend. 1966. *The Trauma of Decolonization*. New Haven: Yale University Press.

Lijphart, Arend. 1984. *Democracies: Patterns of Majoritarian and Consensus Government in Twenty-one Countries*. New Haven: Yale University Press.

Lindblom, Charles E. 1977. *Politics and Markets: The World's Political–Economic Systems*. New York: Basic Books.

Linz, Juan J. 1990. "Transitions to Democracy." *Washington Quarterly* 13.

Locke, John. 1690. *An Essay Concerning the True Original Extent and End of Civil Government*. New York: Hasner.

Lubin, Nancy. 1984. *Labor and Nationality in Soviet Central Asia*. Princeton, NJ: Princeton University Press.

Lubin, Nancy. 1995. "Islam and Ethnic Identity in Central Asia: A View from Below." pp. 53–70 in Yaacov Ro'i, ed., *Muslim Eurasia: Conflicting Legacies*. London: Frank Cass.

Luong, Pauline Jones. 2002. *Institutional Change and Political Continuity in Post-Soviet Central Asia: Power, Perceptions, and Pacts*. Cambridge: Cambridge University Press.

Luong, Pauline Jones and Erika Weinthal. 2002. "New Friends, New Fears." *Foreign Affairs* 81, 2: 61–70.

McChesney, R.D. 1991. *Waqf in Central Asia: Four Hundred Years in the History of a Muslim Shrine 1480–1889*. Princeton: Princeton University Press.

McChesney, R.D. 1996. *Central Asia: Foundations of Change*. Princeton: The Darwin Press.

McFaul, Michael. 1995. "State Power, Institutional Change and the Politics of Privatization in Russia." *World Politics* 47, 2: 210–42.

McFaul, Michael. 2001. *Russia's Unfinished Revolution: Political Change from Gorbachev to Putin*. Ithaca: Cornell University Press.

McKee, Michael. 1988. "In Networks we Trust: All Others Pay Cash." *European Journal of Political Economy* 4: 184–211.

Maravall, Jose. 1997. *Regimes, Politics, and Markets: Democratization and Economic Change in Southern and Eastern Europe*. Oxford: Oxford University Press.

March, James G. and Johan P. Olsen. 1989. *Rediscovering Institutions: The Organizational Basis of Politics*. New York: Free Press.

Masanov, Nurbulat. 1995. Kochevaya tsivilizatsiia kazakhov. Almaty: Sotsinvest.

Masanov, Nurbulat, Erlan Karin, Andrei Chebotarev, and Natsuko Oka. 2002. *The Nationalities Question in Post-Soviet Kazakhstan*. Chiba, Japan: Institute of Developing Economies, Japan External Trade Organization.

Massell, Gregory J. 1974. *The Surrogate Proletariat: Moslem Women and Revolutionary Strategies in Soviet Central Asia 1919–1929*. Princeton: Princeton University Press.

Micklin, Philip. 2000. *Managing Water in Central Asia*. London: The Royal Institute of International Affairs.

Migdal, Joel S. 1988. *Strong Societies and Weak States: State–Society Relations and State Capabilities in the Third World*. Princeton: Princeton University Press.

Motyl, Alexander J., Arch Puddington, and Amanda Schnetzer, eds. 2001. *Nations in Transit 2001*. New York: Freedom House.

Moore, Barrington Jr. 1966. *Social Origins of Dictatorship and Democracy: Lord and Peasant in the Making of the Modern World*. Cambridge: Harvard University Press.

Murrell, Peter. 1993. "What is Shock Therapy? What Did it Do in Poland and Russia?" *Post-Soviet Affairs* 9, 2: 111–41.

Murell, Peter, ed. 2001. *Assessing the Value of Law in Transition Economies*. Ann Arbor: University of Michigan Press.

Nazarbaev, Nursulatan. 1998. "Address of the President of the Republic of Kazakhstan to the People of Kazakhstan: On the Situation in the Country and Major Directions of Domestic and Foreign Policy: Democratization, Economic and Political Reform for the New Century." *Panorama* No. 38, 1.

Nazarbaev, Nursultan. 1995. *Ukaz Prezidenta Respubliki Kazakhstan imeiushchii silu zakona "O Tamozhennom Dele v Respubliki Kazakhstan"* [Decree of the President of the Republic of Kazakhstan Having the Force of Law "On Customs Regulation in the Republic of Kazakhstan"]. Almaty: Zheti Zharhy.

Nazarbaev, Nursultan. 1996. "Vybor – Tsvilizovannoe demokratichskoe Obshchestvo." pp. 19–24 in Nursultan Nazarbaev, *Pyat' let nezavisimosti*. [Five Years of Independence] Almaty: Ilym.

Nazarbaev, Nursultan. 1997. *Kazakhstan-2030: Prosperity, Security and Ever Growing Welfare of all the Kazakhstanis*. Almaty: Ylim.

Norman, Wayne J. 1993. "A Democratic Theory for a Democratizing World? A Reassessment of Popper's Political Realism." *Political Studies* 41, 2: 252–68.

North, Douglass C. 1981. *Structure and Change in Economic History*. New York: Norton Publishers.

O'Donnell, Guillermo, Philippe C. Schmitter, and Laurence Whitehead, eds. 1986. *Transitions from Authoritarian Rule: Comparative Perspectives*. Baltimore: Johns Hopkins University Press.

Oh, John Kie-Chiang. 1999. *Korean Politics: The Quest for Democratization and Economic Development*. Ithaca: Cornell University Press.

Olcott, Martha Brill. 1995. *The Kazakhs*. Stanford: Hoover Institution Press.

Olcott, Martha Brill. 2002. *Kazakhstan: Unfulfilled Promise*. Washington, DC: Carnegie Endowment for International Peace.

Olson, Mancur, Jr. 1971. *The Logic of Collective Action: Public Goods and the Theory of Groups*. Cambridge: Harvard University Press.

Olson, Mancur. 2000. *Power and Prosperity: Outgrowing Communist and Capitalist Dictatorships*. New York: Basic Books.

Onuf, Nicholas. 1989. *World of Our Making: Rules and Rule in Social Theory and International Relations*. Columbia: University of South Carolina Press.

Ostrom, Elinor. 1990. *Governing the Commons: The Evolution of Institutions for Collective Action*. Cambridge: Cambridge University Press.

Pannier, Bruce. 2000. "Central Asia: Kyrgyz, Tajiks Complain About Uzbek Landmines." *RFE/RL Weekday Magazine* (29 November 2000).

Park, A.G. 1957. *Bolshevism in Turkestan, 1917–1927*. New York: Columbia University Press.

Pchelintsev, O. 1989. "Immunitet k izhdivenchestvu." [Immunity against Malfeasance] *Trud* April 25, 2.

Pomfret, Richard. 1995. *The Economies of Central Asia*. Princeton: Princeton University Press.

Popper, Karl. 1971. *The Open Society and its Enemies*. Princeton: Princeton University Press.

Portnikov, Vitalii. 1992. "Ritm reform my dolzhny opredeliat' sami." *Nezavisimaia gazeta* (20 October 1992): 2.

Pryor, Frederic L. 1991. "When is Collectivization Reversible?" *Studies in Comparative Communism* 24, 1: 3–24.

Przeworski, Adam. 1991. *Democracy and the Market: Political and Economic Reforms in Eastern Europe and Latin America*. Cambridge: Cambridge University Press.

Przeworski, Adam and Fernando Limongi. 1993. "Political Regimes and Economic Growth." *Journal of Economic Perspectives* 7: 51–69.

Putnam, Robert D. 1993. *Making Democracy Work: Civic Traditions in Modern Italy*. Princeton: Princeton University Press.

Pye, Lucian W. 1985. *Asian Power and Politics: The Cultural Dimensions of Authority*. Cambridge: Harvard University Press.

Rakowska-Harmstone, Teresa. 1970. *Russia and Nationalism in Central Asia: The Case of Tadzhikistan*. Baltimore: Johns Hopkins Press.

Ranis, Gustav and Syed Akhtar Mahmood. 1992. *The Political Economy of Development Policy Change*. Cambridge, MA: Blackwell.

Rashid, Ahmed. 1994. *The Resurgence of Central Asia: Islam or Nationalism?* Karachi: Oxford University Press.

Rashid, Ahmed. 2001. *Taliban: Militant Islam, Oil and Fundamentalism in Central Asia*. New Haven: Yale University Press.

Rashid, Ahmed. 2002. *Jihad: The Rise of Militant Islam in Central Asia*. New Haven: Yale University Press.

Reddaway, Peter and Dmitri Glinski. 2001. *Tragedy of Russia's Reforms: Market Bolshevism Against Democracy*. Washington, DC: US Institute of Peace.

Regionalnyi Statisticheskii Ezhegodnik Kazakhstana (RSEK). 1997. Almaty: Committee on Statistics and Analysis, Agency for Strategic Planning and Reforms.

Remmer, Karen. 1990. "Democracy and Economic Crisis." *World Politics* 42: 315–35.

Respubliki Kazakhstan: Informatsionnyi Pasport (RKIP). 1998. Almaty: Zhety Zhargy.

Roberts, Sean. 1992. "A Land Divided." *Cultural Survival Quarterly* 16, 1: 45–8.

Robinson, Mark and Gordon White, eds. 1999. *The Democratic Developmental State: Politics and Institutional Design*. Oxford University Press.

Rodrik, D. and R. Fernandez. 1991. "Resistance to Reform: Status Quo Bias in the Presence of Individual-Specific Uncertainty." *American Economic Review* 81: 1146–55.

Roeder, Philip. 1993. *Red Sunset: The Failure of Soviet Politics*. Princeton: Princeton University Press.

Rogowski, Ronald. 1987. "Trade and the Variety of Democratic Institutions." *International Organization* 41, 2: 203–23.

Rogowski, Ronald. 1990. *Commerce and Coalitions*. Princeton: Princeton University Press.

Root, Hilton L. 1996. *Small Countries, Big Lessons: Governance and the Rise of East Asia*. Hong Kong: Oxford University Press.

Roy, Olivier. 1993. *The Civil War in Tajikstan: Causes and Implications*. Washington: United States Institute of Peace.

Roy, Olivier. 2000. *The New Central Asia: The Creation of Nations*. New York: New York University Press.

Rumer, Boris Z. 1989. *Soviet Central Asia: "A Tragic Experiment."* Boston: Unwin Hyman.

Rumer, Boris Z. 2000. *Central Asia and the New Global Economy: Critical Problems, Critical Choices*. Armonk, NY: M.E. Sharpe.

Rywkin, Michael. 1990. *Moscow's Muslim Challenge: Soviet Central Asia*. New York: M.E. Sharpe.

Sagdeev, Roald Z. and Susan Eisenhower, eds. 1995. *Central Asia: Conflict, Resolution and Change*. Chevy Chase: CPSS Press.

Sakwa, Richard and Mark Webber. 1999. "The Commonwealth of Independent States, 1991–1998: Stagnation and Survival." *Europe-Asia Studies* 51, 3: 379–415.

Savas, Emmanuel S. 1987. *Privatization: The Key to Better Government*. Chatham, NJ: Chatham House Publishers.

Schmitter, Philippe C. with Terry Lynn Karl. 1994. "The Conceptual Travels of Transitologists and Consolidologists: How Far East Should They Attempt to Go?" *Slavic Review* 53, 1: 175–85.

Schroeder, Gertrude E. 1988. "Property Rights Issues in Economic Reforms in Socialist Countries." *Studies in Comparative Communism* 21: 175–88.

Schumpeter, Joseph. 1984. *Capitalism, Socialism and Democracy*. New York: Harper Collins.

Schuyler, Eugene. 1876. *Turkistan: Notes of Journey in Russian Turkistan, Khokand, Bukhara, and Kuldja*. New York: Scribner, Armstrong & Company.

Shleifer, Andrei and Robert W. Vishny. 1995. *The Grabbing Hand: Government Pathologies and Their Cures*. Cambridge: Harvard University Press.

Skocpol, Theda. 1979. *States and Social Revolutions: A Comparative Analysis of France, Russia, and China*. Cambridge: Cambridge University Press.

Smith, William C., Carlos H. Acuna, and Eduardo A. Gamarra, eds. 1994. *Democracy, Markets, and Structural Reform in Latin America: Argentina, Bolivia, Brazil, Chile, and Mexico*. Miami: North-South Center Press.

Solnick, Steven. 1998. *Stealing the State: Control and Collapse in Soviet Institutions*. Cambridge: Cambridge University Press.

Sorensen, Georg. 1993. *Democracy and Democratization: Processes and Prospects in a Changing World*. Boulder: Westview Press.

Sperling, Valerie, ed. 2000. *Building the Russian State, Institutional Crisis and the Quest for Democratic Governance*. Boulder: Westview Press.

Starr, S. Frederick. 1996. "Making Eurasia Stable." *Foreign Affairs* (January–February), 80–92.

Staticheskii Ezhegodnik Kazakhstana (SEK). 1997. Almaty: National Statistical Agency of the Ministry of Economics and Trade.

Stiglitz, Joseph E. 1997. "The Role of Government in the Economies of Developing Countries." pp. 61–103 in Edmond Malinvauded ed., *Development Strategy and Management of Market Economy*. Oxford: Clarendon Press.

Stiglitz, Joseph E. 2002. *Globalization and its Discontents*. New York: W. W. Norton.

Strange, Susan. 1988. *States and Markets: An Introduction to International Political Economy*. New York: Basil Blackwell.

Terry, Sarah Meiklejohn. 1993. "Thinking About Post-communist Transitions: How Different Are They?" *Slavic Review* 52, 2 (Summer): 333–7.

Thomas, Vinod and John Nash *et al.* 1991. *Best Practices in Trade Policy Reform*. Washington, DC: The World Bank.

Tilly, Charles. 1992. Coercion, Capital, and European States, AD 990–1992. Cambridge: Blackwell.

de Tocqueville, Alexis. 2000. *Democracy in America*. Chicago: University of Chicago Press.

Transparency International. 2000. Transparency International Annual Report 2000. Berlin: Transparency International.

United Nations Office of Drug Control and Crime Prevention, (UNODCCP). 1999. *Global Illicit Drug Trends*. New York: UN Office for Drug Control and Crime Prevention, UN Printing Office.

Van Atta, Don, ed. 1993. *The 'Farmer Threat': The Political Economy of Agrarian Reform in Post-Soviet Russia*. Boulder: Westview Press.

Van Bergeijk, Peter A. G., and Jarig Van Sinderen, eds. 1999. *Structural Reform in Open Economies: A Road to Success?* Cheltenham: Edward Elgar.

Vogel, Steven K. 1998. *Freer Markets, More Rules: Regulatory Reform in Advanced Industrial Countries*. Ithaca: Cornell University Press.

Wade, Robert. 1992. *Governing the Market: Economic Theory and the Role of Government in East Asian Industrialization*. Princeton: Princeton University Press.

Weber, Max. 1979. *Economy and Society: An Outline of Interpretive Sociology*. Guenther Roth and Claus Wittich, eds. 2 volumes. Berkeley: University of California Press.

Weinthal, Erika. 2002. *State Making and Environmental Cooperation: Linking Domestic and International Politics in Central Asia*. Cambridge: MIT Press.

Wheeler, Geoffrey. 1964. *The Modern History of Soviet Central Asia*. New York: Praeger.

Williamson, Oliver E. 1998. *The Economic Institutions of Capitalism: Firms, Markets, Relational Contracting*. New York: The Free Press.

Williamson, Oliver E. 1975. *Markets and Hierarchies: Analysis and Antitrust Implications: A Study in the Economics of Internal Organization*. New York: Free Press.

Wittfogel, Karl A. 1957. *Oriental Despotism: A Comparative Study of Total Power*. New Haven: Yale University Press.

Woodward, Susan L. 1995. *Balkan Tragedy*. Washington: Brookings Institution.

World Bank. 1997 *World Development Report 1997: The State in a Changing World*. Washington, DC: The World Bank.

World Bank. 2002. *World Development Report 2002: Building Institutions for Markets*. Washington, DC: The World Bank.

Young, Crawford. 1994. *The African Colonial State in Comparative Perspective*. New Haven: Yale University Press.

Index